THE MAHARISHI

Paul Mason learned the practice of Transcendental Meditation after hitchhiking to India in 1970, when he visited the Maharishi's ashram at Rishikesh. He has maintained an abiding interest in Indian teachings. He is also a musician, composing music that integrates influences from both East and West. He has contributed to the magazine *Yoga Today* and to *Behind the Beatles Songs*, a book about the meaning of various of The Beatles' songs.

Other titles by this author:

Via Rishikesh

Mala: A String of Unexpected Meetings

Forthcoming title:

The Teachings of Guru Dev - The Roots of TM

THE
MAHARISHI

The Biography of the Man
Who Gave Transcendental Meditation
to the World

Paul Mason

EVOLUTION PUBLISHING
Lyndhurst Hampshire UK

Cover picture by Rex Features Ltd
Cover design by Gina Dearden
Printed and bound in Great Britain

ISBN 0-9550361-0-0

To my parents

Acknowledgements

I would like to extend my grateful thanks to Kathy and all the many people who were, either directly or indirectly, of assistance to this work, and expressly to: Maharishi Mahesh Yogi, Yolanda Baldi, Raj Varma, Andreas Müller, Bevan Morris, Brahmachari Satyanand, Steve Jeffery, Jerry Stovin, Walt Gibbons, Vesey Crichton, Vincent Snell, Peter Russell, Prem C. Pasricha, Joan Benesh, Mary Lou Jennings, Sarah Rose, Marcus and Phillipa Saint, John Windsor, Jet Fairly, Henderson Davison, Derek Dearden, Bob Rankin, Dinah Demuth, Roger Preece, Dario Ciriello, Sally Bowen, Sarah Buret, Surjeet Husain, S. Guruvareddi, the staff of Dhyan Vidhya Peeth, the monks of Jyotir Math, D. N. Upadhyay, and Swami Ashibananda and the other swamis of Gyaan Mandir Uttar Kashi. Also to the 'Anonymous Devotee of His Holiness Maharishiji Mahesh Yogi', Bob Hopeless and useful feedback from internet newsgroups. A very special thanks goes to all the staff at Element Books, and to my loving family who have provided me with very necessary tea, sympathy, feedback and valued support, Richard for so much assistance in matters computer related. Thanks to Dandi Swami Narayanand Saraswati Ji for his blissful blessings.

Acknowledgement and credit should also be given to the authors and publishers whose works I have quoted within the terms of 'fair usage' and to anyone else who has been of material use or support, and whom I have unintentionally omitted to mention.

Preface

Maharishi Mahesh Yogi is a very famous son of India, so it is a pleasure to be able to offer the first major biography of his life and work. A thorough attempt to profile the man and his teaching has been undertaken.

He is a disciple of the late Shankaracharya Swami Brahmanand Saraswati of Jyotir Math. Since about 1955 he has been popularising meditation. He has been assisted in his efforts by the support of the Shankaracharya's successor Swami Shantanand.

Though today 'The Maharishi' is an old man, he still actively leads his worldwide movement for the promotion of Transcendental Meditation (TM), and frequently appears on his organisation's satellite television channel 'Veda Vision', founded in India in 1998. His broadcasts are transmitted from his permanent residence in Europe.

Until recently some of his followers even tried taking the message of meditation into the world of politics, going so far as standing for election to Parliament in the UK, and remarkably, even fielding a candidate for the US presidential election. However in December 2000 his Natural Law Party was officially disbanded.

His life and work has prompted much attention around the world.

Following the successful publication of the English, German and Portuguese language editions of this biography, it is pleasing to offer this new English language edition (which includes previously unavailable quotations attributed to the Maharishi's 'Guru Dev', Swami Brahmanand Saraswati) and important source material linking Transcendental Meditation with the Shankaracharya tradition.

Contents

PART III: *The Enlightenment Business*

PART I

---★---

The Spirit and the Flesh

1

— ★ —

Mahesh and His Master

I mean look how it all started. I believe he just landed in Hawaii in his nightshirt, all on his own, nobody with him … – John Lennon[1]

For San Francisco Bay Airport, Thursday, 29 January 1959 was just another working day – more flights, more passengers, just like any other day. From Honolulu, Hawaii, came yet another scheduled flight, stimulating another flurry of activity for the uniformed customs men. Baggage handlers attended to their normal duties, unloading luggage from the hold of the plane and delivering it for collection. In the arrivals lounge were the normal complement of eager, expectant faces looking out for loved ones, business colleagues and the like. There was to be nothing out of the ordinary about the passengers today, no famous actors or politicians were due in.

As the new arrivals began to emerge, attention fell on one lone individual, a visitor from somewhere far beyond Hawaii. There, walking self-assuredly upon quaint hessian-banded wooden sandals came a figure of slight stature draped simply in a pure white robe with long, wayward, wavy black hair tumbling about his shoulders. His was a sunny, amiable countenance, with large glistening chestnut-brown eyes, broad flattened nose and cheeks both generous and shining, partially obscured by a flourishing growth of beard. On espying the carpet roll he clutched, any child might have fancied him to be an Arabian fakir come drifting in upon a magic spell. Much more likely was that he was a potentate from some small but wealthy kingdom, maybe a sultan or maharajah from the East who wished to travel incognito. The two Hawaiian nationals that escorted him out of the terminal could perhaps have explained something of the identity and mission of this mystery man.

The United States of America had but scant exposure to representatives of that rich cultural heritage which is India. Some sixty-five years before, the great World Parliament of Religions of 1893 had paid host to the turbaned, corpulent personage of Swami Vivekananda and listened to his monkish philosophy. More recently, in 1920, the city of Boston had planned an International Congress of Religious Liberals which received, from a ship newly arrived after a two-month voyage from Calcutta, India, a delegate that many Americans later took to their hearts, the ochre-robed and deceptively youthful-looking Swami Paramahansa Yogananda.

With no plans to attend either parliament or congress, but nevertheless exuding unbridled confidence and virtually unbounded zeal, came India's latest emissary, known by his followers as His Holiness Maharishi Mahesh Yogi.

At his first press conference in the USA on Wednesday, 29 April 1959, he revealed his intention to spiritually regenerate the entire world, adding:

> My life truly began 19 years ago at the feet of my Master when I learned the secret of swift and deep meditation, a secret I now impart to the world.[2]

Prior to his arrival on Western shores, the man we now know as 'the Maharishi', had spent almost his entire life in India. It was at the age of twenty-three, in his home town of Jabalpur, Madhya Pradesh, that he first met Swami Brahmanand Saraswati, a wandering holy man of some renown. He recalls:

> We were a few men who had gone to visit Guru Dev. We sat outside his door a long time until we were finally admitted. We sat down by the door which had been left open. Guru Dev sat in darkness. We could only sense his presence – he didn't talk to us. Suddenly a car drove by on the road and the headlights momentarily shone through the open door. For the first time I was able to see Guru Dev's face. Oh, it was a wonderful sight! I have never seen anything so wonderful. Immediately I experienced a deep reverence and devotion to him and I decided to do everything in my power to be in his surroundings.[3]

Mahesh evinced a strong desire to offer himself as a disciple to the elderly monk. The spontaneous commitment he felt for the hermit had the young man's parents deeply concerned. Voicing their disapproval in no uncertain terms, they did their utmost to dissuade him from taking to a life of renunciation. This was not the life they wanted for their son, not at all.

If he had overheard these concerned, conscientious parents, it would probably have brought a smile of recollection to the old hermit's austere countenance. As a young child of barely nine years old, he had witnessed a very similar reaction to his own deeply felt convictions.

Let us take a closer look at the life of this old *swami*, for it will be seen that he plays a key role in the story of the Maharishi, namely that of *guru* or master.

The city of Ayodhya, in northern India, is famous as the birthplace of Lord Rama, star of the ancient epic poem *Ramayana*. Lord Rama is worshipped as an *avataar* (incarnation of God), and his name is held sacred by millions.

On Thursday, 21 December 1870 [*Vikram Samvat* 1928, *Marg Shirsh Shukla Dasmi*] in the village of Gana close to Ayodhya, Rajaram Mishra was born. His family were Brahmins (the caste which provided both teachers and priests) and were relatively affluent, being *zamindar* or landlords. They were thus able to offer Rajaram a secure, comfortable childhood.

Perhaps this young boy would never have entered the annals of history but for two incidents which awakened him to the world beyond his playthings. When he was barely seven years old he suffered the loss of his most cherished companion, his grandfather, whose lifeless body was borne away to the chant of 'Ram *naam satya hai*' (The name of Ram – or God – is truth).[4] Rajaram took this *mantra* as guidance in his hour of need. Already of a retiring nature, the young lad became increasingly withdrawn, dwelling as he did upon the transitory nature of existence and its temporal happiness.

A year later Rajaram was enrolled at the Sanskrit Institute, an institution of some standing in the holy city of Benares (an ancient city known also by the names of Varanasi and Kashi). The very atmosphere of this pilgrim centre no doubt deepened the youngster's leanings and yearning towards a commitment to a spiritual life. As it happened he had not studied there long before his next major upheaval. As was the custom in that era, a child marriage had been arranged for him. We can but imagine the boy's feelings, at barely nine years of age, at being informed of his own impending wedding. He was not of a mind to become a victim of his parents' schemes, and being a boy of unusual pluck and determination, he made ready to break free, to do a disappearing trick.

For several days Rajaram journeyed along the banks of *Ganga Ma*, the sacred 'mother' Ganges River, with faith as his only companion. From Benares he made his way to Allahabad (Prayag) and onward as far as Hardwar, intending to travel via Rishikesh to the Garhwal Himalayas, an area steeped in ancient folklore. But discovery could be evaded for only so long and before arriving in Rishikesh a police inspector apprehended the young runaway and returned him safely to his parents.

His family was of one voice in their condemnation of his strange behaviour and unaccountable unworldliness. According to tradition, a young man's future lay in settling down to his duties and in being a credit to his community. Undeterred by such arguments he reasoned with his parents and with the local wise man, until at long last they acknowledged defeat and capitulated to his demand for freedom to seek his own path in life. His mother, in giving her permission to 'go and sing in praise of the Lord', exacted a promise from him not to become a 'begging *sadhu*'[5] and made him agree that should he ever hanker after the comforts of material life, he would return immediately.

Talking to the wise, mixing with the holy, the young truth-seeker drifted where inspiration led him. For food and lodgings the *ashrams* and *dharmashalas* (religious rest houses) would have all been open to him since, then as now, India was always accommodating to sincere seekers of the truth. Notwithstanding this custom of offering alms to travellers in search of holiness, life could not always have been easy for the young boy alone. Excursions into the byways of the Himalayan hinterland threatened many dangers, for wild beasts lurked there, including boars, bears and tigers. Rajaram's steadfast faith in his God held good, and he ventured freely and remained unscathed. In this solitary quest for self-realization, he recognized the need for guidance and thus entertained the hope of meeting someone who might offer him spiritual tutelage.

In his search he encountered many learned and sincere devotees, but met no one with whom he felt comfortable enough to entrust himself. On one occasion after having tracked down a *mahatma* (great soul), he waited patiently for the *swami* to emerge from meditation. After offering his respects and greetings, Rajaram requested him to provide him with fire. The *yogi*, who after his exercises had at first appeared so serene and blissful, exploded in a rage on hearing the boy's request. Perhaps he suspected the youngster's motives, for it is well known that in the tradition of *dandi* (staff) carrying *swamis*, the use of fire is generally avoided. Rajaram patiently endured the heated outpourings before calmly asking him from where this anger sprang, if not from fire. The *swami*, thoroughly abashed, hugged the lad and apologized profusely. Over the next few days he gave time to the precocious aspirant who had so impressed him, familiarizing the young seeker in the fundamentals of *yoga* discipline.

The search for living examples of the spiritual perfection Rajaram sought for himself continued and, at length, at the hermitage town of Uttar Kashi, in the Himalayas, he met Shri Swami Krishnanand Saraswati. In this teacher the boy found the qualities he sought, those of renunciation, celibacy and mastery of philosophy. Believing him to be a man of deep realization, Rajaram offered himself as disciple to this austere teacher, took initiation and received a new name, that of Brahma Chaitanya Brahmachari.

Along with his fellow *brahmacharin*, in surrendering to the rigours and demands of monkhood, Brahma Chaitanya derived great support and love from his *guru*. Dedication to the service of his master in time resulted in a special dispensation being accorded to him. Shri Krishnanand 'banished' the young lad from his *ashram* and ordered him to enter a *gupha* (cave) a few miles away. With only weekly visits to his teacher on the day of *Guruvar* (Thursday), the novice set about the task of attaining enlightenment. His fellow pupils, unaware of the real purpose behind his 'banishment' from their community, believed him to have upset their teacher in some way. At length Shri Krishnanand resolved to address this situation and therefore sent a senior *brahmachari* to seek out the novice and to enquire of him whether there might be some empty cave that the master could come to stay in. The reply came back that there was none.

On the next Thursday when Brahma Chaitanya returned as usual to the *ashram* in order to receive his teacher's blessings, he found himself very unpopular with his fellow *brahmacharin*. It was common knowledge that there were many empty caves thereabouts, so his message that there were no empty caves in which the *guru* might stay, had, not unreasonably, been interpreted by them as untrue and therefore gravely insulting. When they were all gathered before Swami Krishnanand, his fellow pupils couldn't wait for their teacher to punish his insolent behaviour. Surveying the assembly with his large penetrating eyes, Shri Krishnanand remained silent, as if unaware of the ill-feeling that had arisen amongst his disciples. One of them spoke up:

Maharaj, what penance, what atonement is prescribed for a person who disrespects his *Guru*? Disrespect amounts to contempt, does it not? How should such a man be treated who disrespects his *Guru*, shows contempt for him?[6]

The *guru* asked him to provide an example and the questioner hesitatingly revealed his motives for raising the issue. When he had finished, all eyes fell on Brahma Chaitanya and it became clear to him that he was required to speak. He explained that what he had said was the truth and further elaborated:

> Guruji, you do not live in houses made of stone and clay. You live subtly in
> the hearts of your devotees. Shricharan, all the space in my heart is already
> occupied by you.[7]

After his explanation, a prolonged silence fell upon the assembly, and
Brahma Chaitanya's fellow *brahmacharin* now understood something
of the depth of both question and answer. With the master's permission
the shamefaced and deflated pupils removed to their quarters, leaving
guru and *chela* alone.

It is recorded that by the age of twenty-five the runaway had become
fully established in the truth of his inner self and completed his study of
the scriptures. He set off from Uttar Kashi with the *guru* to stay at a
village close to Rishikesh. Here it is alleged that Shri Krishnanand
engaged himself in assisting life to return to a dead youth's body after it
had already been prepared for cremation.

The ensuing years found Brahma Chaitanya dwelling amidst deep,
dense forests pursuing the lifestyle of the religious renunciate that he
was. By habit he did not fraternize with others, least of all with women.
Stories abound bearing witness to his life of contemplation, his habitual
prayer and his crystal-clear thinking and there are even rumours, rich in
content, concerning miracle-working.

We catch up with the God-loving monk just after the turn of the
century, at the famous religious festival of Kumbh Mela in the city of
Allahabad, where his *guru* decided to ordain him formally into the order
of *sannyasin*. Here at Prayag, the confluence of the sacred rivers Ganga
and Saraswati, Brahmachari Brahma Chaitanya took the title of Shri
Swami Brahmanand Saraswati Maharaj and received the symbols of
swamihood, namely *kamaldalu* (a wooden pot) and *kaupeen* (loincloth).
Henceforth, dressed in the flame-coloured robe of his calling, he would
attract much attention as a venerated holy man, even though he was no
more than thirty-six years of age. Audience with him, though sought by
many, was granted only to the few who correctly interpreted his put-offs
as tests of earnestness and sincerity. Those in search of his *darshan* or
'holy look' would find themselves confronted by a hand-painted
message in Hindi reading *Aaj nahin milenge*, meaning 'Today we will
not meet'.[8] If visitors waited long enough, their patience would usually
be rewarded. It seems that on such occasions he would initiate enquirers
into secret *yoga* meditation techniques.

His fame spread, to such an extent that villagers desirous of his
blessings would even attempt to gather dust that his feet had touched.
For Swami Brahmanand, (Brahmanand or Brahmananda means

'Absolute bliss') the lure of the jungle, with its offer of protection and sustenance proved irresistible. A favourite haunt of his was a cave under a waterfall where, living a frugal existence, he practised his austerities. One of his fellow *swamis* sought him out:

> He used to live only on germinated gram seeds mixed with a little bit of salt. He lived on a hillock in a small natural cave near a mountain pool. I was led there by the villagers to that place, but I did not find anyone there and became disappointed. The next day I went again and found a few footprints on the edge of the pool made by his wooden sandals. I tried but I could not track the footprints. Finally on the fifth day of effort, early in the morning before sunrise, I went back to the pool and found him taking a bath. I greeted him saying, '*Namo Narayan*', which is a commonly used salutation among swamis meaning, 'I bow to the divinity in you.' He was observing silence so he motioned for me to follow him to his small cave and I did so gladly. This was the eighth day of his silence, and after staying the night with him, he broke his silence and I gently spoke to him about the purpose of my visit. I wanted to know how he was living and the ways and methods of his spiritual practices.[9]

Such was his spiritual magnetism that some nurtured the hope that he would some day hold a religious post and therefore become more accessible. When offered the immensely prestigious position of Shankaracharya of Jyotir Math, northern India (one of the four key positions in the Hindu faith), he outrightly refused it. Again and again attempts were made to persuade him to accept the *gaddi* (throne) of Jyotir Math that had not been filled in well over a century. The prerequisites for this office are highly exclusive -candidates must be Brahmin by birth and life-long celibates, they must have a profound knowledge of the religious scriptures and be of Indian birth, and they must live in a state of enlightenment.

The passing years produced no change in Swami Brahmanand's refusal of the position of Shankaracharya. In spite of this he acquired many devotees and inspired many to follow a spiritual life. His relationship with his master, Shri Krishnanand, had long since outgrown the formalities of *guru* and *chela* and instead had become transformed into one of mutual regard, each insisting that the other be accorded the greater respect. This did not prevent the silver-haired Shri Krishnanand from urging his fellow *mahatma* to become less reclusive and to share his spiritual knowledge with the masses.

Swami Brahmanand, whilst following his inner stream of inspiration, would occasionally surface in the midst of some town or other, and after becoming ensconced in a devotee's accommodation he would again immerse himself in prayer and meditation. Chances to glimpse him, let alone talk to him, were rare and highly sought after. In Jabalpur in central India there lived one Raj Varma, an photographer and artist, who like many before him, was repeatedly rebuffed before gaining audience with the *swami*. In the ensuing months Raj's nephew also expressed a desire to visit the wandering hermit. He was more fortunate, for when the occasion arose, access was readily provided and, laying eyes on the robust-looking *swami*, he became convinced that here he had found his *guru*.

It is said that Mahesh Prasad Varma (aka M C Srivastava) was born on Friday, 12 January 1917 into a comfortably well-off family, the third of four children. As an infant, Mahesh would have submitted to the customary shaving of the head and the writing (with honey upon a golden pen-nib) of the syllable *om* upon his tongue. It is likely that his father's name was also Prasad for according to custom a new-born male child bears his father's name in addition to his own. Likely also is that he is of the *Kshatriya* (warrior or 'protector') caste, with his father believed to have been a minor official in the Department of Forestry. Although it is thought by many that Mahesh's family hail from Jabalpur, it has been suggested that he was in fact born some little distance away in the village of Chichli, near Gadawara in Madhya Pradesh, some 150 kilometres east of Bhopal.

As a boy Mahesh would have felt the love of his family as his father and mother, uncles and aunts in turn took him upon their knee, generously sharing their sweets and affection. There were stories for 'little Mahesh' to hear, tales of gods and demons, saints and *gurus*, and of people rich and poor. Of these stories, those concerning the mischievous god-child Krishna and the virtuous deeds of god-prince Rama would both have been firm favourites. From these tales the cultural values that were the boy's birthright became transferred, absorbed and reinforced. Mahesh was later to reflect on the process whereby personal values become cultivated:

> The children in India are told when you get up you bow down to your mother, you bow down to your father, you bow down to your elders. You go to the temple, you bow down to the Deity. You go to school, you bow down to your teacher.
>
> It provides a great shield of security and assistance from all quarters for the child to grow on right lines with great energy, with great intelligence, with great accomplishment, very great. And these feelings of love for mother and love for father supported by this ritual of bowing down, this later on develops in devotion to Almighty Great Father.[10]

In this regime of worshipful obedience, what chance of forgiveness could a child hope for should his behaviour become less than impeccable? Some reassurance could be derived from the much-loved stories of Krishna, the mischief-making boy who so easily won the hearts of everyone. When Krishna stole his mother's butter she tied him to a tree. Someone offered to free him, but he refused, preferring to wait for his mother. Perhaps that is how it was for Mahesh:

> It is the love of a mother for her child that makes her look kindly upon his mistakes. In fact, a mother enjoys the mistakes of the child because, when he commits a mistake, she is able to give him more of her love. In that love, the child grows to be better able to overcome the weakness of committing mistakes.[11]

It is said that Mahesh was possessed of a naturally cheerful disposition, but he was later to recall:

> This has been the one question in my mind ever since I was young: God is omnipresent and God is almighty and God is merciful and in the heart of everyone, why should a man suffer having God within himself? And what is the value of oneself if he keeps suffering?[12]

The growing tide of modernity sweeping the world brought with it incitement to disobedience. The cultivation of 'free thinking' was a concept greatly valued by Westerners, but of dubious value to the highly organized structure of traditional Indian society. The suspicion was that political awareness could lead to a weakening in religious values and possibly, given time, it's eventual destruction. The dilemma that faced the educated classes was how they might gain the material advantages of 'progress' without losing their highly valued spiritual culture. Mahesh's parents faced the situation boldly and made sure that he received an above-average education. In a country where English quite literally ruled, they saw to it that he mastered not only the native language but that of the Raj too. Evidently he showed a certain promise in the scientific disciplines, although, as with many other students, the ancient language of Sanskrit posed difficulties for him. Offered the rare opportunity to engage in higher education, he undertook degree courses in both physics and mathematics at Allahabad University. It appears that he was registered there under a different name, that of M C Srivastava – (M C, in all probability stands for Mahesh Chandra). Quite why Mahesh is known by two names, Mahesh Prasad Varma and M C Srivastava, is difficult to establish. But, maybe the rumour is correct which suggests that Mahesh left his family home early in life and, since he appears to have maintained close links with both his Uncle Raj R P Varma and his nephew Girish Chandra Varma, it might be speculated that it was with their family that he spent some of his childhood, perhaps temporarily assuming the family name?

But, now at university, the acquisition of so much information only accentuated his hunger for deeper fulfilment:

> I was completely dissatisfied with what I studied in college. Because I knew – this can't be the whole knowledge. I was searching for something complete whereby I could understand everything.[13]

Perhaps it is true, as some say, that he then took to working at a local factory for a brief period, but it is clear that he had also become enamoured with the subject of *yoga*. Even amongst the most worldly and irreligious of Indian people there is a desire to hear stories of saints and miracle workers. In the busy life of material advancement that Mahesh was witness to, time could always be found to contemplate ideas concerning God and religion, and to hear stories about miracle-working holy men.

> One day someone in the street whispered to me, 'There has come a great saint, but he does not want to be known by the people. If you wish, then we shall go quietly one night.' I said, 'There could be nothing better than that.'[14]

Such was the magic of this 'saint' that just one look at the glowing silent face of Swami Brahmanand had this young man immediately enthralled. He returned again and again, making daily visits all the while the *swami* remained there.

> Then Guru Dev was gone back to the lonely forests ... those who knew him were strictly prohibited to tell others his whereabouts.[15]

Market places in India throng with vitality. The scents of fresh vegetables, fruits and freshly gathered spices, blend with the fragrance of burning *dhoop* (incense) and wood smoke from restaurants and *chaay* (tea) stalls to produce an exotic aroma. The sounds of the barking voices of traders calling attention to their wares, the tinkling cycle bells, the vain hooting of a car demanding the right of way, mixes with the creaking of horse *tangas* (taxis) and groaning grinding heavily laden ox-carts. One particular market place, on one particular day, was busier than usual, thronged with expectant, eager local citizens, swelled by people from out of town. The air crackled with electricity, for not only was this the monsoon season, when at any moment a torrent of rain might fall, but something even rarer, an event of a lifetime, was drawing ever closer.

The occasion that the growing mass of people awaited was the chance to take *darshan* of the Shankaracharya of northern India, the newly appointed head of the Hindu faith. Their religious life had for a century, perhaps even longer, been without its major representative. Amongst the crowd, craning his neck for a glimpse of the parade, could be seen the chubby, expectant features of young Mahesh. It was now some three months since he had met Swami Brahmanand and received his blessings and guidance. On seeing him again, draped in a saffron-coloured silk robe and clutching the sceptre of his office, Mahesh set his heart on becoming his disciple. The young physicist had chosen to turn over the coin of knowledge and examine the spiritual side of existence. What better choice of *guru* could he make than this revered holy man who shunned all personal glory, having no interest in matters of power or material wealth?

Later, the procession over, Mahesh returned home to announce his intention of leaving to become a disciple to the Shankaracharya. This monumental decision, to become a monk and renounce his kith and kin and presumably all prospects of a lucrative career, apparently threw his family into great confusion. When later asked if his parents had not wanted another career for him, he replied:

> I think this is common in the parents. It all depends ... that their son should live happily, and happiness is – he should have the comfort of a home and good family and he should live all the joys, and he should not go to the Himalayas where there is nothing and where will he sleep and do what he has to do and all that ... because monks' life is a very hard life. No home, nothing, nothing – you sleep under the trees and meditate in the caves or wherever, whatever. So there is nothing definite in the life of a monk, particularly in India. Here in the west the monks are more organized and the church is there and they take care of it, but in India when one leaves home – he doesn't take care of himself, because he has no means to take care. He is out of society; no one asks him to do some work and pays him wages or anything – nothing. So now he is all in the faith of God – now that he is left with just his faith. So the life of a monk is a very very hard life. Therefore the parents don't generally like the children to take such hardships now – out of love.[16]

Swami Brahmanand insisted that before accepting Mahesh as a disciple he must fulfil two preconditions: he should complete his studies at university; and more importantly he should receive parental permission before joining him. An eligible bachelor with very good prospects, Mahesh was set to take up a wife and a profession. His father therefore listened to the Shankaracharya with extreme reservations but at length reluctantly consented to his son's departure.

2

---★---

HIMALAYAN HERMITAGE

It might be wondered why Mahesh's *guru*, Swami Brahmanand, had finally been persuaded to take the mantle of Shankaracharya when for twenty years he had steadfastly refused to succumb. The simple answer is that he was not persuaded.

Long, long ago, some say as long ago as 2,500 years, came one who was to be known as Adi Shankara. To him is attributed the mass spiritual reawakening of the people of India at that time. At the age of thirty-three, just before departing from his earthly body, he arranged for the future management of religious guidance by setting up a *math* (monastery) at each point of the compass. The first of these was headed by his disciple Trottakacharya and located at Jyotir Math (modern-day Joshimath) in the Garhwal Himalayas. Shankara is said by believers to have been the incarnation of the god Shiva (also known as Shankar), the only incarnation in human form. Lord Shiva is perceived as Lord of the *Yogis* and worshipped by many anchorites of this discipline. Shiva has many names or epithets, amongst them that of Mahesh (Sanskrit for 'Great Lord' or 'God'). The naming of children in India is taken very seriously and a *pandit* is generally consulted for the purpose. Contemplation of one's own name is thought to encourage specific desirable qualities and tendencies if it has been correctly chosen It is of note that Swami Brahmanand's name at birth was Rajaram (King Rama) and as he grew older he took to the chant of 'Ram *naam satya hai'*.

Adi Shankara, in setting up the *maths* had produced reference points at which the wandering *sadhus* and *swamis* might congregate. It has been suggested that the favoured movement of such people should be in a circular flow, forever passing through the lives of everyday folks or *grihasthas* (householders). It is clear that with the lapse in the lineage of Jyotir Math, coinciding as it did with British rule, the plans of Shankara had been upset, leading to religious and moral decline. All this was known to Swami Brahmanand, no doubt, but though possessing the necessary credentials for office, he preferred to remain in the quietude and anonymity of forests and jungles. Nevertheless the requests had continued. In fact, by 1941 the situation was set to come to a head. Through the efforts of two *swamis*, Gyanandji and Karpatri, pressure was brought to bear on him to comply with their wishes. It surprised all concerned when he appeared to yield. Accordingly arrangements were immediately made to bring about his installation. Only two days before the great event, he did his second significant disappearing trick (the first having been on the eve of his marriage). Taking the seat of Shankara could make incalculable demands on him, and perhaps this was why he so unceremoniously slipped the net. There was much consternation at his conduct, but rather than look elsewhere for a substitute, the celebrations were merely postponed.

When Swami Brahmanand re-emerged in Benares some three weeks later, news of his return brought the representatives running to him, begging for his co-operation. On this occasion he neither accepted nor rejected their offers. No agreements were made, he remained silent. However, since he had not disagreed, the plans for his investiture were re-instituted and out of expediency commenced without delay. The traditional rites were brief but complete. As of Tuesday, 1 April 1941 the nation had as head of Jyotir Math, Badrikashram, Himalayas, the highly respected Jagadguru Shrimad Swami Brahmanand Saraswati Maharaj Ji. Seated within a palanquin atop a mature elephant he allowed himself to be paraded before the people and, it is said, at a conference held in his honour that he was given an outstanding reception. The Maharajah of Darbhanga delivered a speech extolling the *swami's* greatness and amidst the celebrations, with the chanting of hymns in full swing, a feeling of great optimism settled and enveloped those gathered there. For those present it seemed as though a new era were dawning in the history of the Indian people.

During the first months of his ministry, Swami Brahmanand (or 'Guru Dev' – *dev* meaning 'divine' – as many of his disciples addressed him) made a tour of southern India and on his return attended the religious ceremony of Maharudra *yagya*, convened in Madhya Pradesh. Shortly thereafter he took on a new disciple, young Mahesh, complete with degrees in physics and mathematics.

Mahesh's Uncle Raj offered this insight into his nephew's enthusiasm and commitment for his new life with the Shankaracharya:

> He came to the ashram as a youth bubbling over with mirth, full of energy and joy of living. He became so devoted to his master in everything ...
> At night he lay down outside Guru Dev's door.[17]

This vision of the new disciple's devotion to his teacher is echoed in the Maharishi's own recollections.

> Right from the beginning the whole purpose was just to breathe in his breath. This was my ideal. The whole purpose was just to attune myself with Guru Dev, and that was all I wanted to do.18

In undertaking to serve as a disciple, together with the usual vows of service and celibacy he took a new name, that of Bal Brahmachari Mahesh. The relationship of *guru* and *chela*, an ancient time-honoured Indian tradition, is not entered lightly, for the *guru*, in accepting a pupil, assumes responsibility for his welfare. In addition to offering material security he is also expected to render such guidance and assistance as might bring about the latter's spiritual advancement. In return for this total support, the *chela* commits himself completely, dedicating his every thought, word and action to God and *guru*. Demanding and serious though this relationship most certainly is, it is not an act of total renunciation for the disciple. According to tradition those wishing to renounce material existence (and its attachments) fully are initiated into the order of *sannyasin*. Only after taking the vow of *sannyas* is the title of *swami* conferred.

A pressing task for the new Shankaracharya was to address the problem of reconstructing the monastery in the township of Joshimath, which had been destroyed by an earthquake in 1851-2. Before dealing with the rebuilding programme, a primary problem lay in gaining repossession of the Jyotishpeeth land. In this matter the new Shankaracharya was assisted by Sir Joseph Clay, the former Deputy-Commissioner of Garhwal Himalayas and adviser to the Secretary of State. On a hill situated between snow-clad Himalayan peaks lay the ruins of the former monastery, and in the grounds, the ancient mulberry tree (surviving to this day) which Adi Shankara is supposed to have planted with his own hands. Beneath the roots of this now vast tree is the cave or *gupha* which served as his hermitage. Adjacent to this and a little way down the hill, lies the cave of his disciple Trottakacharya, whom Adi Shankara nominated as the first Shankaracharya. On the site of the original monastery an attractive, simple thirty-room structure came to be built. In addition to this work, the construction of a temple in the monastery grounds was completed at the behest of the Maharajah of Darbhanga.

A photograph in Raj Varma's possession shows Swami Brahmanand with his disciples gathered around him. The master sits cross-legged in a simple wooden armchair 'throne', his hair now a few inches long. To one side of him, a man with splendid beard and turban (perhaps a

Gurkha soldier), attired in military-style tunic and bearing a fearsome-looking shotgun over one shoulder, stands guard. The *chelas* vary in age from about eighteen to eighty. Brahmachari Mahesh stands amongst them; clad in white dhoti (sheet) with a shawl around his shoulders.

Although the Shankaracharya was not openly accessible, an audience with him was now generally easier to secure. Gone were the days when the best that could be hoped for was a glimpse of him or the rare opportunity to attend the half-hour prayer evenings he conducted. Now all who took the trouble to find him could partake of his *darshan* and attend his brief lectures.

Joshimath at a height of 6,500 ft, is a halting point for pilgrims undertaking the strenuous circuit of *Uttarakhand Yatra*, a tour of holy places in that region of the Himalayas. Whilst en route to Badrinath, a principal Hindu shrine to the god Vishnu, many pilgrims also wish to pay homage to the Shankaracharya *Gaddi* 'Seat of Shankara'. After the arduous climb towards the monastery, and observing the venerated caves on the way, visitors would make their way on past the small shrine dedicated to the goddess Purnagiri Devi. After making the breathtaking ascent they would arrive at the *math*, climb the stairs at the front of the low, long, two-storey building and be welcomed into a small hall. On a highly polished wooden throne, low and wide, beautifully carved with flowers and Sanskritic texts, and strewn about with cushions, sat the upright figure of the Shankaracharya upon his deerskin. On the walls of the hall large mirrors had been carefully placed, reflecting not only the many adjacent vases of flowers but also the images of visitors as they presented themselves.

Prominently displayed at the entrance to the building, a signboard warned newcomers against trying to offer donations Those perplexed at this unusual request were only more confused on learning that the Shankaracharya's ever-expanding title had been supplemented and prefixed by the words *Ananta Shri Vibhushit*, that is to say 'Bestowed with Infinite Wealth'. A contemporary spiritual teacher, Swami Rama, himself well respected, confirms that Swami Brahmanand was 'unaffected by worldly temptations and distractions'.[19] This assertion finds ample support in the tale of a visit by the Shankaracharya, to the city of Kanpur, when he exhorted those wishing to make offerings, 'I am not one to be satisfied with offerings of rupees and paisas, which are like dust and pebbles to me. Offer to me bagfuls of your vices.'[20]

As a master he was no less uncompromising, as the following account indicates. Brahmachari Mahesh was given an errand to run. His *guru* requested that he urgently run to a location high up and far away (probably to distant Tapoban where the *siddhas*, those with supernatural powers, are said to live), in order that he might deliver a message to a saint who dwelt there. On arriving, the breathless and exhausted disciple waited for the reply. The saint, after reading the message, merely bid him return quickly to his *guru*. Many times did the *brahmachari* find himself on such a mission and on one such occasion, as a result of his undue haste, he tripped and fell. After dusting himself down, he stooped to recover his *guru's* precious message, only to find it had become unsealed. Curiosity gained the better of him and he read it. The message said simply: 'Please instruct this *brahmachari* to return immediately.' One can imagine the novice s amazement as he read this. But how did the *brahmachari* interpret this seemingly purposeless service to his teacher?

> The disciple adjusts his likes and dislikes to the likes and dislikes of The Master, thereby elevating his mind to the status of the master's mind. In this nothing matters except obedience.[21]

For two and a half years Brahmachari Mahesh made it his single-minded task to perfectly attune himself to his master's every wish and whim, for in so doing, he no doubt hoped to acquire his own enlightenment. In time, Swami Brahmanand, apparently pleased with his disciple's spiritual progress, granted him permission to retire to a cave in order to practice his *sadhana* (spiritual discipline) in seclusion.

Swami Brahmanand's description of the spiritual search for oneness was captured on a 'wire' recording:

> The heart went to find *Paramatma* (God) and finished there and caught, and caught for sure.
>
> As if you send a sculpture of salt into the ocean to measure. Or say to this sculpture, "Go and measure!" that, "How deep is the ocean?", "What is the depth?"
>
> So that sculpture can go easily but it will not come back.
>
> There is no difficulty to go but there is difficulty to come back. As it goes to ocean it dissolves. Who will come back when the seeker experiences how / how much is *Paramatma?*
>
> How is it possible for the soul speak of *Paramatma* if *Paramatma* has not been seen?

The Shankaracharya's outward appearance had by now radically altered; his hair, brushed back from his forehead, was now grown long, and he had grown his beard, a full and resplendent growth. From the rare photographs and surviving amateur film footage, glimpses can be gained of his demeanour. Although more frequently caught in solemn mood, there is evidence that he could display a radiant smile and project a lively sense of fun and jollity – an enigmatic combination, perhaps indicating two facets of the same reality, on the one side projecting his inner serenity, on the other his joy of outer existence. He made sure that life was not all duty and tests for his *brahmacharin*; time was also given over to the study of the scriptures, prayer, contemplation and meditation.

In the role of Shankaracharya, Swami Brahmanand performed the function of a religious teacher, bringing out the essence of the traditional Hindu teachings for his flock. It has been said that when the *swami* met sincere seekers he would sometimes initiate them into the mysteries of *yoga* meditation. These teachings were necessarily passed on in a climate of faith and worship, although the precise form of the meditation is uncertain. Reconciling the devotional nature of Hinduism with its myriad forms of God, its multiple and varied forms of worship with the rigors of objective science must have forced Brahmachari Mahesh to more than once ponder that 'man cannot serve two masters'. However, it would be unwise to infer that the techniques the *swami* taught could only survive in a framework of religiosity. It would be equally incautious to assume the opposite. In point of fact a 'science' of the worlds of both matter and spirit has long been studied in India, although quite how closely this discipline accords with modern science is a subject for debate. But before dismissing it, we should at least be aware of our debt in the field of mathematics, for the so-called 'Arab' numerals which we use every day in point of fact originated in India.

The word *Veda* means knowledge, as does the word science. According to many, the *Rig Veda* is said to be the oldest record of human thought, and though its Aryan authors were once believed to be of European extraction, Indians have steadfastly held the *Vedas* as their own. Descriptions of the geophysical environment in which this civilization dwelt offer much support for this latter contention. A key area of Vedic science is in its classification of energy and matter in terms of *gunas* or qualities: *sattvic* (pure), *rajasic* (energetic) and *tamasic* (impure). It is still common practice in India to refer to foods according to this code, hence *tamasic* food would be that which is over-cooked or over-processed, while *rajasic* would be most appetising and tasty, highly seasoned and spiced, but low in nutrients. A *sattvic* diet would naturally include fresh fruit and vegetables, pulse foods, cereals and dairy produce.

When the Shankaracharya was out pursuing his missionary work, the running of the *math* fell to those *swamis* who remained behind. In winter milk was virtually unobtainable, for the cattle were taken to the lower mountain reaches. Fruit and vegetables were scarce too, so that the *swamis*, living their *sattvic* lives out on the mountainside without the conveniences of delicatessens or supermarkets, had to make do on very little. From Herbert Tichy, the European explorer and mountaineer, we gain this insight:

> In Yoshimath the Sherpa Nima and I fought a cheerful but obstinately contested battle with the aged priest Govindanand. For several weeks we had shared the Spartan life of the hermits, eating neither vegetables nor fruit, and we craved vitamins. The bazaar at Yoshimath could supply only onions and garlic, but with these we were content. When the appetising savor of the rice with onions which Nima had prepared spread through the building, however, Govindanand burst into our cell in a rage. Did we not know, he asked, that onions were an 'apple of voluptuousness,' strictly forbidden in the monastery?
>
> No, we did not know it, and we had no voluptuous desires whatever. Hostilities ensued, ending with our eating the onions, which we really did not want to forgo, raw and at a safe distance from the monastery, although this did not diminish the sinful smell that emanated from us. Nevertheless, we departed in peace and with the priest's blessing.[22]

Perhaps we should ask ourselves what had provoked the young Mahesh to give up the comfort and ease of his former life in exchange for such austerities. In later years he was many times to describe the 'Flash' of his 'Guru Dev's' presence. But was this personal magnetism the sole reason for submitting himself to a life of physical and mental endurance (it is recorded that for five years he had to abstain from the use of salt)? We find an answer in the statement made many years later, when he claimed his life only truly began nineteen years before, when he learned the secret of 'swift and deep meditation'. This indicates that even before he became a *brahmachari*, Swami Brahmanand had instructed him in a technique of meditation. It would appear that on receipt of this teaching he became a changed man, so much so that he cut himself off from his former life in order to be with his benefactor.

The location of Jyotir Math was such as to deter all but the most ardent pilgrims from journeying there to take *darshan* of the ancient temples of their forefathers. Periodically the Shankaracharya would, with a few close helpers, take to travelling about the towns of the local districts. Transport for himself and his entourage presented no less a problem than for those intent on pilgrimage to the local shrines of Kedarnath and Badrinath. The solution which was found for conveying the party was, to say the least, novel. Instead of using a small bus or van, a large chassis was obtained and customized. The resultant float or

'Popemobile' (the comparison is a reasonable one), on which the enthroned *swami* could travel amidst a rich array of foliage and flowers, was used as a mobile dais, with space enough for a handful of disciples and a very careful driver.

These excursions gave one and all the chance to partake of the Shankaracharya's *darshan*, and thousands came to see him seated in his silk ochre robe, with his austere gaze, his bleach white beard, his long dark hair intermingled with the garlands of fresh flowers draped around his neck. He would always sit on a throne gilded and carved with images of lions on the arms of the seat. To ward off the glare of the sun, an umbrella shade was placed over him, fashioned from red velvet with intricate patterns, religious symbols and text, executed in golden stitching. His forehead was daubed with sandalwood paste, a measure intended to lessen the effects of the heat, and when the vehicle halted, his disciples brought out yak whisks to cool him. Many of the general populace also took the opportunity to obtain the blessing of *tilak* (a mixture of sandalwood paste, rice and red dye) anointed upon the forehead. On his mission of spiritual revival, he travelled far and wide, presiding over many ceremonies, conferences and the like.

Quotations from Swami Brahmanand were collected together and a selection of them were published by the ashram under the title *Amrita-Kana* (Ambrosia Drop) in 1950, the compilation was accredited to 'Balbrahmachari Shri Maheshji'. Many years later when Raj Varma published a book entitled '*Strange Facts About a Great Saint*' – an English language version of Rameshwar Tiwari's biography of Swami Brahmanand – he included English translations of a cluster of quotations from *Amrita Kana*:

> Having become a devotee of God one can never remain unhappy anywhere. This is our experience.

> The *Jiva* has been going on doing its work from several births. Its tendency to work exists since times immemorial. Therefore, if the work is just started with a little co-operation of the mind, it will continue to go on just like the railway wagon moving a long way off, if it is just jerked and pushed by the engine.

> It is necessary to bifurcate the work of the mind as main and secondary. Thinking of God (*Paramatma*) should be considered as main and giving a little co-operation to carrying on worldly activities (*vyavahara*) as secondary.

> Apply your body and wealth mainly, and your mind secondarily, to run the *vyavahara*.

When the mind is mainly engaged in thinking of God, you shall receive His grace. God is all-powerful (*sarva shaktiman*). Even a little of His grace is capable of bestowing on the Jiva all that is good in its entirety.

The declaration of the Lord that is proved by the Vedic Scriptures is this: "Whosoever thinks of me with one-pointed devotion, I shall conduct his necessary worldly activities also." The experience of the *bhaktas* also goes to prove this declaration of the Lord.

Accumulate wealth (*artha*); but in such a way that it is not against ultimate good (*Paramartha*). That which hinders *Paramartha* and results in accumulation of sin is not wealth (*artha*) but the negation of wealth (*anartha*).

"'As is the cloth so is the price." For carrying on the short-lived activities of *vyavahara*, employ your short-lived body and wealth. Mind is a permanent thing which remains with you always. Even in the other world, it will continue to stay with you. Therefore, connect it with a permanent thing. God, being the eternal existence both in animate and inanimate things, is the only permanent thing of the highest order. Connect your mind with Him.

If the mind is satisfied with wealth, wife or children, why does it go elsewhere? Because, it cannot stick on to anything. From this it is clear, it is not satisfied with anything of this mundane world. It runs after things taking them to be good and desirable but after a short while it leaves them.

Nobody wants your mind in this world and mind also is not satisfied with anything of this world.

The mind is not fit for the world nor the world for the mind.

When the mind realises God, it is permanently established there and shall not desire for other things. From this we can understand that God alone is fit for the mind and nothing else.

Keep this in mind, that your mind which is not wanted by anybody in this world is useful to take you near God.

Therefore, in this market place of the world carry on *vyavahara* with your body and wealth and allow your mind to go towards God. Then your *vyavahara* in this world will get on well and the path to *Parmarth* will also be clear

People are unhappy because they do not have a chosen deity (*Ishta*). Without *Ishta*, people are turning out to be orphans.

It is only the *Ishta* that saves one from *anishta* (untoward happenings).

See your *Ishta* as all-pervading. That is one-pointed devotion (*ananyatha*).

Of the five Deities – Shankara, Vishnu (Ram, Krishna), Surya, Ganesha and

Devi, whosoever is more adorable to you, the *mantra* of that Deity should be repeated by you every day.

You must get to know the *mantra* of your *Ishta*, and the method of meditation (*dhyan*) thereof, through an experienced *Sadguru* and somehow or other, devote some time every day in *japa* of the *Ishta mantra* and *dhyan*. Through *japa*, realisation (*siddhi*) will result. There is no doubt about this. "*japaat siddhirjapaat siddhirnasanshayaah.*"

See your *Ishta* everywhere. There should be no place where your *Ishta* is not seen.

It is absolutely difficult to get the vision of your *Ishta* until and unless you get one-pointedness on your *Ishta*. To cure a disease, both medicine (*oushada*) and dietary restriction (*pathya*) are necessary. To cure the disease of restlessness of mind, *abhyasa* (spiritual practice) is *oushada* and *vairagya* (non-attachment) is *pathya*.

To apply your mind to your *Ishta* is *abhyasa*. To constantly think of *Ishta*, meditate on it, talk always about it, and think always about it, this is *abhyasa*. When the mind is engrossed in the *Ishta*, non-attachment automatically comes. Therefore, we say you need to become a person having attachment (*ragi*). That is to say, there is need for the mind to develop attachment to the Ishta.

After long periods spent in service, seclusion, study and meditation, Brahmachari Mahesh considered himself sufficiciently well attuned to his master's thoughts as to take upon himself the role of private secretary and dealt with the majority of correspondence without recourse to his 'Guru Dev'. It is said that sometimes he would even be sent to some distant town or village to lecture on the scriptures. His Uncle Raj says:

> I can say straight out that Maharishi was Guru Dev's favourite disciple and no wonder – few are capable of such work and few have such unending loyalty.[23]

The Shankaracharya attracted eminent visitors. Dr S. Radhakrishnan, the famous Indian philosopher, sought guidance at his feet, as did the first President of India, Dr Rajendra Prasad, who addressed him as 'Vedanta Incarnate' or 'The embodiment of the scriptures'. A photograph taken in December 1952 shows the President standing beside the barefoot Mahesh. Brahmachari Mahesh, was later to describe his master thus:

> His entire personality exhaled always the serene perfume of spirituality.

> His face radiated that rare light which comprises love, authority, serenity and

self-assuredness; the state that comes only by righteous living and Divine
realization.

His spiritual teachings are simple and clear and go straight home to the
heart. He strictly adhered to the courses of inner development laid down by
the systems of Indian Philosophy and ethic...[24]

Photographs taken at this time show the Shankaracharya to have aged
considerably, his health having for some time given cause for much
concern. Homeopathic and allopathic (Western) medicines were
administered to him but were of no avail, and he declined rapidly. At
1.15 pm on Wednesday, 20 May 1953, after a period of five minutes
absorbed in silent meditation, Shankaracharya Swami Brahmanand
Saraswati breathed his last. Hours before his death he allegedly
summoned Brahmachari Mahesh and explained to him that, as a dying
father's unfinished business is dealt with by his sons, the same is true
for the *guru* and his *chela*. Raj Varma claims that his *guru* directed
Mahesh to:

> ... look around. Many people are dejected. There is a lack of energy in their
> minds. Their minds are not strong enough. What I have taught you also
> contains the knowledge of the technique for the householder, which has been
> misinterpreted and forgotten during the centuries.[25]

After further deliberation on this topic, the elderly swami is supposed to
have added these words of reassurance:

> Don't think of money for travelling here and there. Don't worry and don't be
> afraid of being alone and don't be anxious about anything. Begin working
> and everything will go by itself.[26]

It is said that only after the *swami* had told the young *brahmachari* of
his future work were instructions concerning his last rites then
communicated.

After his death, still seated in the lotus position, he was taken to
Calcutta railway station and transported to Benares, where at
Kedareshwar Mahadev he was committed to the waters of the Ganges:

> The chest was lowered into the Ganga. Brahmachari Mahesh Yogi dived
> alongside and retained a touch of the precious container till it finally came to
> rest on the riverbed. Reverently, he bowed and surfaced again, sharing the
> agony perceptible in the faces surrounding him.[27]

After Swami Brahmanand's untimely death, people were left wondering
who, if anyone, would be appointed in his stead. On Friday, 12 June
1953, according to the will of Swami Brahmanand, his close disciple Sri

Swami Shantanand Saraswati Ji Maharaj was installed as successor to the throne of Shankaracharya.

It will be observed that one of the preconditions of entitlement to the post of Shankaracharya is to be born a Brahmin. Brahmachari Mahesh, being of the Kayastha caste, was not eligible to hold this venerated office, even if he had fulfilled all of the other criteria. In the event Brahmachari Mahesh took leave of the monastery and 'retired to the caves of the 'Valley of the Saints' in Uttar Kashi, high in the Himalayas'.[28] Uttar Kashi (northern place of Shiva) is a town some way north of Rishikesh, frequented by pilgrims on their way to Gangotri, the source of the River Ganges. The town contains numerous temples, of which the largest and most impressive is Vishwanath Mandir, an old-fashioned market place, shops and artisans but few dwellings. The rest are situated across the river and in the hills to each side of the valley. The local populace live a traditional life, preparing their food seated on the broad verandas of their simple wooden-beamed homes and storing foodstuffs for their few animals in hayricks in the upper branches of trees. Overhead fly the crows and large birds of prey: kestrels and even eagles. In former times wild animals roamed, making it unsafe for anyone to venture out after dark.

It was in this remote and ancient place that Swami Brahmanand had found his *guru* and taken initiation into the mysteries of *yoga*. The town is renowned for its community of scholars, *sadhus*, *swamis* and *mahatmas*, most of whom live in an area known as Gyan Suu. Here, where the sight of holy men and saints is considered commonplace, Brahmachari Mahesh, covered only with his loose long black hair and simple white robe would not have attracted much attention. The destination he sought lay on the outskirts of town, an *ashram* by the name of Sri Shankaracharya Gyan Mandir. Located a comfortable distance from the main Rishikesh-Gangotri road and bordering the gurgling Bhagirathi River (an alternative name for the sacred River Ganges), the *ashram* is situated within reasonably spacious grounds whose perimeters are lined with trees (some of them yielding bananas and oranges) which provide a screen from the neighbouring lands. On the sandy banks of the crystal-clear waters of the Ganges, people wash themselves and their clothes, but the river has exacted payment in that over the years successive monsoons have swollen its waters, resulting in significant loss of land to the *ashram*.

The focus of the buildings of Gyan Mandir 'Knowledge Temple' is an impressive shrine, a *Shivalinga* (ancient symbol of the forces of creativity). Surrounding the temple are the buildings containing simple whitewashed cells which provide accommodation for inmates and occasional visitors. A few also contain a *gupha* or cave below floor level.

Having arrived at Gyan Mandir, Mahesh committed himself to prolonged spells of deep silence.

> Where I stay in a small Ashram in Uttar Kashi, the cave is like a very small basement under a room. The entrance is through an opening only big enough for one person to enter. Down there is quiet. No sound. Cool in summer. Warm in winter.[29]

Amongst the hermits thereabouts the prevailing attitude was (and still is) abstention from everyday mundane cares. Seeking direct contact with God or Brahman is believed to be the only worthwhile activity and any deviation is perceived as wasted energy. Brahmachari Mahesh was to spend many months in solitude in his sandy cave. If he wanted to sleep he had only to take to the bed that lay directly above the cave. He would come out only to take exercise, to deal with the normal bodily functions or take the occasional meal which a man from the town would bring and leave outside his door.

For most of the *brahmachari's* time at Uttar Kashi he kept his own company. On those rare occasions when he took companionship it was with a fellow truth-seeker, and even then, more often than not they would spend the time in silence. 'We hardly ever spoke ... After all, there was really nothing to talk about.'[30] After years of devoted service to his master, he had to acclimatize himself to life without the *swami's* living presence. He pursued his *sadhana* and in spite of the isolation (or perhaps because of it), he began to entertain the notion of travel.

He had a friend who came to visit, an extremely elderly monk who wore his hair so long that it trailed along the ground behind him. This growth became burdensome to him and he therefore decided to cut it, preferring a scalp both shorn and shaven. On hearing of the younger man's hankering for travel the old man set about explaining why there was no advantage in leaving the confines of Uttar Kashi. 'This is holy ground,' his companion said. 'All the rest is just mud.'[31] On that note the subject was firmly closed. However Mahesh's wish to travel persisted.

> When I mentioned to him a few weeks later he said, 'I think you have been thinking of it for so long. Why not get rid of this thought, and get rid of this thought means go there and come back and never think of it again.' When he said that, this purpose of not returning or returning didn't come to my mind. But at least he responded to that idea which was coming to my mind – go to Rameshvaram, go to Rameshvaram.[32]

As a *brahmachari*, Mahesh had become used to taking instructions (both implicit and explicit) and must therefore have found it difficult to take responsibility for his own actions. The great wide world, spurned during study under his master, now awaited his return. He might have chosen any destination, but his thought had been to visit Rameshvaram, a place of religious pilgrimage in southern India. With the required permission, Mahesh was soon to commence his journey.

3

---- ★ ----

'THE MAHARISHI' EMERGES

After the year and a half or so spent in seclusion at Gyan Mandir, Brahmachari Mahesh took to the road in order to follow his inspiration to visit southern India. His destination was very close to Sri Lanka, and is renowned for its religious atmosphere, drawing pilgrims from all over the subcontinent. After touring around the temples and holy shrines of Rameshvaram, the lone hermit moved down to the southernmost peninsula of Cape Comorin to spend time at Kannyakumari. From the temple there, he then travelled some way northwards into the state of Kerala, to the coastal town of Trivandrum in search of yet another place of worship. Whilst walking toward the temple of Guruvayur Krishna Mandir in Trivandrum, the footloose traveller sensed that someone was following close behind him. At length he was overtaken and a stranger, after introducing himself, began to question him as to whether or not he ever spoke in public, asking, 'Would you bring some of the wisdom of the Himalayas to us?'[33]

The *brahmachari* explained that he was unaccustomed to giving lectures but told the stranger where he might be contacted. The stranger returned and during the following week a series of lectures was held in the locality. Such was the interest generated by these talks that the local press was alerted and further lectures were arranged. Even after a further six months in Kerala, the *brahmachari* still had no immediate plans to return to his cave at Uttar Kashi. When he was not busy lecturing he would spend much time in the company of the prominent lawyer responsible for arranging his schedule of talks.

Mahesh's master, the late Shankaracharya Swami Brahmanand Saraswati, had many devotees in southern India who had grouped together in the city of Alleppey to found and dedicate to his name the Adhyatmic Vikas Mandal (the Society for Spiritual Development). At nearby Cochin arrangements were made for *yagyas* (religious rituals) to be performed from 23 to 26 October 1955. The numbers of the late

Shankaracharya's devotees who arrived from all over India swelled the already sizeable congregation. Led by Vedic *pandits* daily ceremonies were performed and there followed conferences which took personal development as their topic. These events were accompanied by a grand parade along local thoroughfares in which Brahmachari Mahesh appears to have been the centre of attraction, being the only person present pictured wearing a garland of flowers.

Inside the hall, to the centre of the low wide stage was placed an ornate throne upon which was set a garlanded framed picture of the late Shankaracharya Swami Brahmanand. The framed portrait of the revered teacher was illuminated from above by a standard lamp, its shade shiny and lined with tassels, resembling the parasol formerly associated with the departed *swami*. In festive spirit, coloured paper decorations were suspended from the ceiling and hung about the walls. The congregation, comprising young boys sitting at the front, their elders behind them and women in a group to one side, sat in rapt attention upon cotton matting strewn about the floor. The assembly was estimated at over 10,000, although it is doubtful whether the hall itself contained more than a few hundred. Messages of goodwill were read to them from the current Shankaracharyas of Jyotir and Shringeri Maths.

The star of the show, 'Maharshi' (Great Sage) Bala Brahmachari Mahesh Yogi Maharaj of Uttar Kasi, Himalayas, opened his lecture by saying:

> It gives me great pleasure this afternoon to be in the company of you all here assembled in the close vicinity of the Maha Yagna Mandapam. From the early morning the atmosphere here is being surcharged with the Divine Vibrations of Rig Veda and Yajur Veda Parayanam and the chantings of the Maha Yagna *Mantras*.[34]

As he moved through the formalities of paying homage to the previous speaker (the Maharajah of Cochin) and to those well-wishers who had written to the assembly, he indicated that the occasion was 'graciously sanctified by the presence of the great Lord Shiva and his retinue'. His message of hope centered on the promise that *sat-chit-anandam* (unlimited bliss) is accessible to all:

> Then why waste time in helplessness and suffer any agony in life? Why suffer when you can enjoy? Why be miserable when you can be happy? Now, let the days of misery and peacelessness be over and let their operation become tales of the past. Allow not the past history of agony to be continued in the present. Be happy and gay.[35]

After introducing his philosophy in a general way, he then boldly claimed to hold answers which could solve the dilemma of suffering mankind. In the second of his lectures, he held forth on the physical location of the *sat-chit-anandam* he had referred to previously, stating:

> Electrons and protons of the modern science, seen through the Indian system of analysis of the universe, are manifestations of Agni-Tatwa and Vayu-Tatwa combined. The energy of the electrons and protons is due to the Agni-Tatwa and motion in them is due to Vayu-Tatwa. Thus we find, the present day science has reached up to Vayu-Tatwa in the field of analysis of the universe.[36]

Naming the successively finer strata of creation as *Agni, Vayu, Akash, Aham, Mahat* and *Prakriti*, he concluded:

> And finer than the Prakriti-Tatwa and the very cause of it is the Brahma-Tatwa which is the Ultimate Reality, the subtlest 'Anoraniyan', Sat-Chit-Anandam.[37]

For this audience of exclusively Indian composition, so recently released from the grip of Western rule and knowing the scorn that had been heaped upon their traditional beliefs, this elucidation must have been as pure nectar. Although his explanation must have been confusing to them, they were reassured that here was a man who could reconcile the most modern beliefs with those of their forefathers.

Various other speakers took to the microphone, including the Maharajah of Cochin and the barrister Shri A.N. Menon, who noted:

> The world has known saints performing miracles of various nature, but here is a saint whose miracle works in the inner man to glorify it.[38]

This 'miracle' that 'works in the inner man' is undoubtedly an allusion to the system of meditation that was currently being taught by Mahesh. Although it is difficult to identify the actual technique prescribed, it can safely be assumed that it centered on the use of a personal *mantra* or special sound to be intoned by the practitioner. Mention of the efficacy of certain recommended *mantras* was made, although a warning was given against the use by 'householders' of the magic syllable '*om*'. This advice strongly echoes the counsel of the Mahesh's own *guru* in that he specifically advised women to avoid the use of '*om*' and use in its stead the syllable '*shri*', holding that the repetition of '*om*' could create a potentially disastrous mentality of unworldliness for them. The Mahesh addressed the topic in the following manner:

> 'Om' is the *Mantra* for the Sanyasi. The Sanyasi repeats 'Om Om Om'. It is given to him at the time of 'Sanyas-Diksha', at the time when he has completely renounced attachment to the world. Renunciation and detachment

increase with the repetition of 'Om'. 'Om' is chanted aloud by a Sanyasi to put an end to his desires. Desires are destroyed by loudly chanting the *mantra* 'Om'. And if there is any desire deeply rooted in the mind of a Sanyasi, the chanting of 'Om' will result in the destruction of the object of such desire in order to make the Sanyasi, wholly desireless.[39]

The audience, hanging on every syllable of his words, gazed attentively at 'Maharshi' Mahesh as he continued:

> If unfortunately, the householder begins to repeat the pranava *Mantra* viz. 'Om', 'Om', 'Om' he experiences destructive effects in his material life. The effect starts with monetary loss and then goes on to destroy objects of affection, one by one. Such a man, when he finds loss of money and separation from the dear ones, he is reduced to utter peacelessness and frustration.[40]

He remained all the while seated upon a deerskin in the cross-legged lotus posture, his large dark eyes flashing to the flow of his speech. Simply attired in a white *dhoti*, garlands of fresh marigolds around his flourishing full beard and long black hair, he possessed many outward symbols of his vocation, which emphasized the authority of his words. After the stern warning with regard to dabbling in mystical practices he gave the following opinion:

> It is not at all necessary for the householder to go for direct practice of 'Tyaga' or 'Vairagya' [Renunciation] for realisation. That practice is unnatural for him, antagonistic to his nature and opposed to his way of life.[41]

For centuries the philosophy of detachment has permeated Indian thinking. At a stroke such beliefs had been set at nought! Stripping away the unfamiliar Sanskritic terms, his message stands revealed: 'You don't have to become a monk or adopt a monkish mode of life to experience the highest of spiritual goals.' This was a message that many wished to hear. There were few present who might have found the hermit life alluring. But on the other hand, how could real peace of mind be experienced whilst caught up in the thick of everyday life, with its share of disappointments and unavoidable miseries? There must therefore be a catch!

Mahesh expounded his philosophy yet further by pointing out that attachment to material life lies solely in the area of thought and that since even the greatest material treasures are seldom located upon one s person, it is only the thought of wealth that confers the sense of ownership. He explained that for a householder to experience a state of 'non-attachment' he must first have acquired the ability to transcend or 'go beyond' thoughts related to the outer world.

In less than a year the *brahmachari* had so far distanced himself from his life of abstinence and seclusion as to be lecturing the people of southern India that they were missing nothing that could not be had in the comfort of their own homes. In the search for *sat-chit-ananda*, many took him at his word and asked for instruction into his meditation practices. The end of the three-day conference was marked by a rousing cheer of '*Jai Shri Guru Deva*' (Glory to the Blessed *Guru* Divine) in praise of the *guru* of Mahesh.

To commemorate the conference, a souvenir booklet was published under the name *Beacon Light of the Himalayas*, subtitled 'The Dawn of a Happy New Era in the Field of Spiritual Practices Mind Control, Peace & Atmananda – Through simple & easy methods of Spiritual Sadhana propounded by Maharshi Bala Brahmachari Mahesh Yogi Maharaj of Uttar Kasi, Himalayas'. This publication (now lamentably difficult to acquire) contains a full transcript of speeches from Brahmachari Mahesh, the Maharajah of Cochin and others, including the barrister A.N. Menon. It provides a wealth of interesting perspectives into the early ministrations of the man who would henceforward be referred to as the 'Maharishi'. The booklet opens with a short message penned and signed by Bal Brhmachari Mahsh (sic):

Maharshi's Message to the Peaceless and Suffering
Oh ye of the peaceless and suffering humanity.

My happiness desires to root out your suffering. Will you extend your arm and allow me to lift you up from the mire of misery and peacelessness?

Come on, here is the call of peace and joy for you. Here is an invitation, a cordial invitation for you all to come and enjoy the Blissful Grace and All Powerful Blessings of my Lord the Great Swami Brahmanand Saraswati, the Great among the greats of the Himalayas. I have found a treasure in the Dust of His Lotus Feet and now I invite you to share it with me and make yourself happy.

Come on; I invite you to get into the Blissful Realm of His Universal Benevolence. See, the path is straight and entry is free. Come on with faith and you will find that the very cause of your peacelessness and misery will be eradicated and you will be adorned with lasting peace and real happiness in your day to day life.[42]

It is worth pausing a moment to reflect on the evolving name and title of Mahesh. It has been suggested that Mahesh's own explanation for the genesis of this title is that, when addressed as 'Maharshi' he 'did not resist' it. But possibly his own first name had simply been misheard? This notion is amply supported by the fact that he himself signed his name as 'Mahsh'. So from Mahesh to Mahsh, from Maharshi to Maharishi.

Having been met with so much enthusiasm in southern India, the Maharishi took to propagating his message in the various other provinces of India. He held meditation camps in the cities of Bombay and Calcutta and at numerous other venues such as Hardwar (not very far from Uttar Kashi) and Pahalgam in Kashmir, the latter lasting for two months. How different his daily life was from that of his teacher, who at his age was secluded in a dense jungle, in prayer and contemplation.

According to the International Vegetarian Union the Maharishi addressed the 15th session of the World Vegetarian Congress. This event was held at Madras on 30 November 1957 where he posed a fundamental question:

> How are we going to change the 'Killing world' of today into a non-killing world of tomorrow? How are we going to change the spirit of killing, the spirit of aggression, the spirit of violence into the spirit of kindness and love – overflowing love for the whole creation? How are we going to change hardness and cruelty of heart to softness and overflowing love for everybody?

Reminding his audience that all the major religions condemn killing he then declared:

> The killer knows that he is killing and in return he will be killed. The sinner knows that he is committing a sin and that he will be punished for it. Not that he does not know. He knows it. But, with this information, the cruel is not afraid – his cruelty is hardened still. The killer declares his action is the role of a saviour, he kills in the name of life, he kills in the name of saving life, he kills in the name of maintaining life. He kills and murders ruthlessly in the name of protection and peace. In the name of world peace and protection have been waged the deadliest of wars. In the name of peace and protection are preparations being made for the murder of man and creation. Shame to the greatness of the human intelligence which fails to recognise the Judge Supreme!

An impassioned speech and one which no doubt would have been well received. But, as yet he had not answered his own question of just how he proposed to encourage non-vegetarians to change their habits. Clearly he was leading up to it – his suggestion must have come as a surprise to many.

> Our task of the day is to find a cure for this major ill of humanity. The heart of man is so changed. The inner man has to be transformed.. A direct experience of the Blissful nature of Soul and the inner man is completely transformed. The mind, experiencing the Great Bliss, feels satisfaction and

this satisfaction of the mind results in right understanding and virtuous
action, kindness, love and compassion for all...

Although hundreds, sometimes thousands, turned out to hear the
Maharishi's lectures about meditation (it is even said that mass
initiations were not uncommon), the desire to contact ever greater
numbers of people steered him to ever greater success. After many
months of touring he returned to southern India once more, this time
using the city of Madras as his base, and hatched plans for a rather
remarkable event. Invitations were dispatched with a view to drawing
together disciples of the late Swami Brahmanand for a great celebration
of his memory. The Seminar of Spiritual Luminaries was to be held in
Mylapore, and 'eminent saints and philosophers of all countries' were
exhorted to attend. The stated reason for calling together these people
was 'to contribute their experience in finding out a practical formula of
spiritual regeneration of the world'.

Perhaps this seminar was, in reality, nothing but a gesture of goodwill,
for the Maharishi could not hope to pursue his endeavours without first
gaining the support of the late Shankaracharya's other disciples. Be that
as it may, the wording of the invitation made direct reference to hoped-
for contributions, which seems to imply that the Maharishi's techniques
of 'mind control' were still open to improvement. It is very likely that
he entertained doubts about his methods and hoped that this event might
prove an opportunity to garner important feedback, most especially from
his peer group. In addition to this apparent insecurity, it is likely that he
also looked forward to hearing testimonies in support of his extravagant
claims, thus endorsing and confirming as a *maharishi* the erstwhile
brahmachari, who had promised his audience in Kerala:

> Here is no empty promise of Heaven after death. Here is the positive
> experience of 'Heavenly Bliss' during lifetime. Come on who desires for
> it...[43]

It is said that the Seminar of Luminaries was attended by over 10,000
people and that as it drew to a close the Maharishi felt inclined to ask
those assembled there: 'Why can't we spiritually regenerate the world
through this technique?' Apparently his question drew tumultuous
applause, prompting him to arrange a day's extension to the festivities.
The Seminar's invitation to find 'a practical formula of spiritual
regeneration of the world' proved to be somewhat self-fulfilling for on
Wednesday, 1 January 1958 the Maharishi announced:

> The one aim of the Spiritual Regeneration Movement is to provide a simple
> and easy method of meditation and infuse this system of meditation in the

daily life of everybody everywhere on earth. To meet this end, this Movement had been started to work for the construction of meditation centres everywhere in every part of human habitation.[44]

The Maharishi later explained:

It was the concern of Guru Deva, His Divinity Swami Brahmananda Saraswati, to enlighten all men everywhere that resulted in the foundation of the world-wide Spiritual Regeneration Movement in 1958, five years after his departure from us.[45]

In the following months, in addition to the holding of several more spiritual development camps, a total of twenty-five meditation centres were opened across India. It was at Bangalore in the spring of 1958 that the Maharishi claims to have been inspired to make his next move. After finishing his meditation, he slipped into a state of introspection:

One fine morning I thoughtfully reviewed the work done and calculated how much time it will take for the whole world with this rate and I found out that it will take 200 years (laughter).
    Then I said 'No, I must change my ways of work'; then I thought what to do. Then I thought: I must go to the most advanced country because I thought – the country is most advanced because the people of that country would try something new very readily.[46]

When I met some people in the morning I said, 'I want to go to America,' and they said, 'All right'.[47]

Letters giving news of the Maharishi's desire were quickly dispatched to followers in Bombay, Calcutta and Madras. Within a few days there came a response: 'Send him here, he will stay with us for two weeks, and we will make all arrangements.'[48]

Not long after this generous offer he received other invitations from those with business interests abroad. This was not what the

Maharishi wanted.

No, your connections will be business connections, and they are based on profit – money – so they will not be of any use to me.[49]

Arrangements were made, but the trip to America had to be delayed whilst travel documents were obtained. During the lengthy wait for his passport, a farewell tour of Kerala was arranged during which he met numerous well-wishers, including various dignitaries who made richly worded speeches in support of his mission.

On Sunday, 27 April 1958 the Maharishi made for Calcutta Airport not to catch a flight to the United States of America, but to make a relatively short hop across the Bay of Bengal to the capital of neighbouring Burma. His arrival in Rangoon contrasted greatly with his massive send-off from India; there was only one individual waiting to meet him from the plane. Before long however, the wandering *brahmachari* attracted considerable attention and within a short while several lecture dates were organized. As a result of these few talks, many candidates were found who wished to learn how to practice his style of meditation. An unexpected boost to his popularity came when the prediction of an aged Buddhist monk became known – a year before, he had foretold that a great Indian *yogi* would visit Rangoon on *Bodhipurnima* Day. This prophecy brought forth visits from monks, high-ranking officials and a large complement of local men, women and children. This was the first clear indication that the Maharishi's teachings were capable of attracting people from outside the specifically Hindu world. After ten days of talks and initiations, the Maharishi triumphantly returned to Rangoon Airport ready to embark on the next leg of his journey. A rousing send-off had been organized and a veritable sea of Burmese and Indians thronged the departure lounge to send him on his way, causing the Maharishi jubilantly to consider the truth of an old maxim. 'Then it rang in my mind: "Well begun is half done."'[50]

So it was that in May 1958 he flew to Bangkok and then to the island of Penang. On Thursday, 22 May the *Times of Malaya* carried an interview in which the Maharishi declared:

> My system of meditation is a golden link to connect and harmonize materialism and spirituality. It is a direct process to integrate man's life on earth. I invite everyone to take the maximum advantage of my stay in Penang.

In Penang, he found many Indian expatriates eager to receive his message and notably even found appreciation from the Sikh community, traditionally wary of Hindu doctrines. Whether he spoke at temples or *gurudwaras*, interested individuals would gather to hear of the blessings of 'Shri Guru Deva.'

After spending only a few weeks in Penang, he journeyed some 300 km south to the city of Kuala Lumpur, capital of Malaya. He met with no less success there than he had in Penang. Nevertheless, after staying only ten days there, the spur to travel found him garlanded and bidding goodbye and '*Jai Shri Guru Deva*' to new-found devotees. The touring continued and by 14 June 1958 he had settled in Singapore. Whilst working on plans for the establishment of a meditation centre there, news came that a broadcast he had prepared for Radio Malaya during his stay in Kuala Lumpur was shortly to be broadcast. It was transmitted at 9 pm on Thursday, 24 July, and for five minutes the airwaves resounded to his high-pitched tones as millions listened to his message.

> When we think about the joys of the world and try to locate the permanent abode of greatest happiness, we find that through our senses we are experiencing the charm of gross nature, and the charm of the subtler fields of nature are not being experienced ...
>
> The real joy of life lies in the field of subtle nature, beyond the field of sense perception ...
>
> It is the experience of thousands of people coming in my contact that they begin to feel calmness of mind, more energy and happiness in their daily life within two or three sittings ...[51]

From Singapore the Maharishi returned to Penang where he set about establishing another Spiritual Development Centre and training more Spiritual Guides to continue his work. The ceremonial opening of the centre was performed by the Mayor of Penang, after which the centre's General Secretary gave a speech in which he referred to the Maharishi's technique of meditation as a 'spiritual sputnik from the Himalayas'.[52] The Russians with their Sputnik 1 and the Americans with their Explorer 1 had opened up the space race – was it just coincidence that at the dawn of the space age, the realms of inner space were being newly re-explored too?

By mid-August 1958 the Singapore meditation centre was also ready to be opened and the occasion was celebrated at the city's Victoria Memorial Hall. It was intended that the centre should take as its leader a newly appointed Spiritual Guide who for the past quarter of a century had been President of the Buddhist Union. The role of officiator at this inauguration was to be filled not by the centre's leader, however but by no less a person than the bespectacled Chief Minister of Singapore, Mr Lim Yew Hock. From the *Beacon Light* conference onwards, the Maharishi had shown a marked tendency to court the approval and sponsorship of the powerful and the rich, and at important functions he would ensure that he sat in the company of persons of high social standing. Of those who spoke at the opening on 17 August, the testimony of one speaker, a business magnate, is of particular note.

> Within three or four days of the initiation, I was able to enjoy unspeakable happiness, calmness, and peace. Now I always feel full of spiritual vigour and happiness. Maharishi is grand like the Himalayas wherefrom he comes, but humble like a child, great like truth but simple like love.[53]

Spurred on no doubt by such unwavering support as this, the lone *brahmachari* relentlessly pursued his quest to further publicize his teachings. The next trip was to be his longest yet, for his destination lay in faraway Hong Kong. Again he met with a ready audience, with whom he quickly set about forming a meditation centre, to be called the Happy Valley. At the Chinese Chamber of Commerce on 7 November 1958, a ceremony was held to mark the centre's inauguration. It was officiated by a local magistrate, Mr Hing Shing Lo. Following his speech the Maharishi addressed the assembled crowd and confidently pointed out that 'everybody has the capacity for Deep Meditation'.[54] Clarifying the role of the centre, he told its staff:

> It will be the sacred duty of the management to drum into the ears of the people that here is a place where everybody can get the key to all peace and happiness in life.[55]

Having stayed in Hong Kong only a little over a month, the momentum of the tour caused him to move on yet again and this time not just a hop, but a huge bound, to the island of Hawaii, from which he then intended to fly directly to America. Before he left Hong Kong, a man suggested the name of someone he might contact in Hawaii. There he again met with great success, and although he had planned to spend only two days in Honolulu he was prevailed upon to stay longer, one month longer as it happened. On Wednesday, 31 December 1958 (one year after the formation of his movement), the *Honolulu Star Bulletin* told its readers about this visitor to the island.

> He has no money; he asks for nothing. His worldly possessions can be carried in one hand. Maharishi Mahesh Yogi is on a world odyssey. He carries a message that he says will rid the world of unhappiness and discontent ...

It seemed that the media had found itself a new celebrity, and the Hawaiian newspapers, radio and television stations all gave exposure to his message, although it is doubtful that many fully understood it. No longer was he preaching to the converted but to an ever-widening section of the populace, of diverse denominations and persuasions.

Back in India, devotees were kept abreast of all these new developments. They received hand-written epistles from the Maharishi chronicling the movement's progress. The Madras mission took to publishing a newsletter, known as the *Torch Divine*, and in the absence of their teacher, it played a vital role not only in linking interested parties but in providing meditators with a mutual support system.

So it was that the Bal Brahmachari Mahesh who had toyed so uneasily with the recurrent thought to 'go to Rameshvaram' had not only relinquished the role of hermit but in less than four years had assumed the position of Director of Operations in an organization that took as its goal the spiritual regeneration of the world. Within nine months of travelling, the interest shown in his practice of Deep Meditation was such that its future success seemed fairly well assured.

> I had one thing in mind – that I know something which is useful to every man; therefore no matter where I am people will find in me the commodity that they want. (laugh) With that confidence I left India and gradually I came to the States.[56]

4

---★---

FROM HAWAII TO HOLLYWOOD

Although confident of success, the Maharishi really had no idea how his teachings would be received in the West. Since childhood he had heard much praise for the mentality that produced advancements in economically go-ahead countries such as the USA and Germany and reasoned that in order to have made these advances, these nations must be unusually receptive to new ideas. He therefore hoped to tap this tendency by placing his system of meditation before them. He naturally brought the habit of systematic enquiry which he had learned whilst attending university to bear on the ancient teachings of his spiritual master. As a graduate scientist, Mahesh was no stranger to experimentation and the need for subsequent verification and accreditation of any discoveries. The young *brahmachari* became convinced that amongst the spiritual practices his master taught were simple, practical, easy-to-use techniques which might have a universal application. In travelling around, the Maharishi had found no lack of truth-seekers eager to learn and apply them, and after hearing the numerous glowing testimonies to the apparent efficacy of this meditation, he had felt justified in forming the Spiritual Regeneration Movement. For the most part, initiates were found amongst those already culturally predisposed towards Eastern teachings, but the time had now come to test his methods on those who knew little or nothing of Eastern philosophies and still less about its practices.

So it happened that the Maharishi, after hopping his way across South East Asia, finally arrived at his desired destination on the western seaboard of America. There was no fanfare in San Francisco to greet him, for no herald of his arrival had been dispatched beforehand. However, the very appearance of this slight, foreign gentleman with his flowing mass of hair, billowing robes and graceful step, assured him immediate attention.

When he first arrived in the States he adopted a relatively low profile;

he was attended by no journalists and gave no public lectures. It could be argued that after so much travel he needed time to consolidate and to assimilate his new environment. The two meditators who had accompanied him from Hawaii saw to his immediate personal needs. Once installed at a small local hotel, visitors (mainly friends of meditators) were encouraged to visit him. About a month later, he received an invitation to stay in a couple's large apartment, an invitation which he gratefully accepted. He was henceforth able to enjoy greater space and freedom to conduct his affairs.

> From that day I was speaking every day in one organisation in San Francisco, gave about 29 lectures and every evening the whole thing was full and because people found something which they thought can't be false …
>
> And when they started to meditate, then they became propagandist about it. They spread it …[57]

It was during this stay in San Francisco that the Maharishi received his first press coverage in the USA. He was far from happy when he learned that his meditation had been dubbed a 'non-medicinal tranquilizer'. His comments are worth noting.

> Cruel …! I feel like running away, back home. This seems to be a strange country. Values are different here.[58]

Not long afterwards, on Wednesday, 29 April 1959, the Maharishi took leave of his friends at the Jen Sen Tao Buddhist Association and the rest of his new-found admirers in San Francisco, but he was not 'running away, back home', merely slipping away down the coast to spread his message further.

Waiting in Los Angeles was a crowd of meditators' friends and their relatives ready to bedeck him with floral offerings. After briefly meeting them he lost no time in moving on to the Ambassador Hotel, where a press conference had been organized for him. There bemused reporters from local newspapers were to hear of the Maharishi's intention of bringing about a more loving society and eventually creating world peace:

> I have brought from the land of ancient sages to the modern man of this new world a simple technique of living in peace and happiness.[59]

An evening paper, the *Herald Express*, carried a report of the event with the challenging headline 'Yogi Has Cure for World Ills' above a picture of the Maharishi holding a bouquet of roses. Beneath it they quoted him as saying, 'I will fill the world with love.'

The following weekend, on the back page of the Women's Section of the *Los Angeles Times* a small ad advised:

> Maharishi Mahesh Yogi
> Master from the Himalayas
> Valley of the Saints – Uttar Kashi
> Will speak at the Masquers Club
> May 1 to May 7 – Phone …

On the Sunday evening, at this Hollywood actors' club, an audience of several dozen interested individuals seated themselves in the comfortable armchairs that formed a semicircle around the Master. Initially he sat in silence, fingering a line of beads hung around his neck. One of those present, Mrs Helena Olson, later commented:

> His voice drew one's entire attention. At first it was almost without sound. The quietness of his speech seemed to direct ideas to the mind and not the ear.
>   His voice became more audible and fell gently on the ear. The words were strong with authority. There was no thought of doubting what he said …
>   He singled out a large, red rose and emphasized a few points with it. As the rose waved back and forth I noticed his hands … definite in movement, strong and beautiful. As I watched, he opened the palm and inclined it gently toward the audience.[60]

After this initial exposure to the Master Mrs Olson felt sufficiently moved to invite him to come and share her and her husband's house on palm lined South Harvard Boulevard. Mrs Olson attended all the remaining lectures at the Masquers Club and from Richard Sedlachek, the Maharishi's new helper learned that the Master had once undertaken 'thirteen years of being in the silence'.[61] She was later to publish a very readable account of her everyday life with this rather exotic lodger under the title of *A Hermit in the House*.

On the evening of his arrival at No. 433, the Maharishi was shown his new quarters and after swiftly surveying the bedroom, set about removing the blankets from the bed. He then began to unfurl his mysterious carpet roll.

> Then almost shyly, so as not to hurt our feelings, he said as he drew out exquisite silk sheets, pillow and spread: 'These have been provided for me by devotees in India.'[62]

From the carpet roll he also produced a brown cashmere shawl for extra warmth should it be needed and then proceeded to unpack the remaining contents of his most unusual form of luggage.

> He lifted neatly folded pieces of silk from the rug, a small metal box of toilet articles, a little clock and a fountain pen – and our Yogi was all unpacked.[63]

In the evening, the Olsons invited the Maharishi to join them in their family worship, which consisted of readings from the Bible followed by prayer and a period of silence.

> When it was over, the Master who now sat with us in our family circle, said, 'A good silence, but I will add power to it. I will initiate you, in the morning.'[64]

The following day Mr and Mrs Olson prepared themselves to be initiated into the technique of Deep Meditation. Mrs Olson felt a strong desire to take along some flowers from her garden. Having picked a bunch of fresh white geraniums she handed a few to her husband in order that he too might have something to present to the Maharishi. They found him ready and waiting for them.

> He had us place our flowers on a small shrine. Very quickly we were given our technique, and told to sit with our eyes closed and practice it in his presence.
>
> In the first few seconds I felt my entire being quicken, and then a penetrating sensation of warmth. A flood of delight, of warmth.
>
> After some time, a soft voice whispered, 'Open your eyes.' Roland and I opened our eyes to look into each others'. I gasped at the sight of Roland's face. It was serene, yet glowing. All the drawn, serious lines seemed erased. His eyes were large and shining. I hoped mine were the same.
>
> Maharishi had fulfilled his promise of bliss.[65]

But bliss was not all that he had offered his audiences. He had further whetted their appetites, quoting the words of Jesus Christ: 'Seek ye first the Kingdom of Heaven within.' The meditation technique the Olsons were that day taught centred on a word that 'has no meaning'. Roland Olson sought reassurance that the method of meditation the Maharishi taught them did not conflict with Christianity.

> These words were known many, many centuries before there were Christian words, and the effects of saying these words are well known. This is the ancient Vedic tradition that is passed down through our Masters.[66]

Mr and Mrs Olson's home very soon became a hive of activity with visitors coming and going at all hours of the day and night. It was thought necessary for publicity purposes to take some pictures of the Maharishi. He surprised them as he offered useful suggestions regarding lighting – perhaps as a young man he had helped set up portrait shots in his Uncle Raj's Jabalpur Photographic Studio?

The presence of so charismatic a guest made Mrs Olson begin to

seriously reappraise her lifestyle and even question continuing to work
at her job in a local theatre. The Maharishi, on divining her dilemma,
offered her succinct advice: 'See the job. Do the job. Stay out of the
misery.'[67]

Chance situations would occasionally provide insights into the
Maharishi's views on life, as for instance the time when one of Mrs
Olson's Siamese cats, which freely roamed the house and garden,
caught a bird. Whilst her cat received a scolding for trying to kill the
defenceless feathered flyer, her guest looked on reproachfully, not at the
cat but at its owner. Mrs Olson defended her stance:

> 'Maharishi, this wretched cat would have killed the bluebird if we had not
> caught her. What am I going to do with her?'
>   'Nothing,' said Maharishi, 'that is the nature.'
>   'Why should it be the nature of a cat to kill when it is not hungry?'
>   'Mother Nature determines all these things, and the little animals cannot
> help but mind. Like when it is night all birds must sleep.'[68]

Most of the Maharishi's basic needs were attended to by his devotees,
including being chauffeured about in a Karmann Ghia sports car by
Richard Sedlachek, the one who had placed the small ad that announced
the lectures at the Masquers Club. From Hawaii came Sheela Devi, who
saw to domestic duties such as washing silk *dhotis* and cooking the pure
vegetarian dishes that formed the Master's diet (apart from taking *lassi*,
a yoghurt drink, for breakfast, he ate but one meal a day). With the
notable exception of his casual suggestion that someone might phone
the President, the mere intimation of a whim or desire was enough to
propel his converts into action. The Olsons, having noticed the increase
in telephone calls for their guest, even went so far as to arrange for a
personal extension to be installed in his room. Again, when it was
noticed that there was a lack of space for teaching meditation, helpers
rolled up their sleeves to erect an outdoor centre in the garden. For new
converts, nothing was too much to ask of them.

> When one dives within one's self and finds the Being, the perfect State of
> Being, his being living and thinking become infused with the Being, and then
> all good is automatic. You remember the Lord Christ has said, 'Seek ye first
> the Kingdom of Heaven within. And all else will be added unto thee.'[69]

With statements such as this, it is no wonder that the printed literature
produced at this time referred to the Maharishi as 'Rev.' or 'Reverend',
a term normally reserved for the Christian clergy.

With so much activity being generated at No. 433, it came as no great
surprise when the police came along to investigate. Neighbours had

found the constant comings and goings at the house a nuisance, and a police officer had been dispatched to confront the occupants about the extent of their nocturnal activities. The Maharishi appeared unconcerned, openly sympathizing with the local residents. He resolved that a solution must be found. After the series of talks at the Masquers Club, operations transferred to the basement of the Hollywood Congregational Church.

On 2 April 1959 the theme of the talk was health. In measured tones and with absolute conviction the Maharishi told the gathering:

> Anything that pleases the mind heals the mind. Anything that pleases the body heals the body.
>
> Everything in the world has healing power, has the power of healing to some degree or the other.
>
> Meditation has the greatest healing power because it leads to greatest happiness.[70]

A tape machine recorded his lectures for posterity.

What was really needed, however, was a meeting place that would serve as a permanent location for the Maharishi's mission and at length suitable premises were found in a local ballet school which had a large room badly in need of decoration. In the church hall the congregation had been expected to sit on creaking wooden chairs; after giving the new room a new fresh coat of paint, fifty comfortable chairs were installed, because 'the boss' had decreed that there was 'no need to suffer for the Divine.'[71]

Although No. 433 still remained the headquarters and heart of his expanding operation, the hall did much to stem the tide of visitors. Although the newly acquired premises were better suited to his needs, the Maharishi still dreamed of creating a permanent centre in Los Angeles and to that end commissioned his aides to be on the lookout for a suitable property.

Although the Maharishi himself appeared to have no interest in money, his devotees no doubt privately agonized over how they might meet the not inconsiderable expenditure of hiring halls, printing literature and placing advertisements. Visitors had actually not been unmindful of their duty to try and help, and apart from donating their time and effort in diverse ways, they had already been making monetary contributions which they placed in a basket outside the Master's bedroom. But to the Maharishi this was unacceptable as, in his eyes, it was tantamount to openly begging. The question of how sufficient funds could be found to continue, let alone to realize the Master's desire to acquire property, was quite beyond his followers' imagination. In order to find an answer, the Maharishi sought the advice of his host, Roland Olson, and another meditator, Charlie Lutes. Attention soon turned to the advantages and disadvantages of levying charges for instruction in meditation. The Maharishi's advisers were concerned that if there were a compulsory fee, people on a low or no income would become debarred from learning to meditate. A compromise was eventually reached: it was agreed that any payment for initiation be earnings-related. In October 1955 Bal Brahmachari Mahesh had declared: 'The path is straight and entry is free.' But in 1959 a fee of one week's wages came to be set, apparently on the principle of 'When in Rome, do as the Romans do.'

Over a year had passed since the Maharishi had bade farewell to the shores of Mother India and the news that some of his countrymen had decided to pay him a visit was well received. A brother and sister, Lachsman and Mata-ji (reputedly from one of India's wealthiest families) arrived from Calcutta in the company of Ram Rao, president of a meditation centre in India. Mata-ji, intent on offering service to the Master, spent much of her time preparing specialities for him, including the time-consuming work of peeling and crushing grapes in order to quench his thirst. She was relieved of this particular task when it was found that a variety of commercially produced fruit juices were to be found locally. For the newcomers, excursions to all the local tourist spots were organized, the highlight being a visit to the world-famous Disneyland, which provided an agreeable opportunity for the Maharishi to relax from the relentless pursuit of his mission. The presence of Mata-ji and her companions created a degree of interest in Indian culture amongst the devotees, causing many of the American women temporarily to adopt the fashion of wearing colourful Indian *sarees*.

The Olsons proved themselves capable and thoughtful hosts. Mrs Olson even took it into her head to ask the Maharishi whether his mother had been informed of his welfare and whereabouts. Coming from someone else, this might have appeared a strange thing to ask of the Master, but not from 'Mother' Olson, who had come to look on him almost as part of her family. He did not look up and answered her simply: 'Mother knows son is doing well.'[72]

Unbeknown to all but a few of his closest cohorts, the Maharishi was in constant contact with his many centres by telephone. In addition to maintaining links with his followers he had been preparing the way for future endeavours. It appeared that he was giving his mission his undivided attention. The preparation of publicity material, lectures at the University of California and daily meetings and initiations all tested his stamina, but found his energy undiminished. In July 1959, one of his inner circle, Dr J.S. Hislop (formerly a pupil to another philosopher, J. Krishnamurti) organized an International Convention of the Spiritual Regeneration Movement, which was held in Sequoia National Park California. Seated on woollen blankets a loyal group of devotees surrounded the Maharishi and listened as he unveiled his hopes and plans for the future. Contained within the highly optimistic package of ideas he presented was the proposal that an International Academy of Meditation might soon be started. The followers heard their teacher's response to a man, who after calculating the world's population, asked who was to teach all the new students to meditate. The Maharishi answered him simply: 'I'll multiply myself many-fold.'[73]

As the Maharishi announced his imaginative 'Three-Year Plan' it emerged that he intended to train a large number of teachers (25,000) and establish an equivalent number of meditation centres within the span of this plan. Even the most committed believers doubted his ability to fulfil this ambition, but the plan's strength lay in its power to motivate his followers and to galvanize them into vigorous activity. Further justification lay in the fact that it provided the media with ready-made copy, thereby promising further potential for news coverage of this highly enigmatic Indian visitor.

After the Sequoia Park convention the Maharishi resumed his tour, no longer clutching the curious carpet roll, but now replete with a set of leather luggage and a parcel containing tapes of his most recent lectures. This most modern of mystics was now headed for America's East Coast, to the cities of New York and Boston. From his stay in Los Angeles he had learned a great deal, not least in dealing with the difficult questions which were frequently posed. For example, he had an answer for those who believe that it is necessary to suffer in order to gain self-purification.

> 'We do not even think of giving up anything,' Maharishi would insist.

> 'We do whatever our needs demand, but we are regular in Meditation, and when we become filled with the Bliss, the Being, – the need is no longer there. There is no need to even think of it. Thinking of something we wish to give up drives the desire for it deeper into the mind, and we desire it more and more.'[74]

The topic of suffering proved recurrent and because the Master's homeland was seen by many as being caught in the grip of dire economic problems, he was called on to offer an explanation.

> If the people of India are starving and they are Meditating, then it is Karma

[Law of Cause and Effect], but it does not mean that they are miserable. It is possible to have little to eat and still be happy. In America, where you have so much, people are found to be miserable. It is worse to be miserable in the midst of plenty, than it is in the midst of poverty.[75]

After almost a year in the United States, for reasons as yet unidentified (although it could simply be that his visa expired – visas seldom extend beyond a year), the Maharishi moved on. He again prepared to take to the air and on Saturday, 12 December 1959, he departed New York for London.

The heart of the rapidly disappearing British Empire was undergoing the usual seasonal discomfort of winter and busily preparing itself for the traditional festivities. At what better time of year could one with the outward appearance of a young but decidedly jovial Father Christmas show himself? The long journey of some 5000 miles would have had the average man pining for rest, but the Maharishi had energy enough to deal with a press conference. The BBC World Service also took an interest, booking him for a live transmission later that month. Eight hours after landing on *terra firma*, he was ensconced in the Howard Hotel in London's Bayswater district. Soon after that, readers of *The Times* saw an advertisement to the effect that 'Maharishi Mahesh Yogi has arrived'. Details of his whereabouts were also given and after several days someone responded, a Mrs Marjorie Gill.

The familiar pattern established itself and on 18 December he gave his first public lecture in London at the Caxton Hall in Westminster. Within the context of creating a better, more peaceful society, he stressed the need for the role of the individual to be reassessed, reasoning:

> If we want to make the whole garden green, it is necessary to make every tree green. Talks of the greenness of the garden will not help: every tree has to be attended to – watered, fertilised, and made green. Then with that process the whole garden could be made green.[76]

Although the Maharishi possessed a rare talent for using analogies, his audiences must often have been puzzled about their meaning. But for those who gained extended exposure to his line of thinking, the situation became abundantly clear. Behind every analogy was a reference to the practice of Meditation, Deep Mediation or Transcendental Deep Meditation, as it was variously referred to. Not only was its learning highly commended, the technique was made to sound indispensable.

Before taking a short rest from public life, on Wednesday, 30

December, the Maharishi publicly announced his Three-Year Plan, to commence on 1 January 1960, and told his followers that he would shortly be returning to India via Europe. In fact, after a week of silence, the next place to host the engaging Indian visitor was just a few miles away in south-west London. It was an apartment in Chelsea, which soon became the centre of operations and remained so for some months to come. There he could lecture, initiate and direct his followers. Amongst the steady flow of people interested in his philosophy came the occasional journalist, and there was soon a smattering of articles in local, national and European newspapers.

Soon, as in Los Angeles, his followers advised their teacher to take time off from his work and enjoy the sights and surroundings. Henry Nyburg, a wealthy businessman, even offered to chauffeur him on a trans-European holiday, so together they toured Switzerland, Austria, France and Germany in a Rolls Royce. The success of this trip can be measured by the fact that another was planned very soon after.

When he was not busy becoming acquainted with the roads of the Continent, the Chelsea centre continued to demand his attention. By the summer of 1960 an offer of a rather grand-looking property in Prince Albert Road, north London, gave the impetus to the formal establishment of the Spiritual Regeneration Movement of Great Britain, with its own board of trustees. At about this time he took the opportunity to train about twenty followers as Spiritual Guides. To qualify for this grand-sounding title, it was necessary to have an understanding of how to 'check' other initiates' meditations, together with the ability to re-establish correct practice should it prove necessary. The training of teachers of meditation as proposed in the Three-Year Plan found its first phase in this teaching of Guides.

When Brahmachari Mahesh had taken the initiative to discover the 'active ingredient' that lay within traditional *yogic* practices, the problem of isolating these techniques from the trappings of Hinduism was to prove particularly difficult. For a 'monk of the Shankaracharya Order', as he was frequently referred to, the inculcated and established habit of relating the order of the material world to that of the divine was too hard to suppress. Although the material in his lectures gave few insights into the 'monkish' side of his thinking, the odd chance remark would inevitably surface. A promotional pamphlet formulated in Los Angeles had delineated the many benefits to be derived from meditation. For the singer came the promise of a sweeter voice, and for the salesman an increased capacity to convince prospective buyers. But for seekers of God the Maharishi issued a challenge: 'As long as the

mind is not steady on the name of God, the devotion has not begun.'
From this it can be conjectured that the 'word without meaning'
imparted to new initiates could perhaps equally well have been termed
the 'name of God'.

Listening to his lecture at the Guildhall, Cambridge, on 11 July 1960,
entitled 'The Untapped Source of Power that Lies Within', the audience
might well have missed his mention of the celestial, sandwiched as it
was among fairly down-to-earth observations:

> If we drop a stone in pond the ripples begin to move and they move over the
> whole pond.
>   Similarly, by every thought, word and action, every individual is setting
> forth influence in his surroundings and that influence is not restricted to any
> boundaries. It goes on and on and reaches every level of creation.
>   Every individual by his every thought, word and action shakes the entire
> universe. This is the status of the individual.
>   He shares the responsibility for the life of the whole cosmos. The entire
> universe lies in the individual.
>   Every move of the individual shakes the cosmos. The universe reacts to the
> individual action. Every individual has this power that shakes the universe
> and shakes and saves the gods and angels in heaven. Man has this strength
> that upholds the universe. The individual by his every action serves the
> universe and the great power of nature is ready to serve the individual if the
> individual influences the universe for the progression of the process of
> evolution.[77]

What importance, if any, should one place on this mention of celestial
beings? The Maharishi seems to have anticipated such questions for in
the same lecture he stressed:

> We belong to the realistic age of science. Let us be sure that all we strive for
> and achieve remains realistic. Our age of scientific unfoldment does not give
> credence to anything shrouded in the garb of mysticism. Let us realise the
> Absolute Being through a scientific and systematic method of achievement
> where every achievement will be supplemented by the personal experience.[78]

The Maharishi Bal Brahmachari Mahesh Yogi owed much, if not all of
his spiritual understanding, to his teacher Shankaracharya Brahmanand
Saraswati. Since he did not show much awareness of this, one might
suspect that he had disowned his master. This outward impression, that
he was going it alone, a self-made man, probably made relations with
the general public easier than they might otherwise have been. But, for
those who made the effort to gain greater familiarity with his views,
things became much clearer; his master was far from forgotten.

Before coming for instruction, prospective students were asked to bring a few pieces of fresh fruit, some flowers, a clean white cotton handkerchief and their donation of a week's wages. At the initiation these offerings would be placed before a photograph or painting of an elderly Indian gentleman deeply absorbed in thought. Once the student was comfortably seated (the cross-legged posture most strongly recommended), the Maharishi would then murmur a prayer of devotion which the initiate would be unlikely to understand. If he or she happened to be a scholar of Sanskrit the meaning of this *puja* or ceremony would become evident, but more often than not the student would be blissfully ignorant of the content or meaning. The sonorous chant that was being offered was an invocation, containing the names of those particularly famous in the annals of *yoga* tradition. Roughly translated the Invocation of the Masters of the Holy Tradition begins:

> Skilled in dispelling the cloud of ignorance of the people, the gentle emancipator, Brahmananda Saraswati, the supreme teacher, full of brilliance, him I bring to my awareness.
> Offering invocation to the lotus feet of Shri Guru Dev, I bow down.[79]

Only after the completion of this prayer and the performance of a short ritual involving the offerings was the new initiate taught how to meditate.

Having learned the Maharishi's technique, new initiates were encouraged to attend follow-up meetings in which they were given further practical tips and additional information on the theory and philosophy of meditation. To those close to him, the Maharishi would sometimes narrate stories concerning the life of his teacher. Fortunately, much of the late Shankaracharya's life story had been preserved, as his lectures were peppered with personal anecdotes. Transcripts of these talks were later published in the monastery's newsletter and although it was intended that the material would be shared with a wider audience, they remained largely unavailable to the growing numbers of meditators outside India. The Maharishi wanted his meditators to know and respect his departed teacher and accordingly exhorted them to praise him. He taught them the phrase, '*Jai Guru Dev*' meaning 'Hail the Divine Guru', which soon came to be used in a bewildering variety of situations, including simply to say 'Hello' and 'Goodbye'. For some unaccountable reason the utterance of these words seemed to hold a certain undefinable magic for its users.

5

─ ★ ─

THE DIVINE PLAN, GOD AND SUFFERING

In the summer of 1960, after a spell at his disciple Henry Nyburg's luxurious home, the Old Manor in Wiltshire, the Maharishi decided to resume his favoured policy to 'establish a centre and then go to a new country'.[80] So far, the world tour had gone fairly well, and centres had been established across South East Asia, in Hawaii, on the west coast of America and in England. Rather than return directly to his faithful followers back in India, the Maharishi decided to try for just one more triumph, the winning over of the people of Germany. The Rolls Royce and driving skills of Henry Nyburg were duly pressed into action.

After each of his lectures the Maharishi had the task of initiating the many dozens that heeded to his message. He very soon became a victim of his own successes, for the volume of initiations increased to a point where, on one occasion in Stuttgart, he found himself giving over 100 people instruction. Since he had to check the experiences of all the new meditators to ensure that they had a proper understanding of the practice, his other commitments became delayed. However, when he belatedly arrived for his next introductory lecture, he appeared fresh and vital as ever. His apparent indefatigability had his devotees in awe, but nevertheless a revised strategy was suggested for the remainder of the German tour. The intention was to advertise each lecture in advance of his arrival and then to spend just three days in each location. The campaign more than fulfilled everyone's expectations. As days turned into weeks and weeks into months, the Maharishi still found himself inundated with candidates eager to participate in his Spiritual Regeneration Movement.

In order to deal with the increasing demand for initiation it would be necessary to fulfil his desire to 'multiply himself'. In the meantime he had at least to train someone else in the art of teaching his meditation method. He might have enlisted a fellow *brahmachari* from Jyotish Peeth Ashram, but instead he made the rather surprising decision to use the services of his travelling companion. In the shy, retiring, bespectacled, middle-aged Henry Nyburg, the Maharishi found a clarity of intellect and speech which he felt qualified him for training as a deputy. He did not delay and before long the Spiritual Regeneration Movement had not one but two *maharishis*.

During that visit to Germany, no fewer than nine centres were opened. It might have been a good time to return to India, riding upon the crest of a wave. Instead he headed back to London, to share the news of his triumphant journey.

Utilizing the new and proven tour strategy practised in Germany, the Maharishi announced his next campaign, with lectures arranged in all the major university towns, travelling as far north as Edinburgh. The lecture at the Guildhall in Cambridge found him in strident form:

> It's a pleasure for me to be here this evening, in the company of all of you, in this great seat of learning.
>
> What is needed today is a technique to harmonise the qualities of the head with those of the heart. The head alone going ahead leaving the heart behind, man is found tumbling down. This is what is happening today in the world. All advancements in the field of science and technology and all study of the various subjects in the world leading the man to what …? Increasing state of chaos and tension in the world!
>
> The word meditation is not new, the gains from meditation are not new to be counted, but, the information that it is easy for everyone to meditate and experience the inner glories of life, this seems to be a new message. Although the message is a centuries-old message. The same age-old message of Buddha, the same age-old message of Christ, the same age-old message of Krishna. Get within, experience the Kingdom of Heaven, experience Nirvana, experience Eternal Freedom, come out with that freedom, live a life of freedom in the world, the same age-old message. Only for the past centuries it had been forgotten, as if forgotten, the technique forgotten. And that's why the life, the individual life seems to be suffering, seems to be increasingly suffering. So much so that centres which were responsible to lead the people to the Kingdom of Heaven within began to propound the theories of suffering.
>
> Essentially, life is bliss …[81]

This quotation is of special importance in determining the Maharishi's self-image. He linked himself with the leaders of three world religions with such ease as to raise strong suspicions of messianic tendencies. However, it is unlikely that he found anything unacceptable, let alone dangerous, in his stance. It is important to remember the tradition to which he belonged, for in India unlike the West, it is not uncommon for people to be accorded the status of saint. Likewise it is not unknown for such individuals to be identified with the Supreme and given the title *Bhagavan* (God); the Maharishi's own master was frequently addressed in this way. The important thing to note is that the acquisition of this identification with God is an end in itself and seldom the basis of a new philosophy or religion. Although the Maharishi's words seem to imply that he had personally received the grace of God and experienced some sort of Heaven, he did stress that his message was not new, merely the voice of revival. Since he offered neither prophecies nor claims of divine revelation, he still remained in relative safety, positioned in the role of interpreter.

Such was the gentleness of his manner and the authority of his voice, that he encountered no real hostility. Far from being branded a religious fanatic, his predominantly conservative audiences found him reassuringly reasonable, even democratic. After all, he appeared to be offering something much more than fine speeches, he claimed to be able to reveal the 'Kingdom of Heaven within', not just for the select few, but for anyone who wished it.

Let us examine how this miracle was to be achieved.

Central to his thinking lay his stated belief that the natural tendency of the mind is towards greater happiness. Therefore, he reasoned, given the opportunity the mind would gravitate towards ever greater happiness. To facilitate this expansion of happiness, he offered his method of meditation. Acknowledging that the mind is accustomed to entertain thoughts and that any attempt to purge it instantly of this habit might prove counter-productive, he offered to provide a 'vehicle' for keeping the mind occupied. He warned that the correct selection of the vehicle or 'word that for us is without meaning' was of paramount importance to the success of his method, maintaining that by the correct use of this word, the mind might easily transcend or 'go beyond' the thoughts that prevented the mind from experiencing the 'Kingdom of Heaven'. It all sounded far too good to be true!

Thoughts of returning to India were soon abandoned as plans were made to tour Scandinavia. The tour commenced on Monday, 28 November 1960 in Norway where, after the customary press conference, he lectured at Hoyres Hus Hall, Oslo, to a predominantly student audience. From Norway he moved via Denmark to Sweden. Before the tour had started the Maharishi had been informed that the people of Sweden were more 'sophisticated' and 'conservative' than the British. To this he retorted:

This is good. Conservative means they are self-sufficient, and they don't want any infringement from outside.[82]

In trying to understand the country he was to visit, he inquired into Sweden's mental health and accordingly sought information about their provision for mental hospitals. This seems a strange line of inquiry, but he was no doubt already preparing his sales pitch. However, he spent only enough time for a hurried taste of Sweden before moving once more to Germany to lead a Spiritual Guides course where, between 23 and 29 December 1960 he instructed another twenty meditators as Guides. This course was held in the Black Forest area, from where he travelled back to Stuttgart and Munich in order to resume his lecturing. He subsequently initiated several hundred newcomers. Another busy year had come to an end and to mark the occasion the Spiritual Regeneration Movement's boss decided to take some leave, to be spent in silence at Henry Nyburg's chalet in Kitzbühel, amidst Austria's snowy Tyrolean Mountains.

The New Year, 1961, got off to a good start, with the Maharishi returning to Sweden in order to deal with a backlog of initiations there, followed by a flying visit to Italy and a brief but very effective appearance in Greece. The crowning achievement of this visit came in his televized appearance at the Acropolis, which subsequently became a worldwide radio broadcast heard by countless millions.

He chose this moment to return home, not to a life of solitude but to make contact with his followers across India. As it happened though, he barely had time to catch up with the news and look up old friends before flying out again. Before leaving, however, he found time to see his associate, Dr Hislop, who had been nominated to look for a suitable site for a teacher-training academy.

> He [Hislop] stayed there three months. A man brought up in the American aristocracy, goes to the Himalayas and then stays there for three months, where there is no proper food ...
>
> It is Uttar Kashi, and the surrounding area is a place of poverty, not of luxury ...[83]

The reason for the Maharishi's hasty exit from India was that a date had been set for the First World Assembly of the Spiritual Regeneration Movement. Organized by the President of the School of Economic Science, London, Leonardo Mclaren, this prestigious event was set to be held at London's Albert Hall on Monday, 13 March 1961, and for two days prior to the big event, preparatory sessions were held at the Caxton

Hall. At last the day of the assembly arrived and the Maharishi found himself addressing a capacity crowd of 5000. His lecture comprised the many themes he had been popularizing of late. Following this talk, his second-in-command, Henry Nyburg, made an appearance and proposed a Declaration of the First World Assembly of the Spiritual Regeneration Movement.

Following his successful appearance at the Albert Hall, the Maharishi became rather attracted by the idea of world assemblies and proceeded to arrange a number of similar events across Europe and throughout India. Accompanying him at these assemblies were several dozen meditators who could always be relied upon to testify to the merit of his methods. In India he had acquired something of a reputation and now enjoyed celebrity status, with government ministers eagerly endorsing his campaign. When a three-day assembly was convened in Jabalpur on 5 April, the Maharishi and his family had the chance of a brief reunion. But he had little time for idleness, for on average, 200 people were coming to be initiated each day. The finale of this 'assembly tour' was held on Wednesday, 12 April 1961 at Sapru House in New Delhi, approximately two years after the commencement of his world tour. Clearly at this time his capacity for strategy could have won him employment in virtually any major advertising concern.

In the West the Maharishi's lectures had mainly been attended by people uninformed about India's spiritual heritage. Now, in his homeland, he was addressing his peers. The news of his fame met with a mixed response amongst his fellow countrymen, where even the most unlettered villager could give expert information regarding his or her religion. In a nation governed by tradition, and spiritual tradition at that, the Maharishi had his work cut out to defend his version, his reinterpretation, of age-old beliefs. To many it must have appeared audacious that he should presume to rework any of their most treasured beliefs, and they did not let him off lightly. They demanded scriptural authority for his teachings, forcing him back upon the repertoire of quotations he no doubt learned from his 'Guru Dev'. Many of his critics were appeased by his responses, but others remained unconvinced. Perhaps it was just these entrenched attitudes, the clinging on to philosophies which depended on renunciation and self-abnegation, that had first inspired him to court Western approval before again tackling the bastions of his homeland.

From Delhi he made his way northwards towards Rishikesh, known as the 'Gateway of Uttra Khand', an area connected with the spiritual history of India for time immemorial and containing the towns of both

Joshimath (Jyotir Math) and Uttar Kashi. On his previous visit, a fifteen-acre site had been found on which to erect the International Academy of Meditation. As yet there had not been enough time to get it ready for occupation.

> It is difficult to build in the mountains, especially in the Himalayas - everything has to come on horseback or muleback. Every little bit, stone and brick and all these things, so it is taking a little longer than I expected. Because in my mind everything should be easy and quick. But the buildings have gone up beyond my expectations.[84]

In the meantime, an alternative venue was sought where he might train teachers of meditation. It was decided to hold the course in Uttar Kashi, at Gyaan Mandir, and to that end several simple but capacious wooden buildings were constructed to house the course. But at the last minute an invitation came from another *ashram* to hold the course there.

Whilst work was being carried out on construction of Dhyaan Vidya Peeth (the Academy of Meditation), the training course convened at a spot known as Ram Nagar, at Rishikesh, near to the newly acquired plot. From around the world came more than sixty meditators to study in conditions Spartan but tranquil. The Master would lecture his students as they sat upon the bank of the River Ganges. On moonlit nights the group would gather together to take part in communal meditation. During this course the Maharishi found time to dwell upon the problem of searching the scriptural texts to find material that would bear out his line of philosophy.

A prime source of inspiration to many Hindus is a book entitled the *Bhagavad-Gita*, supposedly the transcript of a dialogue between the legendary Lord Krishna and his friend Arjuna. Arjuna faces a grave dilemma – his family has become divided by dispute and a decision has been made to settle their differences by armed combat. Arjuna is famed for his skill and prowess as an archer but he will not, enter the fray. Lord Krishna, who has volunteered to be his charioteer, counsels him to abandon his uncertainties and get on with the fight. Krishna points out that his friend's reluctance to engage in combat will be interpreted as cowardice. But Arjuna's problem lies not in any lack of courage but in his concern that by wounding or killing his relatives he will suffer guilt and remorse for ever. Lord Krishna, often identified as an *avataar* or incarnation of God, hoping to free Arjuna from his indecisiveness, instructs him in a different philosophy of life. Reviewing the verses containing Krishna's instructions, the Maharishi became convinced that he had found several references that appeared to support his own philosophical contentions and proceeded to test them on his captive audience. He was not displeased with their reactions.

On Tuesday, 30 May 1961, eight years to the day after his master's death, the Shankaracharya of Jyotir Math, Swami Shantanand Saraswati graced the teacher-training course with his presence and was received with all due ceremony. Arriving at the site where the new Academy was being built, he addressed the Maharishi and the gathered meditators:

> Rishikesh is a place where so many saints and sages meditated with a view to attaining Self-realisation. Every grain of sand is vibrating forth the holy influence of saints and sages who have inhabited this part of India since ages past.[85]

He commended the practice of the Maharishi's meditation, describing it as a 'master key to the knowledge of Vedanta' and added, 'There are other keys, but a master key is enough to open all the locks.'[86]

After staying for a while at Rishikesh he announced his intention to move on and offered a parting message to those gathered there: 'We are ever at God's feet. Never forget that we are the sons of Sat Chit Ananda.'[87]

Swami Vishnudevanand, his closest disciple stayed until the end of the course, whilst Swami Shantanand and his retinue, many of whom had also served the former Shankaracharya, departed. They had come at the Maharishi's request and it is clear that his position in India was strengthened by this support.

Although sixty had attended the training sessions, far fewer were ordained as teachers of meditation, but at least it had been a step forward towards the fulfilment of his Three-Year Plan. Whilst at Ram Nagar, the Maharishi also devoted time to a course for saints, *sadhus* and *swamis* interested in hearing his teaching.

Soon the lure of touring drew him again. This time he flew first to Africa, where on 23 August he made an appearance in Nairobi, Kenya, and then on to England for a brief meeting with meditators in London. From England he returned to the United States where, after a visit to his friends the Olsons at their home in Los Angeles, he embarked on a West Coast tour. He extended his journey northwards into Canada, visiting the cities of Vancouver and Victoria.

The Maharishi was undoubtedly very concerned that he had trained so few teachers so far and as a preliminary measure towards the training of the '25,000 teachers within three years' for which he aimed, he set up a Meditation Guides' course on Santa Catalina Island off the Californian coast. In order to become better acquainted with his students, he gathered them together, asking each in turn to stand up and identify themselves, and to say something of their occupations. This course, which was specifically aimed at providing an opportunity for extended meditations, occupied the last months of the year. In late December he followed his custom of taking a few days off for silence, during which he undertook the composition of a revealing devotional poem, which he entitled 'God'. The following is an extract:

> My Lord
> And I know
> When I begin, I begin so abruptly
> I know now
> When I began, I began so abruptly
> From the loudest note I began
> For I could not sing it low
> Thy Grace of Eternity
> The Glory of Eternity
> I could not sing it low
> The Glory of Eternal Life
> I know not how to sing it low
> So I blew my trumpet full!
> It echoed round the world
> How it sounded to Thee, I do not know,
> But to me it has been fun
> A real fun of greatest joy
> A real, good great fun
> Yes.[88]

At the start of 1962, the Maharishi was still in the USA, but was now working on the East Coast. Although the rather optimistic goals of the Three-Year Plan laid down in Sequoia Park were still far from being realized, interest in his meditation method increased daily. He believed that the use of pamphlets and literature was of little consequence in the spreading of his message, but that did not stop a steady flow of publications emerging. The new year was to yield a bumper crop of publications starting with *The Blessing That Awaits You*, a basic introduction to meditation, followed by the provocatively titled, *Discovery of 'Nuclear Life Energy' – Maharishi's Theory of the Absolute: The Fulfilment of Dr Einstein's Theory of Relativity*.

Another publication, a guide to *yoga* postures, was released in March. The genesis of this particular booklet is of some interest. It is told that a vexed and serious meditator asked the Maharishi what would happen if the goal of the meditation, a permanent state of bliss, was not achieved in a lifetime. Uncharacteristically, he was rendered temporarily speechless. When at last he found words to answer his enquirer, he

recommended the daily practice of simple *yogic* exercises to accelerate
the process of expansion of consciousness. The exercises he chose had
been prepared by Prof. K. B. Hari Krishna of the University of
Travancore, India. In his foreword to *A Six Month Course In Yoga
Asanas* the Maharishi said:

> For good health it is necessary for everyone to do something with the body
> so that it remains flexible and normal.
>
> The advantage of YOGA ASANAS over other eastern and western systems of
> physical posture is that they do not consume energy. They help restore life
> force, promote health and maintain normal conditions in the body.[89]

March 1962 was a particularly good month for those in search of
'product'. A long-playing record with two of his early lectures, *Deep
Meditation* and *The Healing Power of Deep Meditation*, were issued on
the World-Wide Records label. And as if his eager devotees had not
been more than amply provided for, more came. In the 'God' poem the
Maharishi had confided that 'I know not how to sing it low, so I blew
my trumpet full!' But was the world yet ready for his new output?

In *The Divine Plan* one can almost detect a deliberate effort to keep
the trumpet blowing to an acceptable level. It would appear that there
exists a Divine Plan devised to assist mankind along the road of spiritual
progress, but as motorways become worn and need repair, so it is,
apparently, with the highway to the divine. To facilitate travel,
engineers must be sent out to assess and improve the route.

That the Maharishi perceived himself as following a divine calling is
implicit throughout, although not actually stated. In describing the
function of the Divine Plan, he offered an insight into his perception of
the purpose of life:

> The whole complex of the Universe is so designed that all must evolve -
> angels, man, animals, birds, insects, and all – must forge ahead on the
> highway of evolution and must reach the ultimate destiny in God
> Consciousness. But when man begins to act in a negative way, in a way
> which would lead him to suffering and misery in life, then the Divine Plan is
> disturbed.[90]

He furthermore indicated that the practice of his techniques could reveal
both the nature and the detail of the divine will.

According to the Maharishi, the lineage of monks known as the
Shankaracharya Order is the 'authentic custodian of the wisdom of the
mantras'. Central to the teaching of his meditation lay the successful
selection and application of these *mantras*. He drew a comparison
between the choice of correct 'medium' and the assessment of blood

groups, pointing out that a doctor could do untold harm by transfusing the wrong blood type. He continued in this vein, asserting:

> There are thousands of *mantras* and all have their specific values, specific qualities and are suitable for specific types of people.[91]

Having spent the early part of the year in the USA, by spring the Maharishi was preparing another trip to India to put in an appearance at Rishikesh. Again the Shankaracharya was on hand to lend his support. After another course for recluses (*sadhus* and *swamis*) the Maharishi undertook a brief tour of northern India.

His mission to spiritually regenerate the world seemed on the surface to be going well, but in reality a divisive undercurrent was already starting to make itself felt. At least two of his prominent followers, Leon Mclaren and Dr Francis Roles, had became disaffected with the Movement and were already branching out on their own. Perhaps this had been their intention all along, for Dr Roles had been a follower of P.D. Ouspensky, who in turn had been a prominent disciple of Georges Ivanovitch Gurdjieff, a notable thinker of his time. It is claimed that Ouspensky had instructed Dr Roles to seek out a simple method of finding inner stillness and offer it to those living ordinary lives. Roles had discovered an unlikely and very useful ally in no less a personage than Swami Shantanand. The venerable Shankaracharya had given a clue to his breadth of vision in his address to the participants of the teacher-training course the previous year, in which he had alluded to the many keys or paths to illumination. In time Roles seized his opportunity and happily found the Shankaracharya willing to offer his group the spiritual guidance it sought. The Maharishi, on discovering the existence of the tear-away group, made every effort to persuade the mutinous Roles to toe the party line, but he was eventually forced to accept the situation. According to Joyce Collin-Smith in *Call No Man Master* (Gateway, 1988) Roles 'announced that he had forged a link with a much greater master'. As Joyce appears to have been a close personal assistant and chauffeur to the Maharishi at this time, she is well placed to confide that he was not particularly enamoured with Roles but believed his meditation movement needed the organisational skills possessed by Roles and his associates from the Society for the Study of Normal Man.

The desire for the rapid expansion of his world movement fuelled plans for training further teachers to teach his meditation. In the summer of 1962 the Maharishi set up yet another course, this time in Hochgurgl,

Austria. His ability to attract influential people never seemed to let him down. This time it tapped a rich seam in finding Prince Giovanni Alliata de Montreale, a Member of the Italian Parliament, who thereafter took an active and high-profile part in detailing the merits of Deep Meditation. At the conclusion of the course, the Maharishi took yet another break at Henry Nyburg's country home in England, and with renewed energy he recommenced operations, travelling to Scandinavia, France and Ireland before returning to Los Angeles.

Whilst the Maharishi vigorously pursued his worldwide campaign, his followers were not inactive. Amongst other things, they saw to it that new pamphlets and booklets were published. Many of the Master's lectures were transcribed and reproduced for public consumption. These generally focused on a particular theme but were united by essentially the same message: meditate and be happy. Although for the most part the Maharishi succeeded in steering clear of particularly contentious or controversial issues this sometimes proved unavoidable. In a question and answer session contained in a short work simply entitled *Deep Meditation* he offered some radical, and therefore provocative, comments on contemporary Christian thinking:

> Q. Maharishi, why is, in the Christian circles, such an accent laid upon the suffering of Christ?

> A. Due to not understanding the life of Christ and not understanding the message of Christ. I don't think Christ ever suffered or Christ could suffer. The suffering man from the suffering platform sees the Bliss of Christ as suffering. Green specks on the glass and everything is seen as green.[92]

6

—★—

TALKING BOOK

The years that had been set aside for the Three-Year Plan were almost up. Aware of the fact that his achievements had not matched his plans, the Maharishi prepared his response, the Second Three-Year Plan, but before revealing this new initiative he decided that another short holiday was in order. Once at the quietly beautiful retreat at Lake Arrowhead, California, however, the ebullient master of relaxation could not restrain himself and threw himself into yet another project. Although he had commenced writing a commentary on the *Bhagavad-Gita*, he interrupted this to work on its successor, intended as a textbook to his teachings. Since he was far better attuned to public speaking, he chose first to speak his thoughts onto tape and then to provide direction whilst the subsequent transcriptions were being edited. The resultant book, *Science of Being and Art of Living*, was finished by late January 1963 and published (in English) soon after. On Saturday, 12 January 1963, his forty-sixth birthday, he wrote these words for its introduction:

> The *Science of Being and Art of Living* is the summation of both the practical wisdom of integrated life advanced by the Vedic Rishis of ancient India and the growth of scientific thinking in the present-day Western world.[93]

The majority of his readers would have had to take his word for the truth of this claim, since the thinking of the Vedic *rishis* was unfamiliar to most of them. Included in the Maharishi's introduction was an acknowledgement of his indebtedness to his Master, His Divinity Swami Brahmanand Saraswati, Jagadguru Bhagwan Shankaracharya, whose picture graced one of the opening pages. Unaccountably no photograph of the Maharishi was included in this first edition.

Science of Being and Art of Living was no small achievement; it addressed a multitude of subjects and pointed to meditation as a practical means to their fulfilment. For those who sought further justification for purchasing the book, what could have been more persuasive than the following declaration?

> This is a book of revival for the age. If the golden era is ever to dawn on human society, if the aquarian age is ever to be on earth, *The Science of Being and Art of Living* will provide a free way for it to come.[94]

Although the Maharishi's Hawaiian followers had apparently already published a volume under his name, this was the first authentic book to become available to the mass of meditators. It afforded a unique opportunity for them to gain a greater understanding of and familiarity with his philosophies. By the thoughtful inclusion of analogies and anecdotes, some lighter relief was provided in what would otherwise have been pretty dry text. The vocabulary of the Spiritual Regeneration Movement posed occasional difficulties for new aspirants, in particular the similarity between the words spirituality and spiritualism. Perhaps it was just this confusion that caused the Maharishi to offer his views on the value of spiritualism:

> There are some who try to make use of the supernatural power of creation by contacting the spirit world through a medium or through invoking spirits. That is on a very limited level of strength because no spirit is in possession of the total power of nature. There may be spirits who may be more powerful than man but invoking these spirits or behaving as a medium for them is not a practice to be encouraged because of two reasons. First, the power gained through these spirits is an insignificant, infinitesimal fraction of the power of almighty nature; second, in order to receive that portion of the power of nature, one has to give oneself completely to the influence of that spirit.[95]

Throughout the book the Maharishi seems to have been intent on urging readers on to a point where they would feel compelled to try out his system of meditation. A vital ingredient in achieving this end was his recurrent and persuasive use of a formula from the Vedic *rishis:* 'I am That. Thou art That, and all this is That.'[96]

In striving to explain man's position in the order of things, he asserted his vision of the scope of evolution:

> At the lowest end of evolution we find the inert states of creation. From there, the life of the species begins, and the creation changes in its intelligence, power and joyfulness. The progressive scale of evolution continues through the different species of the vegetable, the egg-born, the water-born, the animal kingdom, and rises to the world of angels. Ultimately, on the top level of evolution, is He whose power is unlimited, whose joyfulness is unlimited, whose intelligence and energy are unlimited.[97]

Having contended that human beings have the ability to share a close affinity with the very highest strata of evolution, he then took a swipe at established religion, criticizing its inability to unite man with his God.

> The true spirit of religion is lacking when it counts only what is right or wrong and creates fear of punishment and hell and the fear of God in the mind of men. The purpose of religion should be to take away all fear from man. It should not seek to achieve its purpose through instilling fear of the Almighty in the mind.[98]

One way of describing the meditation he promoted to achieve this union was to say what it was not. In surveying the practice of emptying the mind, he warned:

> All such practices of silencing the mind are wrong.
> There are many groups in the world who sit in silence and try to hear their inner voice or the voice of God, as they term it. All such practices make the mind passive and dull.[99]

The modern practice of psychology also met with condemnation.

> If there could be a way to expand one's consciousness in the direction of more evolved states of consciousness, and if there could be a way to enlarge the present stage of consciousness to the unbounded universal state of cosmic consciousness, then the subjects of psychoanalysis would certainly be saved from the unfortunate influence of overshadowing their consciousness by digging into the mud of the miserable past – which suppresses their consciousness.[100]

It might have appeared to some that the benefits to be derived from Transcendental Deep Meditation were of a purely personal, even selfish, nature. Far from supporting this view the Maharishi claimed that it could not only be useful for the individual, but could prove a tool for creating world peace.

> It has been brought out by Charak and Sushrut, the great exponents of medical science in ancient India, that as long as people behave in righteousness, the atmosphere remains full of harmonious vibrations.
> Thus we find from every angle that in order to produce a good, harmonious and healthy atmosphere for the good of all creatures in the world, it is necessary that man live in happiness, peace, and abundance. Every man has a chance to live this way.[101]

Towards the end of this lengthy book, he outlined his vision of future possibilities in which, amongst other advances, he envisaged the provision of a number of structures dedicated to the practice of meditation.

> It seems necessary that sanctuaries of silence be constructed in the midst of noisy marketplaces of big cities, so that people, before going to their

business, and after completing their business of the day, may enter into silent meditation rooms, dive deep within themselves, and be profited by undisturbed, regular, and deep meditations. Apart from the silent meditation centers in the noisy areas of towns, it seems to be necessary that such silent meditation centers also be constructed in the holiday resorts where people go on weekends to stay for one or two days. There they may have long hours of deep meditation and come home renewed in spirit, intelligence, and energy.[102]

He must surely have hoped that by tantalizing the reader with page after page of positive assertions about the benefits to be derived from his methods, a hunger would result that could only be satisfied by a trip to the local meditation centre. Indeed, a coupon was attached to the inside of the back cover giving the address and telephone number of the nearest contact. Unfortunately for those as yet unacquainted with his method of Transcendental Deep Meditation, the book yielded little information, for in spite of the countless references to the technique, there was no attempt to give details of it. However, since the book was published privately by the Movement it is unlikely that it was promoted strongly enough to reach a particularly wide audience.

Having created a textbook to his ideology, the Maharishi felt free to resume his travels. On Sunday, 27 January 1963 he returned to some of the South East Asian locations he had visited on his first world tour. He flew to Hong Kong and then on to Rangoon in Burma, finally touching down at Calcutta Airport on 5 February. He then made for Allahabad, bound for the *ashram* of Shankaracharya Swami Shantanand. The former Shankaracharya, Swami Brahmanand, had secured this property in 1950 a few years before his death, from the former Maharajah of Lucknow, who had initially offered it as a gift. News that the Shankaracharya had been able to pay the market value of 100,000 rupees in cash had made tongues wag. How could one who would accept no offerings of material wealth have access to such a vast sum – and in cash? When the people pestered him for an explanation, he maintained a stoic silence. Eventually in a bid to settle the matter, he declared: 'No human being was involved in this. When God gives, He gives all that is required...'[103] Brahma Nivas, as the converted palace had been named, had been designated as the Shankaracharya's winter residence.

The Maharishi now sought to confer with his former fellow-disciple. Fortune smiled on him in that he received the *swami's* blessing for his new scheme, an All-Indian Campaign. It was intended that it should start in Delhi, continue across the northern provinces and then go on to central India. Perhaps he genuinely believed that he could offer something which would help alleviate the severe problems of poverty and suffering in a country still beleaguered by superstition and caste-consciousness.

One problem dogged the Maharishi, and that was the lack of appropriate publicity material, in particular pictorial evidence of the close relationship he claimed to have had with his 'Guru Dev'. Providentially a photograph showing the former Shankaracharya with Bal Brahmachari Mahesh seated close by was discovered in time for the campaign. It turned out to be exactly the same as one of the Shankaracharya in the company of the first President of India, but with the *brahmachari* in the President's place. However, this dearth of suitable photographs was later remedied by the discovery of snapshots of unquestionable authenticity taken during the years that the Maharishi had spent with his master.

This episode provides unexpected and reasonably conclusive proof that the *brahmachari* had not seriously entertained thoughts of forming his own organization or mission until the very end of the Shankaracharya's life, or even later still. Had he done so he would almost certainly have prepared himself for the event. In fact there is little evidence that the Maharishi ever prepared for the growth of his Movement nor, more importantly, that he had the capacity for predicting its progress. This is not to say that he had no interest in the future. He did. After the *Beacon Light* lectures in October 1955 he had consulted a *jyotishi* (astrologer), who is alleged to have offered an extremely favourable forecast.

Saturday 2 March 1963 was a red-letter day in the All-India Campaign. The Maharishi had been specially invited to speak to Members of the Indian Parliament. In comparison with his early lectures, the style of his delivery was by now considerably more fluent. In measured and self-assured tones he drew from his wealth of ideas, the words flowing almost involuntarily from his lips. The politicians of New Delhi would dearly have loved to have been able to equal his eloquence; perhaps it was in the hope of acquiring such skills that some of them later asked for initiation into his mediation.

The All-India Campaign continued with a tour which embraced the predominantly Sikh cities of the Punjab, the distant north-eastern state of Assam, a couple of cities in central India and a visit to scenic Srinagar in Kashmir.

At the conclusion of the campaign, a forty-day Spiritual Guides' course was held at his Academy near Rishikesh and in late April he made his way there. The course, which was intended to train new teachers, laid a heavy emphasis on gaining greater familiarity of the experience of meditation. Accordingly, the course participants spent much of their time in silent inner communion. These periods of quiet were interspersed with lectures from the Maharishi, a certain amount of study and a certain amount of recreation time.

These courses proved a rare opportunity for foreign visitors to better acquaint themselves with Indian culture, discovering for themselves how the other half lived. In keeping with local custom, only strictly vegetarian food was served to them; even eggs were banned from the Academy menu. For those brought up on 'meat and two veg' this must have been a dramatic culture shock. However, in the search for the 'untapped source of energy within', a change of diet was but a trifling matter.

Whilst the Maharishi was still in India, dates were fixed for courses in both Norway and Austria, which it was naturally assumed he would attend. In this the organizers were to be disappointed, for the Master wanted to remain in India to preside over his All-India Campaign. He delivered something of a bombshell by deputizing his understudy Henry Nyburg to officiate in his absence. Although nobody would admit it, at that time the Spiritual Regeneration Movement was virtually synonymous with the Maharishi, whose personal charm and volubility made him well loved. His meditation, in addition to its proclaimed efficacy, also offered followers a symbol of his presence. In attending courses with the Maharishi, his devotees had a chance to bathe in his reflected glory. The news that he would not be overseeing the Scandinavian and European courses himself meant that, in order to show their allegiance, they must accept his will and settle for tuition from his right-hand man.

There was some consolation, however, in the fact that a gramophone record was released at this time.[104] On one side there was a lecture, and on the other a poem simply entitled 'Love'. Like its predecessor, 'God', it was anything but short. The recording of the *Love* poem began with a dedication sung softly in Sanskrit. The poem itself was a series of impressions on the theme of love, with only one explicit reference to his technique of Transcendental Deep Meditation. But to the initiate the implicit references were many and various. For example, the technique required that one neither dispel nor be held by the thoughts experienced during its practice.

The sun shines, and it shines forever in fullness. It may be that the clouds are gathering. Let them come and go, they go as they come. Take no notice of their coming, you go your way. Make your way through the clouds if they lie on the way. Do not try to dispel them, do not be held by them, they will go the way they have come. They are never found stationary, but if you like to pause to see them wither away, wait for a while. The wind is blowing anyway, it is to clear the clouds from your way. Just wait to see the cloud wither away, and the sun, the same old sun of love will shine again, in fullness of its glory.

He makes some profound and irrefutable observations:

When an ocean flows in love, it flows in peace within. When a shallow pond moves to rise high in waves of the ocean, it only stirs the mud at the bottom, and the whole serenity of the pond is spoilt. When a heart, shallow as a pond seeks to rise high in waves of love, it creates a muddle and brings out the mud that was so far gracefully hidden underneath. To enjoy the ocean of love, we have to improve the magnitude of our hearts and gain the depth of an ocean, unfathomable and full.

Also included in the poem is a prayer, perhaps of traditional origin This was not the first time he had been known to offer up personal prayers for contained in *A Sixth Month Course in Yoga Asanas* is another, related to success in *yoga* practice and a third, concerned with thanksgiving for food, is to be found in *Science of Being and Art of Living*. The prayer which lies within the 'Love' poem is by far the most devotional of the three. I have heard something similar from a *yogi*, apparently unrelated to the Maharishi's order:

My lord, in the temple of my heart, on the altar of thy glory, my God, my love is full, and thy love is treasured safely. My love for thee is safe and full in freshness and purity at the glory of thy altar. My lord, thy lordship is secured in the shrine of my heart, and when my love flows, it spreads the glory in thy creation.

The following passage seems almost autobiographical in content:

In love of God, the lover of life finds expression of the inexpressible. Cosmic life gains expression in his activity. The thought of cosmic life is materialized in his process of thinking. His eyes behold the purpose of creation, his ears hear the music of cosmic life, his hands hold on to cosmic intentions. His feet set the cosmic life in motion, he walks on earth, yet walks in the destiny of heaven. Angels enjoy his being on earth, this is the glory of unity born of love.

The body of the poem is packed brim full with optimism and accordingly finishes in like fashion.

Love shall save us from wrong and guide our path in life. Love shall forever shine on our way and the light will guide our steps whether we go slow or fast. The light of love shall forever be with us on our way. Love shall forever be with us on our way. Love shall forever be the anchor of our life. We shall be in love and love shall be in us. We shall live in love, shall grow in love and shall find fulfilment in love eternal. Jai Guru Dev.

The Norwegian and Austrian courses went on as planned, but without the Maharishi's presence. His plans in the meantime, underwent a dramatic change; instead of continuing his work in India, he left to join his followers in Los Angeles and later presented himself at a course in Canada.

From there he intended to fly to Britain but before doing so, showed his mettle by making an impromptu tour from the west to the east of Canada. On 1 October he set off for Britain where he met up with Henry Nyburg. Together they proceeded to Henry's country home. For the Maharishi, holidays had a habit of turning into 'busman's holidays' and on this occasion he recommenced work on his commentary on the *Bhagavad-Gita*. He enlisted the help of his devotees; Dr Vernon Katz assisted in translating the Sanskrit text, and others helped to put his ideas into 'good' English. Less than two weeks later he was off again in search of new minds, on a whistle-stop tour which took in Norway, Sweden, Denmark, Germany, Italy and Greece.

By Christmas he was in Delhi, facing a barrage of questions from the press. Some topics he would answer with great patience, whilst others he would give but scant attention, as if some self-imposed censorship were at work. For instance:

Q. Why do you choose to propagate this system in foreign countries rather than in India?

A. For India I went out! (laughter)[105]

Over the following months the Maharishi curbed his desire to roam in order to catch up with paperwork. A renewed effort to complete his commentary on the *Bhagavad-Gita* took up much of his time until March 1964, when he was invited to appear at a three-day conference on *yoga* under the banner of the All-India Yogic Sammelan. The conference provided an invaluable chance for the Maharishi to test his new interpretations of old and familiar teachings, for attending the conference would be teachers from a diversity of traditions representing a wide range of philosophies and spiritual practices. Perhaps it was at just such individuals that his commentary on the *Gita* was aimed, for after all, at this time precious few Westerners had even heard of the book.

In late May 1964, news of the death of India's Prime Minister, Jawaharhal Nehru, provoked the Maharishi to urge his followers to observe a meditation week in memory of this celebrated leader. Throughout the country, the days became marked by group meditations at centres of the Spiritual Regeneration Movement. Devotion to Nehru's memory was taken a step further when it was decided to dedicate to him a 'temple of peace' in Bangalore, India.

The organizers of the Norwegian summer Meditation Guides' course no doubt wondered whether events would again conspire to rob them of the presence of the Maharishi. Their fears were confirmed when again they were requested to go ahead without him. In the event, he joined them after the first week of the course, but since it was only a short one, it was just a matter of days before the Maharishi was off again.

The movement in London had its backbone in long-standing meditators such as Marjorie Gill, Henry Nyburg, Jemima Pitman and Vincent Snell, a surgeon. It is said of Vincent that he had a reputation for being somewhat volatile, but after learning to meditate he claimed to find that the temperament of his colleagues improved immensely! The Maharishi entrusted the work of running the organization in Great Britain to Vincent and with the assistance of his loyal devotees another tour of the country was arranged. As in India the greatest barrier to success was the established order of religion. Although much of what he said had a religious flavour, the road to God he described sounded just a little too easy to be believed. Those who had dedicated most of their lives to attempting a union with God were sceptical of his claims. Furthermore there were those who doubted that the God he spoke of was the same as the one they were searching for. In order to muster popular support for his methods, he needed to establish himself as a man whose word could be relied upon. What was desperately needed was some endorsement for his methods, preferably from someone senior in the establishment.

A chance to address some of these concerns came in an offer for the Maharishi to appear in a televized debate alongside a representative of the clergy, the Abbot of Downside, Abbot Butler, on the aptly named 'Meeting Point', which was broadcast on the evening of Sunday, 5 July 1964.[106] After a brief introduction, presenter Robert Kee asked the Maharishi how he had come to his knowledge of meditation:

MMY – I would say a very systematic teaching of my Master in India.

Kee – Who was your master?

MMY – He was Jagad Guru Shankaracharya Swami Brahmananda

Saraswati, a very great saint in the Himalayas, hailed by all the people.

Kee – He is a Hindu saint?

MMY – Yes, a Hindu saint, but what I think is the essence of every religion, is really the same – to enable every man to rise above conflicts and anxieties and sorrows and sufferings in life, and to live a peaceful and joyful and harmonious life.

During the course of the ensuing discussion, the Maharishi outlined the theory behind his system of meditation, after which Kee observed:

Kee – It seems to me though, really what you are saying is that by a simple almost mechanical technique I can show you God.

MMY – Very right, very right, mechanical, because now we are in the mechanical age, this mechanical age – and then these mechanics are easy, because at every step of the subtlety of thought, the charm is increasing, the charm is increasing. So this increasing charm draws the mind automatically. That's why we say to enjoy the grace of God we don't have to do anything, just begin to enjoy, because it is the grace of the Almighty and Merciful.

In Kee's opinion the physiological change associated with meditation – the lessened rate of breathing – could also be brought about by the use of drugs or hypnosis. He chose this point in the discussion to encourage the Abbot to make a contribution:

Kee – And I'd like to ask I think the Abbot at this point, where really he sees the religious content in all this – if at all.

Abbot – Well, I think that of course the great difficulty that the Maharishi and I would find in discussing these matters is that we both have our separate vocabularies, and they come from the different traditions in which we've been educated and grown up. But I must say that I can only sympathize enormously with what he has to tell us about the importance of the recovery of what I suppose we, at any rate, would call the contact with God, which must be a union within us, and for that very reason our heart is restless until it comes to rest in God.

On the surface at least, it seemed that the Abbot and the Maharishi had nothing but respect for what the other had to say, and proceeded to while away the time in pleasant conversation. The presenter could not let this state of affairs continue for too long as there were points yet to be raised. By introducing the topic of the Crucifixion, Kee seems to have been intent on whipping up a controversy, and on cue the Maharishi revealed that in his opinion Christ had not suffered on the cross. Whilst the matter was still being debated the presenter played his ace card. Addressing the Abbot, he asked: 'Would you regard the

Maharishi as a heretic?' At home, glued to their television sets, the Maharishi's followers must have been shocked and alarmed at this dramatic twist in the proceedings. Were they to turn off their sets and avoid seeing their beloved teacher tarred, feathered or worse, or hang on with grim determination and hope for the best? They need not have worried, for the Abbot was in a relaxed and generous mood as he responded:

> I don't think I'd regard him as a heretic, because, technically speaking, a heretic to us is one who has seen the Christian light and has rejected it either wholly or in part. Now, therefore, nobody who is faithful to his own lights should be called a heretic; and I would be far from suggesting (General laughter).

The programme concluded with the presenter putting forward the view that at a time when the church was in the process of self-examination, 'all religions should come together, if only to find out how much they are apart'. That the Maharishi's followers were pleased with his performance was amply demonstrated by the swiftness with which they produced a full transcript of the programme and published it under the title of *The Maharishi and the Abbot*.

For the summer of 1964 two courses had been arranged, the first of which was scheduled to be held in the Austrian Alps commencing on 12 July. During the Maharishi's stay at Hochgurgl, course participants were treated to his personal account of the inception and subsequent growth of the Spiritual Regeneration Movement. Having told of his success in southern India and the consequent decision to tackle the problems of the rest of the world, it appeared that he would continue to catalogue only his own achievements. Quite suddenly, however, he changed tack to reveal a fundamental weakness which he believed dogged his Movement's relentless motion. The problem that so concerned him was what he referred to as 'tension in the atmosphere'; the effect of which would account for the lapses that sometimes beset meditators. It was uncharacteristic of him to dwell upon negative issues, to focus on something as nebulous as 'atmosphere'. He explained:

> A hundred people are initiated, and after a month only about 25-30 are found meditating, and after six months there will be only five, then no one. Even though experiencing peace and happiness out of meditation, the atmospheric influence is such that it takes the people away from meditation.[107]

From this statement one can conclude that, whilst he never lacked an audience for his message, he was increasingly concerned over the number of meditators who strayed from the path during his long absences.

To give the Maharishi his due, he handled the dilemma with amazing alacrity and fairly turned the situation on its head. Instead of making a U-turn and concentrating his efforts on the faithful few, he instead formulated a strategy that might address another concern, his desire to get more and more people meditating. He reasoned that to counter the negative pull of the atmosphere, more meditators were needed, increasing group support and thus lessening the chances of anyone discontinuing the practice. Whilst the logic appears flimsy, it does have a certain appeal in that it shifts the burden of responsibility for the success of the movement to its supporters. Many of his audience were thus encouraged to become 'checkers', whose task it would be to ensure that fellow meditators derived sufficient satisfaction from their practice. In turn, this would give them useful experience which could be built upon should they take the plunge and enrol for teacher-training.

The topic of tension in the atmosphere had the Maharishi sounding decidedly gloomy. What were the chances of averting another world war, which might be brought on by collective tensions? He concluded his speech with a rallying call, exhorting the faithful to busy themselves in spreading the knowledge of his meditation:

> Give this message to people in whatever way you can, but to large numbers and quickly. Then only will you be able to save our present generation and leave a better world for the future.[108]

7

——★——

THE ONE AND THE MANY

If the tendency for many new meditators to become tardy in their practice had begun to worry the Maharishi, it had not prevented him from rewarding loyal practitioners. He achieved this with the introduction of 'advanced techniques'; given to those who were steady in their meditation. The advanced techniques were dubbed 'fertilizers' and were subtle additions to the existing method. Since they were available only from the Master, those desirous of his company were given *carte blanche* to seek him out. A less than desirable spin-off from this situation was the inequality it created amongst his followers. Possession of these 'fertilizers' distinguished the supposedly advanced adept from the ordinary meditator and thus created a situation where a sense of incompleteness might arise in someone who had previously experienced no such dissatisfaction. Nevertheless the Maharishi continued to offer advanced techniques and there was no shortage of takers.

After the courses in Austria the Maharishi returned to Canada and the USA, stopping off in Scandinavia en route. In addition to his normal quota of lecture dates he again dusted off the *Gita* project and seriously considered the formulation of as many as two dozen commentaries, aimed at people in different states of consciousness. Of fundamental importance to his philosophy was this concept of differing states of consciousness. In addition to the basic divisions -waking, dreaming and deep sleep – he added a fourth state, known as 'pure consciousness, which he described as transcendental to or 'going beyond' the other three. By cultivating this state of pure consciousness, by going beyond the thought process, the meditator was supposed to arrive at the Absolute, the Being, or in religious terminology, God. What the Maharishi was teaching was that by the regular practice of his system of meditation, the nature of the practitioner would become sufficiently infused with Being to give rise to a fifth state of consciousness, which he termed 'cosmic consciousness'. In this cosmic consciousness, awareness of Being is said to be maintained even after meditation, during one's everyday life. The promise of this fifth state was the promise of bliss as an all-time reality. A sixth state, termed 'God consciousness', was also postulated.

The more he talked of these different states of awareness, the greater became his followers' yearning for them. Understandably, since the Maharishi described these states, they assumed that he lived a more exulted existence. Believing that he spoke from a high platform of consciousness, it was difficult for his audience to doubt his authority on even the most mundane of issues. Furthermore, they delighted in his unpredictability, his unexpected inspirations, as for instance the picnic he arranged at Big Bear Lake in deep snow.

His work on the *Bhagavad-Gita* inevitably gave rise to many discussions on Indian philosophy and its inherent belief in *karma*, the allegedly inescapable law of cause and effect, which states that one reaps the consequences of one's own actions or inactivity. The Maharishi once likened this process to writing a letter and eventually receiving a response. Whilst addressing the group in Los Angeles he gave another example. Apparently of the few hundred initiated there, many had lapsed in their practice, but this, he stated, was their *karma*, their loss. For those who were steady and were present at the meeting he had a reward.

> For those who persevere, when the leaves begin to appear, we add something to the soil, around the root. When the buds begin to show, we add something more.[109]

He was of course referring to his advanced techniques or 'fertilizers'. His careful substitution of the term 'we' for 'I' was a technique both he and his followers used a great deal. However, one wonders how else he might have given such instructions as 'When we meditate, we experience the finer phases of a thought' without sounding too high and mighty.

Early in December 1964, whilst still with the Olsons, the topic of animal behaviour reared its head again. He had often made it clear to his students that the great distinction between man and other creatures was in man's free will. He now reinforced this idea by stating his conviction that animals were therefore incapable of producing Pollution. He had more to say about the inordinately complex field of *karma*. He set about explaining the very origin of all actions, of creation.

> When the time of creation comes, it is held, almost in all religions, that the

great Lord wishes the creation to be, desires the creation to be. Vedas also say, 'I am One, maybe I become many.' *Eko-ham bahu-ssyaam.* In almost all religions they say, 'In the beginning was the Word and the Word was with God.'

When God desires or in other words when it is time for creation to begin, then in that silent unbounded ocean of life a stir is created. And how is that stir created? If you take water in a big flat dish and the water is all still and then you give a push from one side, with one little jerk the whole water moves, one wave goes over the whole water, hum-m-m-m, like that. That means the first subtlest vibration starts and that is the start of creation ... From that eternal silence a hum starts and hum is called OM.[110]

Om is thus the 'word of God' and also without meaning. It is of note that phonetically, *om* is found to be remarkably similar to other words of power, such as the Christian 'Amen' and the Islamic '*Amin*'. Furthermore, the nasal 'mmmm' or half-nasal 'nnnnnn', whilst commonly used as a means of expression, is in its written form only defined by its context, having no literal meaning.

All this is OM, that hum, which is the first silent sound, first silent wave that starts from that silent ocean of unmanifested life.[111]

According to the Maharishi, not only did creation start with the monosyllabic, primordial sound, so too did all life forms and matter, including the Indian scriptures, the *Vedas*. This is the name given to a group of four texts which some believe to be the earliest records of human thought. Study has yielded interesting evidence that goes some way towards corroborating this assertion. A.C. Das, in *R.g Vedic India*, (Banarsidass) claims that studies of geophysical data contained within the *Vedas* accurately describe the north-western region of India during an epoch formerly relegated to prehistory. Prof. Das further asserts that the Aryan (Sanskrit for 'Noble') people were indigenous to this area. Thus the claim that the *Vedas* are intimately connected with the act of creation raises the question of the origin of human life and the very cradle of man's origin. Although Prof. Das distances himself from this particular aspect, he does propound a theory that the Aryans of Sapta Sindhu (modern Punjab) directly affected the culture of the Western world. Certainly the Sanskrit language is accepted as the parent of a whole array of languages, not least of which is Latin. But how did India come to affect such distant regions as the area now known as Europe? Prof. Das believes that those who could not bring themselves to accept the religious and social customs of Vedic India migrated, establishing themselves in Afghanistan, Iran and beyond.

The *Vedas* appear to have greatly inspired the Maharishi for he said:

The Vedas are a very basic study of the fundamentals of life. That is the reason why, through Vedic hymns, it is possible for those expert in chanting those hymns to produce certain effects here, there or there. The universe is vast, so many worlds and all that. We do something here according to Vedic rites, particular, specific chanting to produce an effect in some other world, draw the attention of those higher beings or gods living there.[112]

At this point, the word *mantra* may require a little explanation. Vedic *mantras* are in fact verses, poetic in content and with definite meaning. The *mantras* taught to initiates of the Maharishi's meditation technique are quite different. Although a code of secrecy governs the selection of suitable *mantras*, it is likely that they are chosen from a limited palette of *bij* or seed sounds. But one might reasonably ask who or what created or initially identified the *mantras*? The Maharishi volunteers this explanation:

Risha yah mantra drishtarah. Rishi is a word that means those who contemplate. Rishis [sages] are the seers of the *mantras* and maharishis are those who apply the knowledge for the good of the world.[113]

Thus it is held that the seers are merely witness to the *mantras*, in other words the verses of the *Vedas* are accorded divine authorship. Certainly, the descriptions of celestial beings to be found in Vedic *mantras* are not to be doubted by the faithful. The beings, the angels and gods, are seen as agencies of God and in no way attempt to eclipse his Glory. To those of us unfamiliar with such beliefs, the mention of gods elicits feelings of incredulity and prejudice. Vedic descriptions of divine beings are commonly dismissed by Western scholars as the poetic and fanciful imaginings of a primitive, aboriginal people. Nevertheless, modern thinking had yet to dispose of the belief in supernatural beings, which still persists the world over. The word 'Hinduism' is used to describe the belief structure to which many in India adhere, but those who worship according to prescribed Vedic custom are more properly termed followers of *Sanatana Dharma* 'eternal law' or 'eternal duty'.

Had the Maharishi been addressing his own kind, they would have been only too pleased to hear him supporting traditional beliefs, but he was in Los Angeles and was thus treading on very thin ice. It should be remembered that he wanted to promote his system of meditation as verifiable by experience and even hoped to find acceptance within the scientific community. Since his arrival in the United States he had been encouraging those with a background in the sciences to produce tangible proof of its effectiveness. With such an agenda, was this the time to be making pronouncements about the existence of gods? True, the naming of the days of the week after gods and their planets were reminders of a belief system that existed in the past, but in the jet age, what could the Maharishi achieve by reviving their memory?

The work of the Spiritual Regeneration Movement had one specific goal, to get the world to meditate; no second step had been suggested. Perhaps with the promised eternal freedom, the access to Nirvana or the Kingdom of Heaven within, it was believed that everything would automatically work itself out. But if this were the case, how could the Maharishi possibly hope to reconcile religious differences? His way of tackling this thorny subject was to minimize its importance, which he did by likening the *Vedas* to a mango tree, describing the various religions of the world as just the branches. Having delivered this graphic analogy he placed meditation at the base, as the supplier of nutrition for the whole tree, claiming that it was not antagonistic to any religion but that by its practice the truth of all the great scriptures would be revealed.

After expounding his belief that the creation was the emanation of a divine hum, he turned his attention to society and its divisions. In India the division of labour is determined by birth; those of a particular family perform a specific type of work. This division by *varna* (caste) is attributed to the progenitor of the human race, whom the Hindus know as Manu. It might be presumed that the Maharishi, being a well-travelled man, would have shied away from such extreme orthodox views. After all, even in India there was a clamour for the removal of these restraints. But his statements on this sensitive and contentious subject were both assertive and unequivocal. The following is just one example:

> It is a very fine scientific discrimination of human values so that each man is allowed to have the maximum spiritual development and thereby the whole society is allowed to have the maximum in a combined manner.[114]

Far from trying to soften or remove the distinctions that preordain the course of individual lives, that prenatally decide that someone will be a peasant or a priest, a pauper or a prince, he gave his unreserved support to the continuance of caste-consciousness. Was he not aware that the people of America and Europe were generally opposed to elitist values and were replacing them with altogether more liberal attitudes? Any remaining notions of class and other divisive mechanisms were being abandoned, and a new order was emerging where everyone could aspire to anything. Employees found themselves on familiar first-name terms with their employers, even the American President and his wife were addressed in this way. It is therefore hard to imagine why anyone should wish to establish a caste system like that which is practised in India. But then, the Maharishi, being something of an enigma, was an exception.

It is hard to understand why the Maharishi expected to be able to estimate the numbers of his followers by attendances at his meetings, since the technique of meditation he taught avoided any need for future contact with him for further guidance. The philosophy he espoused was essentially his own and was therefore separate from the teaching of his technique. Each new initiate was totally free to accept or reject it at will. Only those who wanted to increase their intellectual understanding of his ideas or who were simply desirous of his company needed to attend his follow-up meetings. He had not created a club or society which required repeated attendance to derive the benefits of membership. The meditation was a voluntary activity, so it left the initiate free to continue his or her life outside the framework of the Movement. It was therefore impossible to monitor the number of regular practitioners with any accuracy. In any event, rather than reformulate his relationship with his students and followers he chose instead to pursue a policy of reaching out to the maximum amount of people.

After leaving Los Angeles he put in appearances in San Francisco and Santa Barbara before crossing to New York where, on 19 December 1964, he had the good fortune to meet the Secretary General of the United Nations, Mr U Thant. As I have said, this cultivation of the powerful, rich and influential was a significant part of the Maharishi's *modus operandi*. In *The Science of Being and Art of Living*, he had observed:

> If there is a fort, and the whole territory belongs to it, it is wise to go straight to the fort and capture it. Having captured the fort, all that is in the surrounding territory will naturally be possessed.[115]

This imagery evokes the Maharishi's origins as a *Kshatriya*, the caste traditionally responsible for supplying warriors. But according to his Uncle Raj:

> Let me tell you, Maharishi is so spiritually evolved that he is raised above the worldly. He is free from bondage to caste and everything in the world.[116]

After his meeting with U Thant, and no doubt stimulated by such high level recognition, the Maharishi rejoined his followers, first on a course in Germany, then on another in Britain. In Germany, at BadMergetheim, a new wing of his Movement was unfolding. The new division was formed with a view to aiding the recruitment of young people and was therefore named the Students' International Meditation Society (SIMS). This gave him three principal organizations: the original Spiritual Regeneration Movement (SRM), the SIMS and the intellectually inclined International Meditation Society (IMS).

By now, roughly seven years had elapsed since the Maharishi had avowed his intention to spiritually regenerate the world. His efforts had at least brought the idea of meditation to a very wide audience, and of those who had enrolled for instruction there were many who proclaimed its benefits. Some had a greater feeling of awareness leading to decreased anxiety; some even experienced an improvement in memory. Although the strength of the sales pitch still lay in promises of higher states of consciousness, any new angle on the real or imagined benefits of meditation were hungrily seized upon and quickly worked into the Movement's propaganda machine.

Whilst waiting for Nirvana to become more than a fleeting experience, the more dedicated followers organized themselves into local groups under national umbrellas. To keep everyone informed of the Movement's progress, newsletters were produced, giving details of forthcoming meetings and residential courses. Meetings involved listening to tapes of the Maharishi's lectures, group meditations and occasionally a group *puja*. Weekend courses gave initiates the opportunity to extend periods of meditation which, it was suggested, would accelerate their spiritual progress. Meditators came from diverse backgrounds, but the majority were from the white middle classes, and many had no previous interest in or involvement with spiritual organizations. Those who had been with other teachers attempted to extricate themselves from their former beliefs, for the Maharishi laid great emphasis on the fact that different techniques should not be mixed.

The tape recordings which were played at meetings at that time were generally prepared solely for this purpose. They ranged from general spiritual topics like harmony, purity and fulfilment, to the theory of *karma* and practical dissertations on the subject of meditation. Some tapes were also used to check initiates' meditation. Although every effort was made to maximize resources, to create an ideal atmosphere in which to learn and practise meditation, little could be done to provide a role model. In truth, even the Maharishi himself could not really do so since he was a special case, having spent so much of his life as a hermit. What the meditators desperately needed was a fully 'realized' man or woman whom they could directly relate to. The absence of such an example meant that learning could only be conducted by a process of trial and error.

Rightly or wrongly, meditators tended to ape the Maharishi's habits, even down to his patterns of speech. But his example could not always provide answers to his devotees' problems. There were practical issues such as what to do about diet – were there certain foods that should be avoided? He answered them patiently, counselling them not to make any sudden changes in their lives and to avoid those things which resulted in any dulling of their meditations.

Some wanted to know whether they ought to follow his lead and abstain from alcohol and cigarettes. He had made passing references to these substances advising those who derived financial gain from them to seriously consider making donations to charity (and one can guess which one). On smoking he had more specific advice:

> If one smokes it is very difficult to quit smoking, but very easy to gain God consciousness and thereby not feel for smoking if smoking is bad. It is much simpler to attain God consciousness, much more difficult to go the righteous way.[117]

This clarified his position extremely well. First, he acknowledged the difficulty of trying to improve one's habits, while, secondly, he stated that it is very easy to acquire God consciousness, and thus easy to give up those things that are found deleterious to one's health. Additionally, and more importantly, he suggested that habits such as smoking are not enough to debar one from the attainment of higher states of consciousness. On the other hand, he did not offer guidance as to what activities might best be avoided. So whilst the Master appeared very relaxed about his followers' lifestyles, disciples were left in a quandary about how best to spend their non-meditation time.

Many chose to delve deeper into the mysteries of meditation by visiting the Maharishi at his Academy of Meditation in India. Situated across the river from the market town of Rishikesh, Shankaracharya Nagar had arisen out of the forested hillock and now awaited an influx of visitors. Meditators from the world over came to study at the Academy which, in addition to offering instruction in teacher-training, also promoted custom-made courses for businessmen, ostensibly both to increase alertness and to improve performance levels. Frankly, though, anyone incapable of finding tranquillity in this beauty spot, whether they practised meditation or not, was unlikely to find peace of mind anywhere.

When time permitted, the Maharishi continued his work on his commentary on the *Gita*. Until it was completed, those wanting to read about his philosophy would have to content themselves with his *Science of Being and Art of Living*, which had enjoyed reasonably good sales and was going into its second edition. As is frequently the case with first editions, subsequent rereading of the work brought with it a desire to make additions and corrections. (In subsequent paperback editions of this work the 1966 revisions were not always adhered to, and appear as alternate revisions of the 1963 original). Since his words had not been etched in stone, the Maharishi felt free to modify certain statements and generally to revise his terminology. The word 'Deep' was dropped from 'Transcendental Deep Meditation' and interestingly the list of those who had helped in the book's preparation was cut. He was particularly careful to purge the work of any expressions which might lead readers to associate his philosophies with those of others. This he did in an attempt to distance himself from beliefs in other methods of meditation, such as concentration, contemplation, self-remembrance, surrender and a whole host of other practices. In his bid to make crystal clear his view that meditation did not require effort, he also dismissed those who tried to cultivate a mood of peacefulness on the level of the mind. It was hard to find a single tradition with which he would ally himself. Even Tibet, the Shangri La of mystics, received short shrift.

Q. Are you the same school of thought of *yoga* as Milarepa that Evans-Wentz wrote about?

MMY. I haven't heard his name.

Q. A Tibetan.

MMY. Oh Tibet is far-fetched. All the Tibetan ideologies that you hear, they don't belong to this age.[118]

On Tuesday, 12 January 1965, in the comfort of Henry Nyburg's country home, he felt compelled to write down his thoughts on this question of alternative systems of self-unfoldment, which formed part of the preface to his uncompleted commentary on the *Bhagavad-Gita*. He remarked:

Thus we find that all fields of religion and philosophy have been misunderstood and wrongly interpreted for many centuries past.[119]

What then of the Indian traditions of *yoga*; surely the methods that he taught, ancient as he claimed them to be, must be known by many?

You should also know that there are thousands of people all over the world who are aware of thousands of *mantras* written in India by writers of many books. Do not go by what they say about the *mantras* or about the meditation propagated by the Spiritual Regeneration Movement in different parts of the world ...[120]

Why the Maharishi took up this position is hard to understand, as it left him utterly isolated from contemporary faiths and teachings.

Let us consider the effect of all this on his followers. Having heard how easy it was to unlock the Kingdom of Heaven within, they would be looking for quick success. Having been made to understand that they would be wasting their time trying to cast off bad habits, and having been alerted to the dangers of 'mood making' (affecting an air of spirituality), they would need to see signs that his method worked for them. Since so many had already sung the glories of the Maharishi's meditation, any inability to derive benefits from it would inevitably be construed as personal failure. A very real danger for those under pressure to succeed in this 'simple and easy' method was that they might be tempted to indulge in false eulogies in an attempt to hide their supposed inadequacy, which was something the world did not need.

It was natural that people should be cautious about the Maharishi's claims; after all nobody wanted to find themselves misled. His oft-stated claim that his technique required no faith to make it work was not enough to convince the cynics. Therefore, clear indicators of the real physiological value of his methods were sought. Scientific study was already being conducted into the practice of meditation, the first experiments involving the measurement of light emission from meditating subjects, had started the ball rolling. As the years went by the desire to gain scientific validation became ever more pressing. However, those motivated by faith and spiritual convictions saw no need to convince unbelievers, but kept their peace most loyally.

8

——★——

FLOWER POWER

The Maharishi's appearance easily fulfilled people's expectations of a Master from the Himalayas, and the passage of the years only enhanced his image. Gone was the youthful countenance. His oiled jet-black locks were losing their spring and fast becoming shot with streaks of silver. The first significant patch of grey facial hair had already begun to spread around and about his mouth. He was starting to look as ancient as the hills and this image served him well, since people found it easier to accept the teachings knowing him to be of some age and to have spent many long years in study and quiet contemplation. The ability to remain fresh, calm and patient yet retain a lively sense of humour was rare, but there was no doubt that he possessed it. Presumably he developed these traits in the decade and more he spent with his *guru* and the time he spent in silence at Uttar Kashi. Why therefore was he promising immediate success to his students?

> Q. You have been studying all your life, how can we possibly learn in a matter of so many minutes?

> MMY. I have not learned it in many years. I got it through the Grace of my Master.[124]

This response raises the question of precisely how he actually gained this 'grace'. How much had devotion and surrender to his teacher achieved? Was the practice of meditation the key factor in his progress? Since his Master, Swami Brahmanand, was no longer alive, could not his disciple, Brahmachari Mahesh, confer his Grace, instead of teaching meditation?

The memory of the old Shankaracharya was still burning strong in the hearts of his devotees and in 1965 came the publication of his biography, compiled from *ashram* newsletters by his devotee Rameshwar Tiwari. Most of the work was in reality autobiographical, since the Shankaracharya had been eager to teach by example and would often use his life experiences to illustrate spiritual discourses. The story of his life came complete with various colour plates, including an artist's impression of Adi Shankara, a photograph of the aged and white-haired Swami Krishnanand, two more of Shri Brahmanand and one of his successor, Swami Shantanand. The problem is the book's relative inaccessibility, since it was written entirely in Hindi. Perhaps by coincidence, perhaps by design, the Maharishi himself had also decided to publish an account of his master. In a small slim volume entitled *Love and God*, he offered versions of his two poems of the same names and a piece entitled 'Our Guiding Light', a tribute to his late master. Of great interest is his description of the process by which his master as a young *chela* had, through the aid of his *guru*, Swami Krishnanand, found enlightenment.

> To that realized soul, the young ascetic surrendered himself for being initiated into the mysterious realms of the spirit, whose key practices are attainable not from books and treatises, but only from perfect spiritual masters, who silently pass these top-secret practices from heart to heart.
>
> After some time, with the permission and order of his master he entered a cave at Uttar-Kashi with a resolve not to come out before he had realized the Light Supreme. His desire to attain the Highest knowledge was not merely an ideal wish or intention; it was a mighty, overpowering determination that burned like fire in his heart. It permeated every particle of his being and bade him not to rest or stop before the complete realization of the Bliss Eternal.
>
> Soon he arrived at the Heatless Smokeless Effulgent of the Self and realized the Divine Truth, the Cosmic Consciousness, the Ultimate Supreme Reality, Sat Chit Anandam, the Nirvana.[122]

The quest for liberation from disharmony has led many to shun the fleeting and transitory experiences of material existence in favour of a more enduring spiritual serenity. Having attained this blessed state, what did Swami Brahmanand, as young truth-seeker do? Apparently, the answer lay in his destiny, for the Maharishi disclosed that 'his hour of nativity claimed him for the recluse order ...'[123]

The first hard evidence of the *Gita* project was the limited publication of the Maharishi's commentary on the first three chapters. His justification for the release of such an incomplete commentary lay in that these opening chapters contain verses which refer to a philosophy or method aimed at gaining liberation. In the second chapter, whilst counselling his friend Arjuna, Krishna postulates the existence of a state of existence beyond the reach of worldly energies, a state of purity and self-possession, a condition called *yoga* (union or completeness), which he

explains as a state from which action can be undertaken in complete
freedom.

In recent years a new order had begun to make itself felt within Western
society, the effect of which would soon be felt by the Maharishi. In the
wake of a call for greater attention by their children, adults had begun to
re-examine their outlook on life. This reappraisal resulted in a shift in
the *status quo*, along with the coining of a new word, 'teenager'.
Youngsters demanded greater involvement in decision-making about
education, choice of employment and above all their recreation time.
After meeting with a certain measure of success, some took their new-
found freedom further, feeling free to challenge certain inherited beliefs.
Religion, which for so long had largely been responsible for dictating
moral and social attitudes, could no longer demand unquestioning
allegiance. For those who came to doubt and in turn reject the pre-
digested truths of orthodox religion, the evaluation of right or wrong
became merely a matter of personal preference. Without the moral
restrictions and injunctions imposed by religion, there was little to stop
the newly 'liberated' from gorging themselves upon forbidden fruits.
The ensuing years saw an increase in pleasure-seeking on a grand scale,
one by no means limited to the younger generation. One consequence of
this new morality was a pronounced increase in interest in sense
gratification.

In America black musicians had created a stir by developing a
compulsive and exciting new dance music which they called rock 'n'
roll. The outrageous and extrovert antics of its exponents coupled with
the music's sexually explicit lyrical content had caused an uproar among
many self-appointed guardians of public decency, who sought to restrict
its performance. But there was no shortage of white musicians willing to
ape the style, the most able of whom was Elvis Presley, who became the
most famous teenager in the world. Through radio broadcasts, the music
of Elvis and other rock 'n' roll artistes reached out to the shores of Great
Britain, causing a lot of teenagers to try their hand at the new craze. In
next to no time, the youth market became saturated by groups of young
musicians who, whilst they were in possession of no more than a
rudimentary command of their instruments, were intent on success. Of
these, The Beatles were to prove by far the most popular.

The Maharishi had acknowledged the youth revolution by offering
young people their own separate organization, the SIMS, run by his
trusted assistant, Jerome Jarvis. With his dark suit and conventional
hairstyle Jarvis looked to be anything but a typical rock 'n' roll

teenager, but since it was assumed that only the more serious types would be drawn to meditation, his appearance did not seem inappropriate.

The teenage craze for instant enjoyment did not confine itself to music, alcohol and sex but found increased momentum in the ready availability of modern mood-altering drugs. In their search for sensation and excitement teenagers were increasingly turning to the new stimulants, especially the so-called pep pills, which enabled partygoers to forgo sleep and stay 'high' all night long. In addition to artificial stimulants like amphetamines and barbiturates, some sought out the outlawed herbal drug, marijuana, and its resin derivative, cannabis or hashish. With the use of these drugs, unusual experiences of altered states of awareness became fairly freely available. In time, some of the more studious drug-takers began to seek information on cultures where drug-taking was prevalent. They found particular satisfaction in reading certain Eastern scriptures which contain fascinating descriptions of altered states of consciousness. An increased interest in South American culture resulted from the discovery that it possessed a knowledge of extremely powerful mind-altering drugs. By the ingestion of a certain cactus known as peyote, a state of otherworldliness was brought about, and although extremely unpleasant side effects, such as nausea and vomiting, were attendant hazards of such experimentation, for the serious experimenter it proved no great deterrent.

By the mid-sixties, a discovery made in 1938 by an Austrian chemist called Albert Hoffman made its impact felt on the youth of America. In researching the circulatory problems of pregnant women, he undertook a study of fungi which produced an unforeseen effect, the isolation of an acid known as Lysergic Diethylide Acid or LSD. It is said that in 1943 Hoffmann accidentally touched the acid and through its absorption into his skin found that his perception of reality became greatly changed. He found the experience overwhelming. In the early sixties official studies into the effects of LSD resulted in a certain amount of the substance 'disappearing'.

Those hungry for greater sensory experiences had found in it the active ingredients of the peyote without the nausea. This drug spread like wildfire and its users evaded apprehension as it had yet to be made illegal.

Ardent users of the drug claimed that they encountered profound experiences whilst 'tripping' on the drug, making some wonder whether they had discovered a direct path to enlightenment. In their pursuit of greater happiness they had discovered drugs, which in turn had stimulated them to question the very nature and existence of reality. These were 'acid heads', hedonists in search of a constant high , who unsurprisingly tended to congregate together, sometimes living communally. The first outward signs of this phenomenon came in the city of San Francisco and down the Californian coast, with the emergence of the phenomenon of 'flower power'. The 'flower children' or 'hippies' believed in free expression, reflected in their individual and frequently bizarre clothing and their preference for wearing their hair long. The Maharishi, with his long hair, his obsession with flowers and his unusual garb, might well have been taken for their founding father. It was not unusual for people to become confused about his image; he had on occasion even been mistaken for a flower-seller! But the hippies, with their predilection for drugs and the attendant quest for mysticism, had already found themselves a mystic 'guru' – Aldous Huxley.

In 1954, Huxley had written of his experiences whilst experimenting with the drug Mescaline (a derivative of peyote). A flavour of his writing is to be found in this extract:

I took my pill at eleven. An hour and a half later I was sitting in my study, looking intently at a small glass vase. The vase contained only three flowers – full-blown Belle of Portugal rose, shell pink with a hint at every petal's base of a hotter, flamier hue; a large magenta and cream-coloured carnation; and, pale purple at the end of its broken stalk, the bold heraldic blossom of an iris. Fortuitous and provisional, the little nosegay broke all the rules of traditional good taste. At breakfast that morning I had been struck by the lively dissonance of its colours. But that was no longer the point. I was not looking now at an unusual flower arrangement. I was seeing what Adam had seen on the morning of his creation -the miracle, moment by moment, of naked existence.[124]

Huxley was no drug-crazed hippie but a respected writer, and it is very likely that, as a young man, the Maharishi had pored over his *Brave New World.* Furthermore, Huxley had more than a passing acquaintance with Indian techniques of meditation, concentration and contemplation.

My eyes travelled from the rose to the carnation, and from that feathery incandescence to the smooth scrolls of sentient amethyst which were the iris. The Beatific Vision, *Sat Chit Ananda*, Being-Awareness-Bliss – for the first time I understood, not on the verbal level, not by inchoate hints or at a distance, but precisely and completely what those prodigious syllables referred to.[125]

This was surely what the Maharishi was saying?

Huxley had also written a second book on the experiences he had gained through the use of Mescaline, entitled *Heaven and Hell.* The title was quickly used by the media to describe the scope of the altered states of consciousness which LSD supposedly induced. Less than enamoured with the prospect of further brushes with hell, some LSD users set about achieving the experience of heaven alone. The state of endless heavenly bliss they sought was precisely what the Maharishi appeared to be offering; he therefore attracted many who saw a kinship between his teaching and their perception of India, of a country where pleasure, drug-taking and the search for God all coexisted happily together. Since the Maharishi made no explicit attempt to exclude them, the assumption was that they were welcome to join his movement. It is likely that had the Maharishi chosen to abandon the brightly-coloured blooms and taken on the appearance of his associates, these new followers, being very image conscious and not a little suspicious of 'straights', might well have looked elsewhere.

A fundamental ingredient in the hippie lifestyle was music, either to listen to or to play. Hippies were quick to latch on to Indian music, observing that it offered a ready-made exotic aural tapestry to augment their experimentation with drugs. The sitarist Ravi Shankar, shortened traditional *ragas* in order to accommodate the expectations of Western audiences, and soon Indian music was found filtering though to the mainstream of popular culture by way of incidental inclusion in pop songs. Jazz musicians, too, saw great promise in its use of melody as a vehicle for unlimited extemporization and one such musician, a flautist by the name of Paul Horn, went so far as to work with artists chosen by Ravi Shankar to produce some exceptional and inspired music. Working with these musicians had alerted Horn to other aspects of Indian culture, namely its philosophy and its *yoga* teachings. In response to this new stimulus, he rapidly became interested in the idea of learning to meditate and sought a *mantra* from the SRM.

Another musician with $35 to spare was drummer John Densmore, who reasoned that a less hazardous path to peace than that offered by psychedelics might be the use of meditation. In the spring of 1965 he set off to find out more.

> Meditation sounded a less shattering route. We went to some preliminary meetings in LA's Wiltshire district and listened to a mellow man in a business suit. His name was Jerry Jarvis, and his eyes seemed to express a remarkable inner contentment.[126]

John Densmore decided to take the plunge.

> They asked us to bring flowers, fruit and a white handkerchief. We would each receive an individual *mantra*, an Indian Sanskrit word that we were

supposed to repeat mentally. Our teachers instructed us not to speak it out loud or write it down; it would lose its power if we did.[127]

He recounts how he became a little dizzy during his first experience of meditation and attended the second meeting eager to try and rectify the problem. Jerry Jarvis was again in charge.

He talked about how the mind's nature was to have one thought after another. Mind-chatter. He said that the *mantra* was a vehicle to take a thought from the surface of our mind down to the source of thought below. Still, not too much happened when I meditated. There were no colored lights or explosions. Though I was expecting the same quick, startling effect as my LSD experiences ...[128]

But although he was initially disappointed, he did not complain. Rationalizing the situation he realized that it would probably be some time before he gained the full benefits of the practice and so decided to persevere. But one of his fellow meditators was not taking it so easily.

During the follow-up meeting, a blond guy with a Japanese girlfriend by his side kept raising his hand and saying to Jarvis, 'No bliss, no bliss!'

It was very embarrassing. He acted as if he had been ripped off. I think he expected to become Buddha on the first day. We had all hoped it wouldn't take too long, but he was especially impatient.

After the meeting the same guy came up to me and said, 'I hear you're a drummer. Want to put a band together?'[129]

Soon after this event, a group of youngsters with interests in pleasure-seeking, music, 'mind expansion' and meditation, sprang up on the Los Angeles 'scene'. They called themselves The Doors after Aldous Huxley's book *The Doors of Perception* and John Densmore and the heckler from Densmore's group, Ray Manzarek, were members. The Maharishi's directions on to how to meditate found their way into the group's songs: phrases like 'take it easy' and 'take it as it comes'. Doors soon became one of the 'house bands' of the new culture, whose favourite buzz words, 'bliss' and 'cosmic' were quickly adopted by the pop generation. The Maharishi and his brand of Eastern promise were daily gaining increased popularity amongst the youth market.

In 1966 the Maharishi was still hard at work on his mission to spiritually regenerate mankind, still travelling the world, still lecturing, and in his spare time still continuing work on the unfinished *Gita* project.

The occasion of the Kumbh Mela in Allahabad, India, which is held only once every twelve years, is a rare opportunity for *sadhus*, *swamis* and other holy men and women to gather together. Writer Ved Mehta describes the scene he beheld there:

> By the camp fires, beneath the open sky, were huddles of squatting *sadhus*
> and milling or motionless crowds of pilgrims. Now and again, I passed an
> elephant, festooned with flower garlands and embroidered rugs. All along the
> way, beggars held out their bowls, into which pilgrims dropped coins or
> grain. There were naked *sadhus* and *sadhus* opulently robed. There were
> *sadhus* wearing *dhotis* and marigolds, with horizontal stripes of ash on their
> foreheads. There were *sadhus* with ash-smeared naked bodies, offering *ghi*,
> *jaggery* and *sesamum* to a sacrificial fire that crackled in a brazier, and
> chanting '*Hare Ram. Hare Krishna. Hare Om.*'[130]

Amongst the endless sea of pilgrims attending the *mela* were exponents
of the many sects, cults and disciplines comprising modern Hinduism.
In addition to the smoke spiralling up from the campfires was that of the
ganja (marijuana), used by many *sadhus* in their quest for a taste of
heaven. Some pilgrims camped beneath the stars whilst others sought
the comparative comfort of a tent colony. Mehta met many *swamis*,
saints and *yogis*; he also met a follower of the Maharishi.

> A man in a brown lounge suit and with a vermillion mark on his forehead
> comes up to me. He tells me his name and continues, in English, 'I am
> America-returned. I am MA and PhD in public administration from the
> States. Guruji has fifty-four *chelas* from distant foreign lands here at
> Kumbha. I myself am going to be initiated on this Amavasya, when Guruji
> will recite some *mantras* to me by the side of Mother Ganga, and I will recite
> them back. I met the Guruji only a month ago. After I set eyes on Guruji, I
> left my five children to follow him.'[131]

The Maharishi's Western *chelas* directed the writer to speak to their
'Guruji'. He found him in his tent, surrounded by a group of disciples
and no less than three tape recorders. Ved Mehta asked the silk-robed
teacher about his philosophies. After ascertaining the identity of the
newcomer, the 'Guruji' answered him:

> All I teach is a simple method of meditation. We are all conscious on a
> mundane level, but beneath that consciousness, in each one of us, there is an
> ocean vaster than any in the world. It's there that most new thoughts
> originate. The bridge between the mundane level of consciousness and the
> ocean is meditation – not reading, because if you read you can have only
> second-hand thoughts.[132]

He further explained that the test of his meditation was in its utility,
indicating that a result of its practice was increased material welfare and
achievement. Emphasizing this point, that his meditation technique had
a place in a world far beyond the *mela*, he added:

As I said when addressing a meeting in the Albert Hall, in London, my technique does not involve withdrawal from normal material life. It enhances the material values of life by the inner spiritual light. My method is, in my London example, 'like the inner juice of the orange, which can be enjoyed without destroying the outer beauty of the fruit. This is done simply by pricking the orange with a pin again and again, and extracting the juice little by little, so that the inner juice is drawn out on the surface, and both are enjoyed simultaneously.'[133]

In spite of spending several hours with the Maharishi, Ved Mehta claims he came out feeling dissatisfied with what he had heard. It was not so much the message of meditation that bothered him, but the attitude the Maharishi adopted whilst speaking to his audience. According to Mehta the 'Guruji', in addition to being unreasonably dismissive of their questions, also ridiculed the questioners. Perhaps this was true, perhaps Mr Mehta himself had had a particularly rough ride. Rather than hearing stories of a cure-all formula, as yet unproven, he sought more tangible answers to the world's problems, and in that he represented the views of many people.

When the Maharishi embarked on his seventh world tour, he returned to Europe and to North America, where he targeted university campuses in his bid to capitalize on the noticeable increase of interest in his meditation amongst the young. In his lectures he would liken thoughts to bubbles rising from the depths of the mind, giving an enhanced perception of thoughts at progressively more subtle levels. This would, he assured his audiences, enable meditators to think more clearly and more powerfully. Some students who already used his technique supported this view, claiming an increased ability to study, and, in so doing, turned attention away from the rather nebulous area of altered states of consciousness. When all was said and done, the Maharishi was no longer particularly concerned about *why* people turned to his methods; any reason was good enough.

Towards the end of the year he set out to conquer new territories, specifically Trinidad and South America. He was accompanied on these forays by Charlie Lutes, head of the SRM in the United States. Arriving in Caracas, the Maharishi was particularly happy. To Nancy Cooke de Herrara, who had organized the South American tour, Charlie Lutes confided:

He is radiant because he has left behind the heat, humidity, and low vibrations of Trinidad. He didn't like that place at all.[134]

The tour, on which he was billed as a famous philosopher, was relatively successful. It was arranged for him to meet some dignitaries, and his message was on the whole well received. In Rio de Janeiro, however, he found himself being heckled by a French *yoga* instructor who ranted 'Don't listen to him! He is a fake! He is telling you nothing but lies!' When the Frenchman was finished the audience showed their disapproval, and the Maharishi commented to his critic:

> You should call yourself a professor of exercise. *Yoga* means 'union'. You will never achieve union with God just by twisting the body.[135]

The tour continued with dates in Argentina, Chile, Peru and Colombia.

Of the many thousands initiated into the Maharishi's technique of meditation, relatively few felt the compulsion to train to become a teacher. Amongst those who were tempted to get a little closer to the Maharishi was flautist Paul Horn, who as I have said, first became interested in meditation after working with sitarist Ravi Shankar. When given the opportunity to attend the latest Guides' course in Rishikesh, Horn fairly jumped at the chance.

> I met the Maharishi in September 1966. On his then yearly travels around the world, he came through Los Angeles to talk. He was such a beautiful man I really felt very strongly to be with him, to spend some time with him. I just packed up and left it all behind. Unequivocally and without hesitation I can say that this was the greatest experience of my life. In the midst of relative success I was feeling empty and unfulfilled. I was at a major crossroads. The Maharishi gave me back my life. I was reborn. I became a teacher of Transcendental Meditation in April 1967 in Kashmir, India. Teaching such a beautiful technique for unfoldment and inner peace adds another dimension to my life. The balance between that and music is very rewarding.[136]

Whilst he was training to become one of the first twelve meditation teachers in the USA, an idea for a new musical venture offered itself. In a bid to find a balance between long periods of meditation, study and attending lectures, visits by local entertainers were arranged. Soon plans were hatched for a recording session.

> It just so happened that I had my flute along and joined them at Maharishi's request ... I mentioned to Maharishi my desire to make a record with these musicians and have the rest of the world hear their fine talents. Nothing more was said. Then one evening two weeks later I was called to Maharishi's room. There sitting on the floor at Maharishi's feet were the assembled musicians. He proceeded to plan an album with the insight of an experienced record producer.[137]

The result of this meeting was a recording session that resulted in the release of an album of material by World-wide Records entitled *Cosmic*

Consciousness, with a colour photograph on the cover of the musicians performing before the Maharishi at his houseboat on a Kashmir lake.

After this teacher-training course the Maharishi embarked on what seemed to be his last tour of the world. His avowed intent had been to give ten years to the founding of his worldwide movement, and he had only a few months left to put the last finishing touches to his handiwork. In his lectures he showed no sign of diminishing pace or energy. One of them, subsequently released on record, gave an example of his tendency to rework and expand his teachings. Entitled *The Seven States of Consciousness*, and recorded live in Los Angeles, it showed him again delineating the various states of awareness accessible to those who used his Transcendental Meditation:[138]

> Those who meditate, they retire from the outside, they take their awareness from the outside and gradually go deep into the thinking process and eventually go beyond the thought. Transcend thought and then the thinking mind, the conscious mind becomes consciousness. When it goes beyond thought then it transcends thought and becomes consciousness. This consciousness is pure consciousness. The nature of this pure consciousness is bliss. It is non-changing sphere of life because we have transcended all the variable section of relative life and gone to the Absolute. This is called Being, Inner Being, Absolute Bliss consciousness.[138]

The relative order of the universe he termed the 'gross and subtle levels of creation'. The object of his meditation lay first in appreciating 'subtler phases of a thought' and then in transcending thought altogether, in order to arrive at the very source of thought.

> Transcendental Meditation is that process which has made the realization of the Absolute a scientific phenomena. Scientific phenomena means it can be explored in a very systematic manner and it is open to experience by everyone. It only needs taking our attention from the gross field of activity in the relative life to the subtle fields of activity in the relative life, eventually to the subtlest field of activity in the relative life and transcending the subtlest of the relative, we get to the Transcendental Absolute.

The Maharishi was only too aware of the other spiritual organizations which used the word transcendental. He was quick to make fun of its alleged misapplication in the term Transcendentalism, pointing out in his lecture that 'the Transcendental field of life is that which is free from "isms"'. He had to establish the significance of his theory regarding the need to transcend thought in order to go beyond the realms of the waking state of consciousness. Having pointed out that this transcending would lead the meditator to discover pure consciousness, he then went on to identify other states of awareness accessible to those practising his

Transcendental Meditation. Apparently, in order to raise one's level of consciousness from the familiar 'waking state of consciousness', repeated contact with the Transcendental Absolute or pure consciousness is needed. According to the Maharishi, the result of such inner activity bestows 'cosmic consciousness', an enhanced mental condition with a corresponding physiological condition brought about by the repeated lowering of the metabolic rate. It might well be concluded that this description could be applied to the sleep state, where suspension of thought and lowering of the metabolism are common occurrences. However, the Maharishi refuted this notion by making the distinction that the meditator, unlike the sleeper, is in fact wide awake.

> As long as the thinking mind is experiencing a thought, so long the mind is a thinker and the thought becomes finer and finer, then the thinker becomes more and more alert in order to experience the finer thought, and then the thought becomes finer and finer, it becomes finest and when the thought drops off, the thinker remains all by himself and this is self-realization.
>
> What I have to do to realize myself? I have only to stop realizing things from within and see that I don't go to sleep.

To underscore his message that the condition he referred to was not a state of inertia, he added: 'How to be? Stop being active but don't become passive. This is how to be.'

Whilst his directions clearly refer only to the action of thoughts in meditation, to the less attentive they might be construed otherwise, leading some to believe that enlightenment was found merely by refraining from action.

Although the Maharishi could generally talk very fluently, on the odd occasion, his delivery would be marred by an unexpected blip in the cosmic script, as in the following instance during the same lecture, which found him momentarily uncertain of his facts: 'For thousands of years, maybe hundreds, self-realization has been declared to be a difficult thing.'

His change of mind was quickly spotted, producing a peal of laughter from his audience. Although rare, such instances, in addition to providing necessary light relief for his students, served as reminder to the Maharishi that he was still human and prone to faults.

Faulty or not, he made extensive and imaginative use of colourful analogies in order to get his points across. He likened the process of meditation to visiting the bank where, after having collected some cash one would be in a better position to enjoy the market place. The process of repeatedly targeting the state of pure consciousness he would liken to a traditional method of fabric dyeing, where cloth, once dipped in colour, is made fast by long exposure to the sun. By repetition of this process the colour becomes extremely fast. These and countless other analogies showed a fertile creative function at work, which at times proved curiously informative.

The Maharishi had set himself the task of clearly enumerating and describing the various states of consciousness open for exploration. Towards the end of this lecture, which lasted almost an hour, he announced:

> For about four years at the beginning of my Movement I was only devoted to establishing the value of the Absolute into the relative life, value of the Absolute into the relative. It's only from about the fifth or sixth year that I started to speak about the Light of the Celestial. And it's only since last year that I have started to explain about God consciousness in a systematic manner. And it's only from about this year that I have started to speak about that state of Supreme Knowledge. These things cannot be understood clearly enough to bring satisfaction on the intellectual level even without the experience. A few days of experience in Transcendental Meditation when the mind begins to retire in a very systematic manner from the gross thinking to the subtle thought to the source of thought, a few times one has known this, this march of the mind from out to inwards and a few flashes of inner pure bliss consciousness, then one is able to understand this whole philosophy of development of the realization of the self and development of self consciousness to become all-time reality and then from there glorification of cosmic consciousness into God consciousness and from there the rising to Supreme Knowledge.

One can only wonder at all these labels. What could they possibly mean for the uninitiated? For instance, what was this 'Supreme Knowledge', and more importantly, would it ever prove a match for the normal pleasures and sensations of everyday life? And even if it were, would it really be worth the time and effort needed to find it?

Until then, he had never talked about a seventh state of consciousness; even meditators firmly established in their practice had heard nothing of this area of his thinking. He now offered his audience his vision of a life lived in enlightenment:

> One could rise to that Supreme Knowledge beyond which there is no possibility of any more expansion of consciousness, beyond which there is no possibility of any development of life, and having risen to that most developed state of human life so that one lived that high state of life where everything is easy and one's life is fully supported by nature, every thought will be materialized. Just, we don't do anything and enjoy everything. One should live life and enjoy life on *that* level.

——— ★ ———

TIME FOR A SONG

The Maharishi's fundamental purpose in writing a commentary on the *Bhagavad-Gita* was apparently to win over his critics at home. It was therefore odd that he chose to write this work in English and arrange for it to be published outside India. A commentary on another, more familiar work might have better met the needs of his Western devotees.

> One day a very sweet man asked me, 'Why you are writing a commentary on *Bhagavad-Gita*? What is your idea?'

The Maharishi gave him this answer:

> If you hear a song of a good music sung by someone and if you have a good voice, when you are alone you'd like to imitate this song, wouldn't you? Some beautiful song heard some time and in your loneliness, if you have a good voice, you try to imitate that song and try to sing it and try to fill the whole atmosphere with that song. *Bhagavad-Gita*, it means the Song of God, the Song of Truth and the embodiment of truth, Lord Krishna, sung this Song of life and he sung the Song of Eternal Life. And in my loneliness I try to imitate or copy the rhythm of his song. Certainly I am commenting on *Bhagavad-Gita* for the joy of my own writing.[139]

This simple statement (delivered between peels of uncontrolled laughter) was unfortunately absent from the printed pages of the finished work.

In 1967 the SRM published the commentary on the first six chapters of the *Gita* to a market almost wholly unfamiliar with the sacred writings of the East. A handsomely produced book, it contained two plates (one of the author and one of his 'Guru Dev'), and almost 400 pages of text interspersed with Sanskrit verses, with accompanying translation and commentary. In the Preface, readers were alerted to the existence of other commentaries and cautioned against them:

Interpretations of the Bhagavad-Gita and other Indian scriptures are now so full of the idea of renunciation that they are regarded with distrust by practical men in every part of the world.[140]

In the *Bhagavad-Gita*, as we have seen, a discourse is presented between the Lord Krishna (frequently referred to in the text, as the 'one with long hair') and an archer named Arjuna. Their conversation was witnessed by one Sanjaya, a charioteer with alleged powers of clairvoyance, clairaudience and perfect memory. It soon becomes clear that Lord Krishna, far from being a mortal of common stock, is perceived as a superior being, insofar as he not only identifies himself with God but also wishes to be recognized as an *avataar* or godly incarnation. The actual writing of the *Bhagavad-Gita* is attributed to an immortal sage called Veda Vyasa, who is also held to be the author of numerous other Hindu scriptures. Since, to some extent, it is implicitly assumed that the reader accepts certain peculiarly Hindu beliefs, it might be well to avoid further reference to the content of the *Gita* in favour of the issues raised in its commentary.

Hindu concepts of time, reincarnation and the existence of gods take time, imagination and patience to understand, let alone accept. The Maharishi however, spoke as one without doubts:

> Time is a conception to measure eternity. Indian historians base their conception of time on eternal Being; for them eternity is the basic field of time.
>
> To arrive at some conception of the eternal, the best measure will be the life-span of something that has the greatest longevity in the relative field of creation.[141]

To those educated in the West, the being with longest life-span might be believed to be a tortoise or a tree perhaps. From a Hindu perspective, however, an altogether different answer would be forthcoming. The Maharishi wisely, and presumably rightly, attributes his explanations of the longest measure of time to someone else.

> This, according to the enlightened vision of Vyasa, is the Divine Mother, the Universal Mother, who is ultimately responsible for all that is, was and will be in the entire cosmos.
>
> The eternity of the eternal life of absolute Being is conceived in terms of innumerable lives of the Divine Mother, a single one of whose lives encompasses a thousand life-spans of Lord Shiva. One life of Lord Shiva equals the duration of a thousand life-spans of Lord Vishnu. One life of Lord Vishnu equals the duration of a thousand life-spans of Brahma, the Creator.[142]

According to this school of thought, measurement of time has as its fundamental units the life-spans of the principal Hindu deities, of Divine Mother and the trinity of Shiva, Vishnu and Brahma. Each life of Brahma (the god of Creation) is said to be 100 years long, and is broken into lunar months. Each day in the life of Brahma is known as a *kalpa* and is equivalent to fourteen *manus* or *manvantaras*. Each *manvantara* is equal to seventy-one *chaturyugin*, and one *chaturyugi* comprises a period of four *yugas*. These four *yugas* are not equal; *Treta-yuga* is three-quarters of *Sat-yuga*, *Dvapara-yuga* is half of *Satyuga*, and *Kali-yuga* is a quarter of *Sat-yuga*. This smallest unit, the *Kali-yuga*, is said to equal 432,000 years!

The Maharishi was outspoken in his condemnation of historians who 'reject as non-history any series of events for which they fail to find a proper chronological order'.[143] Presumably he was referring both to the *Mahabharata*, from which the *Gita* is supposed to originate, and to the numerous other texts, which modern scholars either dismiss as fiction or, at best, date within the last two millennia or so.

The mention of Hindu gods inevitably leads on to speculation about where such celestial bodies might dwell. Were they to exist, they would presumably live in a heaven or heavens somewhere far beyond the reach of man's sensory apparatus. If this were so, it would not be unreasonable for people to hope that one day they might obtain entry to such regions, or at least to aspire to reaching planes higher than that on which they presently exist.

> When righteous people who have not been able to gain cosmic consciousness die, they enter one or other of these planes, for human life is regarded as the gateway to them all. Here life is longer and very much happier because these planes correspond to higher levels of consciousness. The highest level of consciousness is absolute Being, which has eternal life. At the other end of the scale, where purity is least, life is infinitely short.[144]

What about those who had not yet gained the state of awareness referred to as cosmic consciousness? Did they not have a chance of this higher life? The Maharishi was remarkably coy about broaching the subject of reincarnation, preferring instead to let Lord Krishna do the talking. Although understandably reticent about his beliefs in this rather touchy area, he was not completely silent on the subject. In offering his alternative reading of the word 'birth', he cleverly redirected the reader's thoughts from the subject of the soul's transmigration into countless forms, back to his favourite topic of meditation:

> The Lord says: 'perfected through many births'. By this He means perfected

through the continued practice of repeatedly gaining transcendental consciousness and thus being re-born to the world many, many times until cosmic consciousness is gained.[145]

Although his meditation might be described in such terms for some people, it left the topic of the afterlife unanswered. Elsewhere, however, he came closer to committing himself.

> The result of being engrossed in worldly desires is that one remains in the cycle of birth and death. For the joys of the senses can never satisfy; they involve man more and more and thus keep him in bondage. There being no chance of lasting contentment, the cycle of birth and death continues.[146]

This would suggest that the whole of humanity is caught up in a process that can only be interrupted by the loss of worldly desires, although this concept is tangential to the main thrust of the Maharishi's stated philosophy, which sees no problem in man having desire so long as it finds its way to satisfaction. Perhaps he is suggesting that without the experience of transcendental consciousness, bondage to worldly desires hampers success and in consequence leads man to repeated worldly experiences until he finally gets the message! For those who are inextricably caught up in worldly affairs, who have not seized the chance of attaining cosmic consciousness, the Maharishi offered some reassurance:

> Death as such only causes a temporary pause in the process of evolution. A pause like this is no real danger to life because, with a new body taken after the pause, more rapid progress of life's evolution becomes possible. A greater danger will be something that actually retards the process of evolution.[147]

This introduces us to a peculiarly Indian concept, that of *dharma*. Although *dharma* is most often translated as 'duty', a fuller definition is needed. The Maharishi, in fact, preferred to use the expression 'guiding principle'. In practical terms one could interpret *dharma* as living one's life to the best of one's abilities, being a credit to one's family and friends and of use to society as a whole. Conversely, to live a life of selfishness and greed, to be inconsiderate and heartless, or worse still, to live a life of delusion, would all be termed *adharma*. These concepts of *dharma* and *adharma* offer a basis to establish a self-imposed value system, a framework of reference where one might determine right from wrong.

The problem of defining and providing a clear moral code has always posed its own problems. Laws and rules which were held to provide absolute frameworks of reference have found themselves reviewed, amended and repealed because of their incompleteness. Could there ever be a set of laws that held true in all situations, at all times? The Maharishi viewed the subject from a completely different perspective:

> If, in the absence of any scriptural authority or tradition, a criterion of natural duty has to be found, it may be said on the basis of common sense, that an action which is necessary and does not produce any undue tension or strain in the doer and his surroundings is his natural duty.[148]

He proposed that in his technique of meditation could be found the means to live a life in harmony with all the laws of nature. The suggestion that by using a technique of relaxation, the practitioner of meditation might spontaneously gain the ability to perform only right action, seems extremely far-fetched at first sight. But the idea is also very attractive since, when all is said and done, it would be wonderfully reassuring to know that one always took the right decisions and made all the right moves. But who is to say that such an ideal condition could ever be attained? Was the Maharishi not in danger of offering his followers the chance to create nothing better than self-fulfilling, self-gratifying, fool's paradises for themselves? Indeed on what basis did he make this grandiose claim? Where was the evidence? The theory he advanced was that by transcending the relative states of thought, by going beyond the *gunas* (the three aspects of relative energy), one becomes robbed of all impurities and 'freed from duality'. In his commentary to Verse 45 of Chapter 2 of the *Bhagavad-Gita*, he pointed out that Lord Krishna:

> ... wants to assure Arjuna that this state will always prove right, in accordance with dharma, ever furthering the process of evolution for the good of all. Nothing wrong can possibly result from it, because that is the state of fulfilment.[149]

This facility, to be able to perform only right action spontaneously would on its own be a tremendous incentive for anybody to take up the practice of meditation. Imagine a life free of criticism and dangers.

Of the many alluring benefits promised to those who took up meditation, that of access to a world of the gods must rate especially highly, and the Maharishi was offering just that, explaining that his meditation was also a *yagya* (offering).

> When, through the practice of transcendental meditation, activity is realized as separate from the Self, then all of life's activity is said to have been given over as an offering to the gods. This means that activity continues in its sphere of relative life, over which the gods preside, while the Self remains in the freedom of the Absolute. This is the way to please all the gods through

every activity at all times. A situation is created in which every activity automatically becomes a yagya.[150]

The assertion that not only do higher beings or gods exist but that they can be contacted is, to say the least, quite astonishing! Who are these gods he refers to and what activities are they supposed to perform?

> They are powers governing different impulses of intelligence and energy, working out the evolution of everything in creation.[151]

If we were to accept this notion that gods do exist, then we would want to know more about their characteristics and personalities. For instance, are all or any of the gods Asian in appearance or Hindu by religion? What language do they speak and how do they get about? If all this is not already perplexing enough, there is also the question of how they could live multiple existences as claimed by Veda Vyasa. Are they, along with the rest of creation, involved in a cycle of transmigration from one life to another? If this is indeed the case, then the various names of the gods and goddesses are but job-titles, positions that in the fullness of time, *all* could hope to aspire to. If this is so, then the position becomes further complicated in that the lure of celestial status would, in itself, provide new snares for a mankind already caught up in too many worldly desires.

Whether the Maharishi conceded it or not, his attempts to find, in the words of the *Bhagavad-Gita*, any direct reference to his *mantra* meditation, were unsuccessful. Notwithstanding this defect in his work, he provided many thought-provoking insights into Hindu thinking and much that is of interest to practitioners of his technique. However the overriding self-evident message of the *Gita*, that the Lord Krishna extols us to perform his worship, is all but overlooked. Perhaps the Maharishi secretly acknowledged this for he wrote:

> Only when he has become himself can he properly surrender to the Great Self of the Lord. If he remains in the field of the three gunas, in the many sheaths of gross and subtle nature, then it is these sheaths that prevent direct contact with the Lord.[152]

10

—★—

THE BLESSING OF THE BEATLES

There could have been few people, including his strongest critics, who wanted all of the Maharishi's pronouncements to be discredited. For if he was correct about nothing else, his assertion that no one really wants to suffer seems to hold true, for apparently even those who deliberately indulge in suffering do so only in a search of greater enjoyment. But as for his claims regarding higher states of consciousness, nobody had yet appeared on television claiming to have entered into the cosmic consciousness that he spoke of, least of all the man himself. The race was now on to see which of his followers would be the first to proclaim and demonstrate the existence of these elusive states of awareness. Speculation as to the existence of gods and 'counting the number of angels that can dance on a pinhead' could wait, indefinitely if necessary.

Meanwhile, a pop-group called The Beatles had been enjoying unprecedented success, performing to sell-out audiences around the world, their records selling in ever greater quantities. The inevitable pressure of so much acclaim had led them always to want to do better than their last achievement, and to meet the ever-increasing expectations of their public they stopped touring to concentrate on their recorded material. Out of the glare of publicity that surrounded their tours they were free to indulge themselves in whatever way they felt inclined. They dabbled with new ideas as a means of finding new material and alternative directions for their music. Experimentation with drugs was one avenue, which led to unexpected altered states of mind, stimulating fresh ideas. The public now began to see them as spokesmen for the new generation and attached ever greater importance to them as 'thinkers'.

The making of *Help*, The Beatles' second feature film, in 1965, though primarily intended as a showcase for their new material, also gave The Beatles a chance meeting with Indian culture. The film's lightweight plot has as its theme the story of an Indian cult in pursuit of a ring indispensable to their rites. In an effort to reconcile the actors' comic escapades with The Beatles' music, the soundtrack includes occasional passages of their songs played on Indian instruments. From then on George Harrison's appetite and interest for things Indian burgeoned. His liking of Indian music led him to try and master playing the sitar under the guidance of Pandit Ravi Shankar, and through his familiarity with a wide range of 'new' sounds, was able to make an increased contribution to The Beatles' music. He also developed an avid interest in Indian philosophy, and given the opportunity he would devour any literature he could get his hands on. In these pursuits he had the support of his wife (former model Patti Boyd), who shared his enthusiasm for the magic of the mystical East. Mrs Harrison, who had by now discovered that marriage to a wealthy celebrity left her with more than enough time for herself, on hearing of the Maharishi's promises of increased relaxation and serenity, decided to give his teachings a try.

In February 1967 she attended a lecture on meditation at Caxton Hall in London, and subsequently went with a female companion to the Maharishi's meditation centre in fashionable Belgravia to be initiated. Although they were warmly received by the volunteer helpers there, they must have sensed a certain disapproval of their clothes. The problem lay less in the fact that they were inappropriately dressed for winter but that they wore high 'Jesus' boots which consisted of long strips of leather thong plaited neatly up the leg. A precondition for initiation, with its roots in Indian tradition, is that footwear must be removed. The mini-skirted women struggled long to disentangle themselves from the forbidden footwear, before being allowed entry to the *sanctum sanctorum* of the shrine-room.

When in June 1967 The Beatles launched *Sergeant Pepper's Lonely Hearts Club Band*, their latest record, the cover was festooned with the faces of the famous, the infamous and some less familiar. Included in the mock 'class' photograph, was a selection of pictures of Indian mystics whose deeds and exploits had been immortalized in a fascinating book by Indian *guru* Swami Paramahansa Yogananda. In an interview with Alan Aldridge, Beatle Paul McCartney enthused:

Those Indian people have amazing stories. There's one called Yogananda Para Manza, who died in 1953 and left his body in an incredibly perfect state. Medical reports in Los Angeles three or four months after he died were saying this is incredible; this man hasn't decomposed yet. He was sitting there glowing because he did this sort of transcendental bit, transcended his body by planes of consciousness. He was taught by another person on the cover and *he* was taught by *another*, and it all goes back to one called Babujee who's just a little drawing looking upwards.

You can't photograph him – he's an agent. He puts a curse on the film. He's the all-time governor, he's been at it a long time and he's still around doing the transcending bit.[153]

In *Autobiography of a Yogi*, the book to which he referred, the principal interest for many people is the inclusion of innumerable tales of miracle-working. Although the author makes a commendable effort to explain away such phenomena and cautions readers against becoming distracted and therefore obstructed in their search for spiritual experience, he none the less fuels such interest. Yogananda's work has elicited much interest and praise in academic and spiritual circles for its attempt to provide rational and scientific explanations for mysticism and *yoga* practice.

The Indian instrumentalization that had surfaced on The Beatles' previous two albums continued on their latest offering. The sounds of sitar, tabla, tampura etc had become ubiquitous and formed a swathing sympathetic texture behind their new songs. On the subject of self-realization, George Harrison had even penned an all-Indian piece entitled 'Within You, Without You'.

> I think George's awareness has helped us because he got into this through Indian music-or as he calls it, 'All India Radio'. There's such a sense of vision in Indian music that it's just like meditation. You can play it for ever; there's just no end to what you can play on a sitar and how good you can get.[154]

Wherever The Beatles ventured their fans followed. News that the group had lately been dabbling with psychedelic drugs had only recently broken and already it seemed that they might be tempted to go beyond such induced ecstasies by pursuing the road of *yoga* philosophy. Would hordes of fans be joining the growing number of people eager to share the teachings of Swami Paramahansa, Sri Yukteswar Giri, Lahiri Mahasaya and Babaji? Interviewer Alan Aldridge asked Paul McCartney more about these *gurus*.

Aldridge: These are all George's heroes?

McCartney: Yes. George says the great thing about people like Babujee and Christ and all the governors who have transcended is that they've got out of the reincarnation cycle: they've reached the bit where they are just there; they don't have to zoom back.[155]

When George had been interviewed by Barry Miles of the *International Times* in London, he had readily spoken about his passionate interest in matters Eastern. He was especially eager to espouse the cause of Paramahansa Yogananda, and his autobiography.

It's a far-out book, it's a gas. Through *Yoga*, anybody can attain; it's a God-realisation; you just practise *Yoga* and if you really mean it, then you'll do it. You'll do it to a degree ... there's *Yogis* that have done it to such a degree that they're God, they're like Christ and they can walk on the water and materialise bodies and they can do all those tricks. But that's not the point; the point is that we can all do that and we've all got to do that and we'll keep on being re-born because for the law of action and reaction; 'What-so-ever a man soweth, that shall he also reap'; you reap when you come back in your next birth, what you've sown in your previous incarnation.[156]

Had Paramahansa Yogananda been alive he could have counted on The Beatles to seek him out, but in his absence they tried to make the best sense they could of his ideas. Admittedly, his book was no substitute for the man himself and the search was on for a living, breathing, blissful, miracle-working *yogi*.

The Beatles were by now aware of the existence of the Maharishi and, through George's wife Patti, had some impressions of his philosophy. There was something that upset John Lennon about his teaching.

I didn't believe it at the time. She said: 'They gave me this word but I can't tell you, it's a secret'. And I said: 'What kind of scene is this if you keep secrets from your friends?'[157]

However, in time, and in spite of his reservations, John became so taken with the idea of learning to meditate that, according to his lifetime friend Peter Shotton, he set about persuading many of those about him to join him in his new interest.

John's enthusiasm was so contagious that on the day of his initiation, a large group of his friends and associates ended up accompanying him to the London headquarters of the Maharishi's Spiritual Regeneration Movement. Each of us in turn received a personal *mantra* in exchange for a clean white handkerchief, three pieces of fruit, and – last but not least – a full week's wages. (In my case, this worked out to £25 – which, I reckoned at the time, must have amounted to a tiny fraction of John's fee.) Among those present for this great occasion were Cynthia Lennon; an assortment of Beatles; Mick Jagger and his girlfriend, Marianne Faithfull; my wife Beth, and myself... and Yoko Ono.[158]

It was becoming increasingly fashionable to be seen as a 'deep' thinker and since John had now taken to meditation, it was not surprising that he should wish to borrow ideas from the Maharishi, especially those that sounded profound. He would dazzle acquaintances with lines such as the one imperfectly lifted from the Maharishi's commentary on the *Bhagavad-Gita:* 'Time is a concept by which we measure eternity.'[159]

Such was John's commitment to his new interest in meditation that he envisaged The Beatles playing a substantial role in recruiting new converts, and he addressed his fellow musicians on this topic. 'If we went round the world preaching about transcendental meditation, he said earnestly, 'we could turn on millions of people.'[160]

When the opportunity arose to hear the Maharishi in person, The Beatles made sure they attended. By some inexplicable coincidence or quirk of fate, it transpired that this was to be the last public engagement the Maharishi was ever to make. On Thursday, 24 August 1967, almost three months after the release of *Sergeant Pepper*, three of the group, John, Paul and George, arrived at a London hotel.

Arriving at the Park Lane Hilton, where the maharishi was residing, The Beatles found an overflow crowd in the ballroom. Indians in garish Terylene suits and nylon saris rubbed shoulders with drably attired British folk. The Beatles were ushered to the front of the assembly, where a flock of earnest devotees sat in lotus position, holding their hands cupped upward with their eyes cast down. The holy one came onto the stage dressed in Indian robes that contrasted sharply with the dark business suits of his British disciples. Seating himself on a deerskin in the center of a semicircle of straight-backed chairs, the Maharishi called for five minutes of silent meditation. As The Beatles looked on self-consciously, consciously, embarrassed by the *sotto voce* gossiping of the old ladies about them, the suspense built, until, at last, the *guru* spoke.

Talking in a high-pitched voice, interspersed with odd little giggles, he launched into an endorsement of transcendental meditation. 'This practice,' he warbled in a high reedy voice, 'will alone bring one to the complete fulfilment of one's life.' Demanding but 'one half hour a day', transcendental meditation's effect could be detected immediately. 'Rejuvenation is there!' enthused the monk. 'Within two or three days, the face of a man changes.' The maharishi's claim must have made every Beatle zoom in on the old man's face. God knows, he wasn't any beauty. His complexion was dusky, his nose broad, his hair long, greasy, and unkempt, his beard a cotton boll stuck on his chin. Yet the man was right! He *had* a glow in his face.[161]

At the Maharishi's invitation The Beatles decided to join him at a Spiritual Guides' course to be held two days later in Bangor, Wales. The group seems to have been of one mind in wanting their interest in meditation to be publicized, for instead of travelling to Wales by limousine they took the unprecedented step of using public transport. It is alleged that when the 'Mystical Express' train arrived at Bangor carrying The Beatles and their spiritual teacher, the Maharishi assumed that the waiting crowds had turned out to see him. Perhaps it really had not yet dawned on him how extraordinarily famous the group were and as such how great was his fortune in meeting them.

The new apostles lost no time in communicating their enthusiasm for this new craze, and contacted their manager and friends. Soon Paul McCartney's brother Mike and the Rolling Stones' singer Mick Jagger and his girlfriend Marianne Faithfull were making a beeline for Bangor. Peter Hazlitt reported in Pageant magazine of a meeting he attended with the Maharishi after which Mick Jagger observed:

> What the Maharishi teaches is this. When a man's mind is not peaceful, whatever he does or thinks creates vibrations in the atmosphere. The sum of these tense vibrations finally explodes into calamities like war. There is only one way to neutralise the atmospheric tensions, he believes, and that is to reduce them at source – in individuals.

The prospect of wealthy pop-stars contributing to the cause begged the question of how their money would be used. The Maharishi was openly defensive:

> It goes to support the centres, it does not go on me. I have nothing. But my wants are simple. I do not drink or smoke. I have never been to the theatre or to the cinema.

Naturally enough, the press lost no time in relaying the details of meeting with the 'holy man'.

> For more than an hour they sat cross-legged in a semi-trance listening to an old man from the East expound his theories. Earlier The Beatles had sat with 1,500 other people for more than two hours at a Think-In, a lecture on transcendental meditation – given by the Maharishi Mahesh Yogi, leader of a Kashmir cult.[162]

The 'old man' was very much in demand by the press, who wondered at the attention he commanded.

> Interviewer: People think of you as a saint. What is it that you preach?
>
> MMY: I preach a simple system of transcendental meditation which gives the people the insight into life and they begin to enjoy all peace and

happiness, and because this has been the message of all the saints in the past, they call me saint.

Interviewer: You seem to have caught the imagination of the pop stars in this country.

MMY: What is this pop stars ...? You mean The Beatles? I found them very intelligent, and young men of very great potential in life.[163]

Those who had previously been initiated into the Maharishi's method of meditation had done so unannounced, and had usually taken time to weigh up its benefits in the privacy of their own minds. It is unclear why any new initiates should behave been given special dispensation to attend this course, reserved as it was for serious students already committed to his philosophy. Why The Beatles and their companions received the 'red carpet' treatment therefore remains something of a mystery. After all, they did not easily fall within the Maharishi's Vedic world view. Far from having followed their fathers' professions, they had taken their lives into their own hands and in doing so had become the very antithesis of this philosophy. They were children of the *laissez-faire* society, rebels against orthodoxy. It could not have escaped the Maharishi's notice that whilst he spoke with the group, McCartney felt no compunction at lighting up a cigarette.

The Maharishi in his eagerness to 'capture the fort' of the younger generation was prepared to overlook a great deal. Having gained the attention and support of such celebrities he must have been very pleased for he told them:

'You have created a magic air through your names. You have now got to use that magic influence on the generation that look up to you. You have a big responsibility.' The Beatles, all twiddling red flowers, nodded agreement.[164]

The Beatles' stance on drugs had stirred a certain amount of controversy, what with their signatures on a petition for the legalization of 'pot' and the admission of at least one of the group that he had experimented with LSD. Under the influence of meditation, perhaps, they decided to clean up their image and John Lennon made a surprise announcement:

We don't regret taking drugs but we realise that if we'd met Maharishi before we had taken LSD, we would not have needed to take it.[165]

In truth, disenchantment with the effects of drugs had set in before they met the Maharishi. A trip to San Francisco's hippie community earlier in the year had upset George, who was appalled at the squalid conditions of the Haight-Ashbury district, making him rethink his views on the hippie ideology, centred as it was around drug-taking in general and the use of LSD in particular. John Lennon explained:

> We'd dropped drugs before this meditation thing. George mentioned he was dropping out of it and I said: 'Well, it's not doing me any harm, I'll carry on.' But I just suddenly thought, I've seen all that scene. There's no point and if it does anything to your chemistry and brains? Then someone wrote to me and said that whether you like it or not, whether you have no ill-effects, something happens up there. So I decided if I ever did meet someone who could tell me the answer, I'd have nothing left to do with it.[166]

The course members at Bangor were a far cry from the hippie set. The strongest drugs most of them took were tea and perhaps the occasional aspirin. In their company the only temptation there was to revert to the habit would have been rebellion, and that for the moment was out. After lessons they returned to their dormitories in the appositely named Normal College. Their attention was firmly on the teachings of their new-found 'saint' or *guru* and distractions were out of the question. Whilst at Bangor the Maharishi wrote a message for a new teen magazine, taking great care to position himself in such a way as to capitalize on his association with The Beatles and yet avoid saying anything that might make youngsters wary of him.

> The interest of young minds in the use of drugs, even though misguided, indicates their genuine search for some form of spiritual experience.
>
> With the interest of The Beatles and the Rolling Stones in Transcendental Meditation, it has become evident that the search for higher spiritual experience among the young will not take long to reach fulfilment. But it is for the older generation to provide facilities for the teaching of Transcendental Meditation.
>
> It is an indication of progress that The Beatles are thinking of having their own academy for teaching, in London to start with, and I congratulate the Archbishop of Canterbury who has expressed his satisfaction with The Beatles' interest in Transcendental Meditation.
>
> The youth of today need the support of their elders and I hope they will extend their grace.[167]

Both The Beatles and the Rolling Stones were both renowned for their self-opinionated attitudes. Were they really going to subdue and surrender their personalities in order to bathe in purity and righteousness? How were the fans to respond to their idols' sudden switch in ideology? Where would meditation and its surrounding philosophy fit into their own lives? Alarm bells started ringing, and there was a wave of cynicism in certain quarters of the media. The satirical magazine *Private Eye* lampooned the rising interest in Indian

mysticism with outright cynicism by introducing a character named
Veririchi Lottsa Money Yogi Bear.

Only two days into the ten-day course at Bangor the news broke that
The Beatles' business manager had died in mysterious circumstances,
whilst under the effects of barbiturate drugs and alcohol. Brian Epstein
had long been more than a business associate of the famous foursome,
much more a close friend and confidant. The group tried hard to make
sense of the loss of their friend and mentor. From habit the Maharishi
shied away from any mention of negative topics, but in this situation he
was forced to speak out and counsel his protégés in their time of need.
When at last The Beatles emerged, their comments underlined just how
far they had travelled in the direction of their new teacher. John Lennon
told the waiting journalists:

> He told us not to get overwhelmed by grief and whatever thoughts we have
> of Brian to keep them happy because any thoughts we have of him, they will
> travel to him wherever he is.[168]

Thus it seemed that Epstein was still alive, and sensitive to the thoughts
of his departed friends. George Harrison echoed these sentiments:

> There's no real such thing as death anyway. I mean it's death on a physical
> level but life goes on everywhere and you just keep going. Really! But... So
> the thing is, it's not so disappointing ... it is and it isn't ... you know? And
> the thing about the comfort, is to know he's ... okay![169]

It seemed that in the hands of John and George the message about the
ideology of the meditation was in danger of becoming blurred by other
strands of philosophy. The message the SRM wanted to get across was
altogether more accessible and at a press conference the Maharishi tried
to clarify it.

> MMY: One sits down comfortably in a chair or wherever one wants, and he
> uses a thought that he has been given specially for himself and he starts
> experiencing the subtler state of thought.

> INTERVIEWER: Are you experiencing this subtler state of thought at this
> moment?

> MMY: No I am out in the gross field.

> INTERVIEWER: What do you have to do in order to obtain this state of
> thought?

> MMY: Just a few instructions from a trained teacher and one begins to

experience it.

INTERVIEWER: How long does it take?

MMY: About half an hour.

INTERVIEWER: But how do you know when it's happened?

MMY: Ah, one begins to feel relaxed right from the beginning one begins to enjoy some improved level of well-being.[170]

Though many people became interested in meditation, there were many, many more who were left totally confused as to what The Beatles had become involved in. To the watching world they appeared to have surrendered themselves as disciples to an unknown ageing Indian and worse still might yet find themselves caught up in a make-believe world of mumbo-jumbo mysticism. Had they tuned in to the BBC on 17 September 1967, they might have become better informed. The programme, entitled *The Spirit and the Flesh*,[171] featured His Holiness Maharishi Mahesh Yogi in top form, interviewed by seasoned wordsmith Malcolm Muggeridge.

The recorded discussion had as its subject Muggeridge's assertion that in order to grow in spirit one has to abstain from temptations of the flesh. Muggeridge himself confessed to having a 'greedy sensual nature' and believed that if he were to follow this nature he would be 'like a pig in a trough'. He thus decried the popular trend to stimulate the practice of self-indulgence as alien to spiritual growth. The advance of American and Scandinavian cultures he saw as wholly unwelcome, describing them as 'bestial and degraded'. In stating his belief that the story of spiritual teaching in both the Christian and Hindu traditions had their basis in practices of abstention from desire and self-control, he opened the way for debate. Unlike its predecessor, 'Meeting Point', this discussion promised to be altogether more sparky and contentious.

The Maharishi responded to Muggeridge by readily agreeing that 'greediness' needed controlling but said that that control should be natural, cultivated by his method of meditation. Muggeridge wanted him to clarify the precise formula used in meditation and asked whether the 'Uuuum' syllable might be used. The Maharishi indicated that whilst he instructed people to use a specific sound, he favoured syllables other than *om*. In the Maharishi's teaching Muggeridge thought he detected elements of the 'pill doctrine' and flippantly suggested that his meditation might therefore be likened to taking a 'spiritual capsule', cynically putting forward the recommendation: 'Take three drops of the *swami's* essence and you'll be in tune with the infinite.'

Far from taking offence at these comments the Maharishi readily agreed with his line of reasoning but went on to point out that the injunction to shun or turn one's back on the world should be understood in the context of meditation. He pointed out that to permanently shun the world gave satisfaction only to those few who had chosen the reclusive life, whereas most people needed only to set aside a few minutes to meditate. He claimed that 100,000 people had already derived enormous benefits from its practice, and went on to say:

> The thing is it's just not possible to check the increasing fast tempo of modern life. It's just not possible. What is possible is to supplement this fast life of the outside activities in the world by the inner silence, by the inner bliss consciousness. And this will not only give man stability in his outer life but give him ability for greater progress. This is the need of the modern age.

The mention of progress had Muggeridge interrupting, saying 'The idea of any more progress fills me with unspeakable horror.' The progress he seemed to be referring to was the erosion of values, the casting out of the old world and the replacement of conservatism with suspect and untried new philosophies. He in turn was then interrupted by the Maharishi's bubbly tones.

> I want to make progress more fulfilling and more useful to life by the impact of inner silence and increased energy at the same time. We want peace, but not at the cost of progress and peace, but peace that will the basis of greater activity and yet life in greater fulfilment and more joyfulness. This is what the Spiritual Regeneration Movement has brought -this philosophy – and this is not a new philosophy, I count it to be just the interpretation of the original text of the philosophy of life contained in the books of every religion.

He went on to say that he believed it was hard if not impossible for a modern man to entertain concepts of abstention and detachment. In these words Muggeridge found more fuel for his argument.

> That is maybe why modern men of action have made such a disgusting mess of the world. Isn't that so?

The Maharishi, in restating his position on the need to prioritize inner values, pointed out a basic dichotomy. He observed that even those who advocated the path of renunciation had, of necessity, to abandon their lifestyles in order to come out and speak. Muggeridge did not want to debate this point, preferring instead to lay down a challenge, asking whether the kingdoms of the outer material world were not those of the devil. The Maharishi, careful as ever to avoid conflict, chose to pursue a comfortable middle ground:

So what we want is to regenerate the spiritual value of the devil and then all the kingdoms are fine. And ... yesterday I was very happy to see The Beatles, they were so deeply interested in this deep thought of inner life. I was just surprised to find their interest in this Transcendental Meditation.

Muggeridge, a past master in the role of interviewer, used this change of topic to launch an attack on the use of drugs. It was unacceptable, he claimed, that the nature of God could be understood by taking a drug, as one of The Beatles had allegedly remarked. He was openly contemptuous, saying: 'But do you imagine that sucking a drug is going to, is going to produce the result? No, no, no, no, no.'

It is strange how this lively debate had so soon gone aground after mention of The Beatles. The Maharishi had no need to shore up his arguments with the names of fashionable celebrities and had, until then, been doing admirably in marshalling his ideas. Evidently, he had mentioned their name in order to impress, but in this he had failed, for his host held no brief for the permissive society in general or for the use of recreational drugs in particular. But now Muggeridge too had let himself down, for this linking of the Maharishi and his meditation with the use of drugs was spurious in the extreme. Demonstrating his capacity not only to deal with opposition but also to turn a situation to advantage, the Maharishi replied:

No. But then we must supply them with some tangible, simple, natural means to glorify all aspects of their personality and life. If the religious people and religious practices and churches and all that goes with it, if they are not able to satisfy the need of the youngsters for that experience of higher consciousness then they must fall into this and into this, into this. But what is important there for us is the desire in the youngsters for some experience of higher nature or experience of some bliss consciousness. If Christ has said that Kingdom of Heaven is within you, a young man of today wants to verify where is that Kingdom of Heaven within me.

Somewhere deep in the Himalayan foothills lay a small dry cave, a cave that the Maharishi had left in order to follow a thought, a thought that had in time led him to leave India and take his brand of philosophy to the people of the West. The time he had allocated for his mission had almost expired. Somewhere, in the recesses of his mind he knew that one day soon he might return to that cave. Perhaps that was a part of the unfathomable source of strength that kept the erstwhile *brahmachari* empowered in his public speaking, whilst carefully befriending his adversaries.

But was his method of meditation all that it was claimed to be? How could anyone really answer that? For the moment the world would have to take at face value the words of 'His Holiness' and his devotees. John Lennon, seldom at a loss for words, some weeks later conveyed his feelings about meditation with admirable clarity and succinctness:

> You just feel more energetic, you know, just simply for doing work or anything. You just come out of it and it's, 'who-o-oaah let's get going.'[172]

11

—★—

INDIAN SUMMER

S ome months before The Beatles met the Maharishi, they were invited to become involved in the world's first international satellite transmission. and had performed John Lennon's song-with-a-message, 'All You Need is Love'. They appeared wearing Indian *kurta* shirts hung with love beads. The East was well and truly 'in' with the 'in crowd', and Indian garments, crafts, incense and accessories were selling like proverbial hot cakes. With The Beatles now interested in the Maharishi and his meditation, the re-release of the Maharishi's 'Love' poem, with the addition of a sensitive and lyrical accompaniment on sitar by Amiya Das Gupta, could not have been more appropriate. The cover of the American release proclaimed 'Maharishi Mahesh Yogi, The Beatles' spiritual teacher, speaks to the youth of the world on Love and the untapped source of Power that lies within.' The record opens with a Sanskrit prayer, a fragment of the *Guru Pranam*.

agyaanatimiraandhasya gyaanaanjanashalaakayaa,
chakshurunmiilitam yena tasmai shriigurave namah.

(He removes the dark blindness of ignorance, with the light of knowledge,
Salutation to the *Guru*. Who has opened my eyes.)

There was much speculation about how the alliance between The Beatles and their 'spiritual teacher' would affect their music. Would they turn their skills to creating a eulogy to the marvels of meditation? No doubt the Maharishi was hopeful of this, perhaps envisaging a 'Top Ten' million-selling paean to his methods. As it was, The Beatles were commendably cautious about making such a move, and instead went on to weave their 'magic' spells by pooling their creative energies in a film project entitled *Magical Mystery Tour*. However, as individuals they were pleased to endorse meditation.

A popular British television show, hosted by the famous interviewer David Frost succeeded in persuading John and George to appear for the

first time on a chat show and present their case for meditation. The
Frost Report of Saturday, 30 September 1967, in addition to these star
celebrities, included an interview which Frost had fitted in earlier that
day at Heathrow Airport whilst the Maharishi awaited a flight to
Scandinavia. Frost showed himself to be a reasonable and capable
interviewer, unafraid to ask the questions that just begged to be asked.
He started with the more obvious. Why did the Maharishi always
surround himself with flowers? What was the power of the flower?[173]

> MMY: Flower also presents my message. The message is – enjoy all the
> glories of outer life and also enjoy the honey of life present in the inner
> being. Bliss consciousness should not be lost when enjoying, when one is
> enjoying the outer material glories of life.
>
> Frost: And how does a flower sum that up?
>
> MMY: The outer beauty attracts the honey bee and it knows the technique of
> going deep, enjoys the honey and goes out.

Frost then dug a little deeper and asked what the difference was between
the Maharishi's meditation and 'just sitting around and thinking'? The
answer came clear: 'Other methods try to concentrate, control the mind.'
Expounding on this idea he went on to brand such control as unnatural,
and therefore undesirable, explaining:

> Transcendental Meditation uses a natural faculty of the mind to go deep and
> that natural faculty is to go to a field of greater happiness.

Still pursuing his question, Frost asked for further elucidation on the
actual technique that was being proposed.

> Experiencing the subtler state of a thought takes the mind to the source of
> thought. Here thoughts start as an air bubble from the bottom of the sea and
> coming up it becomes big enough to be appreciated on the surface.

Following a discussion of the nature of the teaching given to new
initiates the Maharishi then said:

> Someone one day started to meditate and next day he came for checking and
> he said: 'I feel wonderful, I slipped very deep and the whole thing is good
> but tell me what you have taught me?'
>
>   I told him: 'Nothing, because the process of thinking has not to be
> learned.'

These comments drew forth a great deal of mirth from the Maharishi
and his associates, and rightly so. It would have been an interesting line
of thought to pursue but Frost instead raised another issue entirely. He
wondered whether, if this meditation could confer greater power of

thought, it might not be possible for this additional power to be misused. The Maharishi usually preferred to side-step the subject of morality, since it was such a potential philosophical minefield. By habit he avoided explicit negative vocabulary; adjectives such as bad, evil and the like he expressed in terms of lesser happiness. It appears that Frost sensed something amiss with this language.

> Frost: Do you, to the people that come to you, say that certain things are right and certain things are wrong?

> MMY: No, nothing, nothing. Only we tell them just start experiencing the subtler state of thought, and experiencing the source of thought which is a tremendous reservoir of energy and intelligence. When I say that the source of thought is a reservoir of energy and intelligence, what I mean is ... See a thought has energy due to which it flows and it has intelligence due to which it takes a direction. So the source of thought must be a tremendous reservoir of energy and intelligence. Conscious mind going to that field becomes filled with greater energy and intelligence and this is what makes a man more efficient in life.

Frost quickly divined the message to be that one should meditate and therefore, automatically, act rightly – to which the Maharishi readily agreed. Perhaps Frost's Methodist upbringing found this formula a little hard to swallow, for on detecting the Maharishi's reluctance to offer clear moral guidance, the otherwise easygoing interviewer began to despair of committing him to even 'just *one* example of wrong doing'. Undeterred, he persevered and was at length rewarded by this rather hesitant offering:

> I think, if a man ... if a child is very careless and the mother takes his book and puts it somewhere else – it is stealing.

Since the interview was destined to be seen by countless thousands of television viewers he might have done better to explain his reluctance to elaborate his beliefs further. Why was he being so openly evasive? Some crimes are obviously unacceptable, and avoiding admitting it made him appear ineffectual and even dim-witted. There seem to be two main reasons for his reticence on the subject: one, that he wished to maintain an image of forgiving saintliness; and two, that he wanted to avoid any risk of identifying with others' misdeeds. This sort of thought avoidance is commonly perceived as 'sticking one's head in the sand' or even superstitiously avoiding 'bad magic'. Years of habituation to this practice could not be overturned in a moment of pressure.

In an effort to keep the interview going, Frost moved on and asked the Maharishi more about the actual technique of meditation. How many *mantras* were there? This question also made the Maharishi uneasy, but when pressed, he answered evasively: 'You could say thousands.' But he did elaborate and explain that the 'sounds' or *mantras* were chosen 'to accord with the rhythms or impulses of the individual'. By repetition, the intitiate would resonate in harmony with the 'sound' and a state of fulfilment would be gained.

In addition to being a capable *agent provocateur*, Frost was a gentleman, and having got the interview that he had come for, allowed the Maharishi the last word, a statement of his claims for the efficacy of his system of meditation. After a brief interval for commercials came the live interview with John Lennon and George Harrison. For meditators of only a few weeks' standing they represented the Maharishi's philosophy extraordinarily well. George Harrison, once known as the 'quiet one' was now almost loquacious, whilst John Lennon seemed uncharacteristically attentive and self-controlled. Frost quizzed them both about the Maharishi's claim that meditation could provide serenity and increased energy, to which John replied that he had now learned to tap his energy and reassured viewers that 'the worst days I have on meditation are better than the worst days I had before, without it.'

When asked to comment, George showed a powerful grasp of the subject:

> The energy is latent within everybody. It's there anyway... meditation is a natural process of being able to contact that, so by doing it each day you contact that energy and give yourself a little more. Consequently, you're able to do whatever you normally do just with a little more happiness maybe.

In this evaluation of the meditation process, George had demonstrated a little of his ability at Maharishi-speak, whilst John, speaking in everyday terms, continued to do his level best to show just what meditation might mean to ordinary people:

> You just sort of sit there and you let your mind go wherever it's going. It doesn't matter what you're thinking about just let it go and then you just introduce the *mantra*, the vibration, just to take over from a thought. You don't will it or use your willpower.

Thereupon George came in:

> If you find yourself thinking, then at the moment you realize you've been thinking about things again, then you replace that thought with the *mantra* again. Sometimes you can go on and you find you haven't even had the *mantra* in your mind, you've just been a complete blank. But when you reach that point, because it's beyond all experience, then it's down there and that

level is timeless, spaceless so you can be there for five minutes and come out. You don't actually know how long you've been there.

Though he spoke with evident enthusiasm and obvious sincerity, there must have been viewers who felt uncomfortable at the prospect of deliberately creating such feelings of disunity with time. But for anyone who had already experienced an excessive amount of outer (or for that matter inner) experiences, 'switching off' for a while might appear a very welcome option. However, were these the descriptions of a Kingdom of Heaven within, or Nirvana that the Maharishi had promised his audiences? As John and George continued and the subject unfolded, it became obvious that they had been led to believe that the benefits of meditation were not to be expected within the actual process, but would show themselves in the quality of the meditator's outer life.

Frost asked what evidence they had of tangible benefits since starting the practice of meditation. It was again George who answered.

> We've only been doing it a matter of six weeks maybe, but there is definite proof I've had that it's something that really works. But in actual fact it'll take a long time to arrive at the point where I'm able to hold that pure consciousness on this level or to bring that level of consciousness into this level of consciousness.

At this point Frost took the opportunity to discuss other topics with them, ranging from their views on taking drugs, to questions about morality and religion. He asked whether they had come to revise their views about religion in the light of their meditations? From their answers, it appeared that they had. It was now John's turn to indulge in a display of Maharishi-speak in order to discount the proposition that meditation necessitated a change of religion. But Frost wanted evidence of their *own* religious beliefs. He asked what difference they saw between Jesus Christ and the Maharishi. John Lennon was extremely quick to reply:

> Well I don't know, you know. Maharishi doesn't do miracles for a kickoff. I don't know how divine or how, you know, superhuman or whatever it is, he is at all.

George, on the other hand, evinced a belief that certain spiritual leaders, such as Buddha and Krishna, were born as divine incarnations of God, whilst others acquired realization of their divinity having had only ordinary birth. John could not resist interrupting him: 'So Maharishi's one of *them*. He was born quite ordinary but he's working at it!'

His remark was greeted by a storm of applause. It was now re-assuringly evident that John, far from having succumbed to a cult whose mind-numbing practices would bring the downfall of The Beatles, was still a jolly, good-humoured chap and a long way from losing his grip on reality.

It might have been a good moment to begin winding up the show, but Frost was still in pursuit of answers to the questions about morality he had posed to the Maharishi. In particular he wanted to know if the effects of meditation were always positive. John retorted:

> We don't really know what would happen to a sort of a killer or something that did it. You know maybe he'd change his mind. You can't ... we don't know about that, you know, you should have asked him that side of it. But it's for the good you know, it's simple, that's the main bit about it, so, they're bound to be a bit better than they were.

He had rightly put the interviewer in his place, but one sympathizes with Frost in that the Maharishi had contributed nothing by his stubborn unwillingness to discuss the matter properly. Overall, The Beatles had put in a sparkling performance, proving on top form. After the interview they withdrew to the recording studio to spend the night recording 'I am a Walrus' with its message about the unity of all: 'I am you, as you are me, as we are all together.' The following Wednesday they re-appeared, on a successful follow-up show for Frost, entering into a debate about meditation with invited guests, a convert and a sceptic.

One might have expected their fans to follow their lead, turning out with their week's earnings (or pocket money) and bunch of flowers and taking the *mantra* that would help them to reach untapped levels of energy and serenity within. Certainly some did just that. However, the majority remained ignorant of the mysteries of meditation and not a little suspicious of The Beatles' aged Indian friend. The sovereign right to determine one's own life and think one's own thoughts was one of the main goals of modern ideology. For many, the very idea of surrendering oneself to a teacher, least of all a mysterious Hindu monk, in order to receive lessons in how to think was singularly unacceptable. In addition, unlike their idols, most fans had had relatively little experience of the sensory overloads that had precipitated The Beatles' involvement with meditation. Some still enjoyed the experiences, excitement and personal prestige that drugs promised, and took exception to anyone who sought to straighten them out.

Although it is true that newspapers in general tended to emphasize and sensationalize the negative side of drug-taking, the degenerative effects had also begun to become apparent to users, even amongst the flower-power hippies. The time was right to rethink the pivotal force that drugs had become amongst the young. Richard Neville, founder journalist of the 'underground' organ Oz, put the situation like this:

> A generation took LSD having discovered that the values of the world they inherited were bankrupt. (Later, some took to the Maharishi, having discovered that it was not the world which was spiritually bankrupt, but themselves)[174]

So, was the Maharishi's meditation just for the burned out, for the disillusioned 'druggies'? To say so was to ignore ten years of the Maharishi's activity. Nevertheless, in view of his current influential position with The Beatles, the press felt free to adopt an altogether more sceptical attitude towards the man and his meditation.

Earlier that year, at the beginning of August, immediately before visiting Britain, the Maharishi had visited Sweden to conduct that country's first summer course at Holmsby Brunn. Then, after his extraordinarily successful stay in Britain, he flew to Bremen, Germany, to be present at the inauguration of the newly built Academy for Development of Personality. He spent the autumn of 1967 back in Sweden at Falsterbohus, which became the temporary European headquarters of the Movement.

It was here that The Beatles' representatives visited him, in order to sort out a minor misunderstanding. The story goes that, having gained the interest and attention of the group, the Maharishi had rather rashly counted on their willingness to do his bidding, and had committed them to media appearances without their consent. The task that now confronted Paul and George was to inform their spiritual teacher that they would not tolerate him making claims on their time without prior arrangement. As aide Peter Brown recalls, George put the situation all down to his teacher's unworldliness.

> I went to Malmo again, this time with Paul and George in tow. We met the Maharishi and tried to explain to him that he must not use their names to exploit his business affairs, and that they definitely would *not* appear on his TV special, but the Maharishi just nodded and giggled again. 'He's not a modern man,' George said forgivingly on the plane home. 'He just doesn't understand these things.'[175]

Towards the end of the year the Maharishi was on the move again, this time on a trip to Paris in the company of John Lennon and George Harrison. By an unexpected coincidence, John's friend Pete Shotton was also in town. At a private audience with the Maharishi, he heard John ask his teacher what could be done to bring a halt to the American war in Vietnam.

> He delivered his reply in the soothing tone of an over-indulgent parent to a
> wayward child. 'You're all very fortunate,' he said, 'to be living under a
> democratically elected government. You have every right to voice your own
> opinion, but in the end you must uphold your country's democratic system
> by supporting your government, which represents the will of the people.'[176]

Also at the meeting was an associate of John Lennon's, Alexis Mardas,
whose father is alleged to have worked for the Greek secret police.

> 'I know you!' he exclaimed suddenly. 'Didn't I meet you in Greece, many
> years ago?'
>   'No, no,' the monk tittered. 'I've never even been to Greece.'
>   'I *know* I've met you,' Alex persisted. 'Only you didn't call yourself the
> Maharishi then. You were travelling under another name, doing something
> completely different from what you're doing now.'[177]

After the meeting Mardas continued his accusations insisting:

> 'I'm *positive* I've met him, John,' Alex insisted. 'He's *not* what you think he
> is. He's just an ordinary hustler. The man's only in it for the money.'[178]

On Monday, 18 December the Maharishi attended rehearsals for a
concert at the Palais Dc Chaillot, in aid of UNICEF, at which sitarist
Ravi Shankar was due to appear. The American group, the Beach Boys
were also due to perform at the benefit, and their drummer, Dennis
Wilson, arrived in time to see John and George in the company of their
Indian teacher watching Ravi Shankar's recital.

> Dennis shook the Maharishi's hand. 'All of a sudden,' Dennis said, 'I felt
> this weirdness, this presence this guy had. Like out of left field. First thing he
> ever said to me [was] 'Live your life to the fullest.'[179]

Wilson became very smitten with him and before long had assembled
the rest of the Beach Boys, intent on having them all initiated into
meditation.

> And then I got my *mantra*, and as the Maharishi was giving them to us he
> said, 'What do you want?' I said, 'I want everything. Everything.' And he
> laughed and we meditated together. It was so wild.[180]

A few weeks later, The Beatles' *Magical Mystery Tour* was released,
and the group found themselves subjected to unexpectedly hostile
criticism. Just why the reviews were so disparaging is not clear, for the
television film and the music it contained were very much products of
their pre-meditation personas, and the fooling and surrealism were very
much in keeping with the times. The explanation most likely lies in the

fact that this was the first opportunity since the release of the 'psychedelic' *Sergeant Pepper's Lonely Hearts Club Band* album that the establishment had had for giving the group a good dressing down. No longer did they qualify for instant and unconditional approval; instead they were to be chastised for their flagrant use of drugs and involvement with mysticism – the principle of action and reaction, the law of *karma*, perhaps?

In January 1968, whilst the Maharishi was in America, George Harrison flew from Britain to Bombay, to the EMI Studios to work with Indian musicians on the soundtrack of a film he was scoring called *Wonderwall*. A by-product of these sessions was a composition entitled 'Inner Light', a song with a meditative feel based on a poem from the Taoist scripture *Tao Te Ching*. On his return to London he and John worked on a track called 'Across the Universe' (later to become a personal favourite of John's), with the repeated refrain: 'Nothing's gonna change my world – *Jai Guru Deva Om*'.

With the endorsement of his teachings by pop 'royalty', the Maharishi found it particularly easy to woo the youth of America. When he arrived for a short stay before returning to India, he was given a hero's welcome, and was greeted by a couple of thousand people at Los Angeles International Airport. He gave a lecture at the Santa Monica Civic Auditorium, which was full to bursting point, and is said to have met prominent musicians such as Mick Jagger and members of the groups Grateful Dead and Jefferson Airplane. Everywhere he went, he spoke to packed houses, extolling the power of the young generation to turn the world on to his meditation. He took his message to national television. His face was even to be found for sale on mass-produced posters alongside pop stars and folk heroes such as Che Guevara.

Not everyone was caught up in the adulation; some people wanted to dig a little deeper before committing themselves. In a particularly revealing interview, published by *International Times* in December 1967, the Maharishi had spoken out against the politics of Communism, claiming that they sounded like 'weakism'. On reading this, and hearing also that the Maharishi equated poverty with laziness, 'beat' poet Allen Ginsberg felt impelled to go and see him. Having gained a personal audience with him, Ginsberg alarmed his disciples by being far from starstruck and sycophantic; indeed positively hostile. He harangued their teacher for nigh on half an hour, quizzing him about his attitudes to the use of the military, the US involvement in Vietnam and specifically on the compulsory drafting of young people into that war.[181]

> Maharishi hadn't covered the problem satisfactorily. He said Johnson and his
> secret police had more information and they knew what they were doing. I
> said they were a buncha dumbells and they don't know and his implicit
> support of authoritarianism made lots of people wonder if he weren't some
> kinda CIA agent. He giggled 'CIA?' His devotees began screaming so I said
> it was a common question so it should be proposed and they shouldn't stand
> around silent and fearful to speak.

To any problem that Ginsberg presented, the answer came back that
everyone should meditate. To a question about LSD, the Maharishi
responded by claiming that meditation was stronger. It is unlikely that
he had himself taken the drug, for had he had detailed knowledge or
personal experience of the overpowering sensory effects experienced by
people on it, he would not have made such comparisons. If this was his
way of enticing a wider interest in his meditation then it was doomed to
fail. To the user of drugs, stronger means more intense, and the drug-
user was thus being misinformed. Moreover, the Maharishi went on to
warn that LSD could damage the nervous system and mentioned that
some half a dozen hippies had visited him in a room in Los Angeles and
had smelled so bad that he had had to take them into the garden.
Ginsberg was outraged.

> I said *WHAT?* you must have been reading the newspapers. He said he didn't
> read newspapers. I said he likely had a misconception from his friends (at
> that point, I guess I said acid hippies were the largest part of the day's
> audience). He insisted that hippies smelled.

Ginsberg was left with mixed feelings about the Maharishi and his
tendentious' statements, and was certainly less than impressed with his
lack of social commitment.

> Judging from voicetone of his business manager – a sort of business man
> western square sensitive – sounds like he is surrounded by a conservative
> structure and he would come on unsympathetic in relation to social
> problems.

But although far from won over by the Maharishi, this ambassador of
hippiedom was not completely dismissive. He concluded his report by
saying:

> The main burden that everyone should meditate half hour morning and night
> makes sense. His blank cheque claims that his extra special meditation form
> is more efficient than any other is something I haven't tried so I can't judge.
> His high powered organisation method of advertising meditation is getting,
> like Pyramid club of people meditating and massive enthusiasm application

which would certainly tend to accomplish general peacefulness if it caught on massively and universally. His political statements are definitely dim-witted (and a bit out of place).

The Maharishi image as a spiritual statesman-cum-*guru*, was fast becoming tarnished as he gained a reputation for being unwilling (or unable) to offer useful guidance on contemporary issues. He appeared to prefer to dwell in a comfortable bubble of neutrality. Perhaps a clue to the situation lies in his own definition of his responsibilities: 'Maharishi's are those who apply the knowledge [of the *mantras*] for the good of the world.'[182] This seems to imply that those seeking guidance on mundane matters would do better to look elsewhere. Each individual would have to determine his or her path through life.

The situation was not improved by pronouncements which frequently antagonized and alienated potential converts. How could he assert that poverty is a direct result of laziness without acknowledging the many situations in which even despite their labours people are frequently forced into impoverishment? Similarly, in his rejection of Communism, presumably in favour of an ideology of self-sufficiency, he completely ignored the difficulties that cause people to pool resources and stand together.

On the basis of his remarks, it would have been ill advised, therefore, to surrender one's thoughts to him. The problem lay in the assumption that because he *looked* like a saviour, he was expected to speak and act like one. None the less, he was not heard to complain at the attention he received, so one might well be forgiven for suspecting that he relished it. The donations of a week's salary and the $35 a head paid by students still came in. Viewed in a purely material light the Maharishi undoubtedly possessed the Midas touch.

12

———★———

RETIREMENT PARTY

The last weeks of January 1968 found some sixty or so meditators preparing to embark on a sort of magical mystery trip which would eventually take them to the Academy of Meditation, Shankaracharya Nagar, in the Himalayan foothills of north-western India. They were to go first to Delhi in order to attend a conference and then travel northwards, via Rishikesh, oven the River Ganges by means of the Lakshman Jhoola suspension bridge. They all had one purpose in mind – to take *darshan* of the Maharishi and under his guidance train to become teachers of his Transcendental Meditation. For musician Paul Horn, who was planning on filming the three-month course for posterity, additional excitement came with the news that, according to the *cognoscenti*, there was strong reason to believe that The Beatles might also put in an appearance.

When the Maharishi flew out of New York on this last journey home he was accompanied by a female admirer, the estranged wife of entertainer Frank Sinatra, actress Mia Farrow, with whom he had earlier spent time in Boston, Massachusetts. The flight took them not to India but to London's Heathrow Airport where, on 24 January, a waiting photographer snapped a shot of them alighting. The Maharishi later flew to Bombay and from there made a belated arrival in New Delhi on the eve of the Eighth World Congress. The congress, which was held on Sunday, 28 January, went without a hitch, and a line-up of speakers commended meditation to solve a variety of problems including health, education, social behaviour and world peace. Indian people, however, tend to distrust the proclamations of the rich and famous, and reserve particular contempt for religious leaders who appear to be too comfortably off. A guest appearance the following day at the University of New Delhi, found a portion of the audience openly sceptical of the

Maharishi's message and, on this occasion, he bad his work cut out to deal with the unwelcome hecklers and their loaded questions. But he was a veteran campaigner with a rare talent for keeping calm. Before leaving Delhi he made one more appearance, this time in a particularly public place in the open air, and to the surprise and consternation of his Western devotees, addressed the many thousands of assembled Indians in Hindi. But the following day he was to journey to Rishikesh, and then his followers would have him to themselves.

Boosted by a $100,000 donation from a wealthy heiress, the building programme at Shankaracharya Nagar had by now come a long way, and the small patch of land on the wooded hillock boasted many new buildings. As a surprise for the Maharishi, his devotees had planned and constructed a squat white residence in which it was intended he should stay. Surrounded by trees, the purpose-built residence had, on the ground floor, two fair-sized adjoining rooms and a comfortable veranda lined with pillars, with a further two rooms, ventilated by fanlights, in the basement. On the flat roof of the building was an additional room surrounded by a low-walled terrace and overlooking an ornamental pond and beds of flowering plants. Canadian actor Gerry Stovin, recalls that the Maharishi's first instinct was to spurn the use of the new building in favour of the grass hut he usually occupied, but he appears to have relented.

Further up the hill from the bungalow, and on the western perimeter of the Academy, lay a row of six stone dwellings for the exclusive use of guests. The other buildings that had been built included 'blocks', single-storey whitewashed residences, but the most notable was a spacious subterranean lecture hall. Pathways had been made joining the various buildings, and a certain amount of landscaping was also in hand. Access to the site was via a pedestrian gateway near which a sub-post-office and a branch of a national bank had been built, or by the roadway which had been cut through the dense surrounding jungle to the rear of the Academy.

The overcrowded, dilapidated black taxis negotiated the final part of their journey, the short passage through the jungle track, during which the excited travellers were able to catch glimpses of the broad River Ganges snaking its way past the *ashrams* and temples of nearby Swargashram village, and to hear the calls of local wildlife. From the drivers and from the bearers of their luggage, the foreign passengers found themselves gaining faltering familiarity with a few words of the Hindi language. As they approached the Maharishi's *ashram*, they could see festive bunting hanging from the trees. They had arrived and the

Maharishi's *brahmacharin* were waiting there to greet them. The air rang with the sound of constant and repeated chanting. Pervading the thoughts and ears of all were but three magic words: '*Jai Guru Dev.*'

Many of the visitors must have worried that the climate in India would be far too hot for them. They were relieved to discover that although the sun shone brightly throughout the day, the air was fresh and cool. The nights however could be really cold, which explained the fireplaces the newcomers found in their rooms.

Every bedroom was simply furnished, with a bedstead and bedding, a chair and a table, shelving and a mirror. All basic facilities were laid on and there was even hot water, which was heated up in disused oil drums by servants. The *ashram* breakfast was definitely not to be missed, comprising as it did of cereal, porridge, toast with jam or marmalade, fruit juice, coffee and tea. In general main meals consisted of generous helpings of simple, strictly vegetarian dishes. Guests were expected to eat the same food as the Master – traditional north Indian fare of rice, *dhal*, curds (soured buffalo milk), boiled vegetables, *puns* (small flat breads) and fresh salads. This fairly basic diet could be supplemented by anything the visitors wanted, orders being processed through the *brahmacharin* or made directly to the servants. It seemed that everything had been thought of, and that a good time was going to be had by all.

The main reason that such a diverse collection of people had come together at this remote place was of course to learn to become teachers of meditation. In addition to meeting many like-minded people, course participants could also indulge in ever-increasing periods of meditation. But the real benefit was to be able to be with the Maharishi, who was to hold lectures twice daily, at 3.30 and 8.30 pm. At these sessions the audience would be encouraged to recount their experiences of meditation, thus providing reference points from which the Maharishi could expound his theories.

As everyone settled into their new environment and became better acquainted with their fellow students, they began to look forward to the period between noon and mid-afternoon when they were free to do as they pleased, although there were some restrictions. There were wire fences to keep out unwanted intruders, and they were constantly patrolled by guards, both day and night. No one was allowed to wander beyond the confines of the *ashram* and the adjacent river bank. One thing the Maharishi (and indeed, the Indian authorities) did not want was an incident with the locals, so those who wished to bathe in the chill, snow-fed waters of Mother Ganges were to be watched over by conveniently positioned soldiers. The Maharishi's Uncle Raj, resplendent with his white military walrus moustache and high-collared Nehru jacket, was also about. He had his residence in the quarter set aside for Indians, from which he dispensed homeopathic medicine and turned out oil paintings of 'Guru Dev' for the new teachers.

A couple of weeks into the course, the 'jungle telegraph' carried news that gave the meditators cause for speculation. One of the Maharishi's three principal *brahmacharin*, Swami Satyanand, had been seen leaving for new Delhi by car, something he usually did only in order to welcome new visitors and accompany them back. The rumour circulated was that he had gone to meet The Beatles. As it turned out, it was only half correct, for when Satyanand returned it was with only half the group, John and George, along with their wives and the group's road manager, Mal Evans. After a welcome by the Maharishi, they spent their time settling into their quarters and meeting fellow meditators. It was some days before the rest of the group, along with their partners, joined the course.

The presence of The Beatles in India brought the world's press in droves to the *ashram* gates, hopeful of getting the photographs, footage and interviews their paymasters had sent them for. The Maharishi responded to this invasion by issuing instructions that no one should enter the Academy without his express permission and barred the use of professional film cameras. In a bid to outwit this strategy, the journalists were forced to attach powerful telescopic lenses in order to photograph their prey, and they were thus able to convince their public that they had been allowed in. Without the fences and guards, the course would almost certainly have ground to a halt. In her book *The Way to Maharishi's Himalayas*, Swedish author Elsa Dragemark recounts what it was like to be on the receiving end of this unwelcome attention:

> After a few days of zealous waiting outside the gates without any result, the journalists took matters into their own hands and forced down the three gates towards the Ganges and stormed into the area. Without respect for people's integrity, they stormed into The Beatles' rooms, chased by the despairing guards, who were now forced to be a little tougher.
> Maharishi knew what to do. Rather than letting them stay in the area, Maharishi went out to them, while we had lunch, and had a press conference under the large trees in the open space near the post office and the guest house. Maharishi tried to calm the excited men by saying: 'The Beatles are meditating and can't be disturbed.'[183]

In a piece of interview footage, the Maharishi is recorded as saying:

> See. In the midst of all these activities and the world's interest for

Transcendental Meditation, I don't get a moment to think of silence.[184]

But the hounds of the world's press were less than satisfied with his parsimonious offerings and took revenge by dispatching cynical and disparaging reports.

> The music reporters, whose jobs depended on promoting The Beatles, were properly respectful, but the general press ridiculed the goings-on at the camp as hokum and struggled to expose the maharishi as a crook. The Beatles defended their saint, John remarking, 'They had to kill Christ before they proved He was Jesus Christ.'[185]

The futility and expense of maintaining surveillance on the *ashram* could not be endured forever, and eventually the editors recalled their men, at which time the Swedish scribe drew a sigh of relief:

> The days soon became calmer on Shankaracharya Nagar's hill and the days passed as usual with lectures, meditations, meals and an enjoyable co-existence.[186]

In addition to boasting the presence of the world-famous Beatles, the Academy also played host to other musical talents. It soon found itself with a house band, comprising the famous foursome augmented by folk singer Donovan Leitch, the Beach Boys' lead vocalist Mike Love and flautist Paul Horn. Apart from the celebrities, which also included the pretty young Mia Farrow (with her sister Prudence and brother John), were the 'ordinary' people, the housewives, the hairdresser, the nurse, the railway signalman, the pilot and the German physicist taking time off from work on the American space programme. According to Donovan, the Maharishi on hearing one of the singer's recent compositions 'Isle of Islay' turned to him and observed 'You are a transcendental musician then?'. He also recalls an incident offering an insight into the difficulties faced by adults going 'back to school':

> You see, Maharishi was quite a relaxed guy, but there was an embarrassed silence in the room. It was the four Beatles, Mia Farrow and myself, or was it Mike Love? We'd all just arrived and nobody was saying anything we were all wondering what to say.
> John was so funny and so direct that to break the silence he went up to the Maharishi, who was sitting cross-legged on the floor, patted him on the head and said, 'There's a good little *guru*.' We all laughed. It was funny. John was very funny and he always said exactly what he felt.[187]

Cynthia Lennon was particularly happy with life at the *ashram* and later took time to write her account of the 'blissfully happy days':

> As one day merged into the next, the weather altered dramatically. The sun

shone and the heat created a marvellous feeling of well-being. Meditation and its effects began to show on us all. The Maharishi was a wonderful teacher. His lectures and talks were humorous and enlightening and provided truly halcyon days. John and George were in their element. They threw themselves totally into the Maharishi's teachings, were happy, relaxed and above all had found peace of mind that had been denied them for so long.[188]

John Lennon's 'good little *guru*' proved a thoughtful host, sparing no effort in attending to his guests' needs, making sure that they were not only comfortable but also suitably entertained. No chance for 'a bit of a do' was missed. If anyone had a birthday, and there were many, it would be turned into a big celebration. On 15 March Mike Love had the pleasure of hearing 'Happy Birthday to you' sung by the all-star scratch band, led by Paul McCartney in ebullient form. The lines were delivered in the style of the Beach Boys, with additional lyrics, several verses of which were dedicated to the Maharishi's teachings and ran something like this:

> We'd like to thank you Guru Dev
> Just for being our guiding light
> Guru Dev, Guru Dev, Guru Dev
> We'd like to thank you Guru Dev
> For being up through the night
> The Spiritual Regeneration Worldwide Foundation – of India
> A-B-C-D-E-F-G-H-I.Jai Guru Dev.[189]

George Harrison's twenty-fifth birthday was also celebrated in style. Partygoers were entertained by a local band of performers, starring a man attired in turban and a costume of shimmering crimson, and were treated to a specially prepared cake. The Beatles were dressed in pyjama-style Indian clothes (*kurta* shirts and elephant trousers) and the women in colourful saris, and the Maharishi presented his famous follower with a plastic globe, inverted so as to confuse the polarity. By way of explanation he told him:

This is what the world is like today – upside down. It is rotating in tension and agony. The world waits for its release and to be put right. Transcendental meditation can do so. George, this globe I am giving you symbolises the world today. I hope you will help us all in the task of putting it right.[190]

George responded by quickly arighting the orb and declaring, 'I've done it!', for which he received the applause of all those present.

The Beatle who was least enamoured with this intense exposure to the meditation ideology and the relative austerities of *ashram* life was the down-to-earth drummer of the group.

> It was only Ringo Starr, who found the time in the ashram completely useless and no wonder, since he mostly walked around kicking his heels. Apparently he found it boring to meditate and after having been in the ashram for only a short time, he left with his wife to visit places less spiritual and peaceful.[191]

Ringo stayed only two weeks before excusing himself on the grounds that he missed his family and that the diet did not agree with him.

The Maharishi had himself said that no one should suffer for the divine; he had also said that it was only necessary to meditate for a few minutes morning and evening. But for those hungry for higher experience, his suggestion during the course that they should prolong their sittings was met with enthusiasm. He told them:

> 'Now go to your rooms and meditate as long as you can. For the time being we will cancel all lessons, but remember one thing that is important – if you want to talk to me about anything, come to me, even in the middle of the night.'[192]

This suited his dedicated followers, but more recent converts found the discipline a little demanding, as Mal Evans recorded.

> The students gradually built up their periods of meditation with Maharishi explaining at discussion sessions what our various experiences meant and how we might progress from there to the next stage of the course. John and George were meditating for anything up to eight or nine hours each day. The record for the course was a non-stop forty-two hours! Then as the course drew towards its end, the idea was to decrease the length of time spent in deep meditation so that everyone would come out of India ready to return to routine life at home.[193]

There were times when the temptation to 'play hookey' could not he suppressed. Truancy took various guises, with some simply idling whilst others wandered beyond the *ashram* grounds, only to be brought back by pangs of conscience. But the main distraction was with the stars in the impromptu music sessions upon the flat roof of the lecture hall. These work-outs were highly productive with Donovan coming up with new ditties, including one to the Maharishi and another to George Harrison's sister-in-law 'Jennifer Juniper', and an ode to meditation, 'Happiness Runs'. Paul worked out new material such as 'Back in the USSR' with a little help from Mike Love. Sometimes the abrasive vocal tones of John Lennon were deployed to comment, as in 'Everyone's Got Something to Hide Except for Me and My Monkey' which dwelt on the carnality of the local species, to challenge 'Dear Prudence [Farrow], won't you come out to play', and to mock 'Bungalow Bill', who had come on the course with his mother.

The Maharishi was not slow in recognizing the need for other diversions and arranged sing-songs by the River Ganges, a moonlight riverboat trip and a day trip to the nearby town of Dehra Dun. A film exists which shows community singing of 'When the Saints Go Marching In', led by John Lennon. An additional distraction was provided by the comings and goings of the helicopter loaned by industrialist K.S.Khambatta. The course also received visits from some distinguished holy men. For Paul Horn one particular visitor stood out from the rest.

> Now this man came to visit us at the Academy. He's just beautiful – 115 years old with pure white hair and very firm skin. He couldn't speak English, only Hindi, but through an interpreter I remember him saying, 'the Almighty created only Bliss, man created everything else.'[194]

It is difficult to visualize a well-known entertainer becoming a teacher of meditation, least of all a chart-topping pop phenomenon or a highly attractive film star like Mia Farrow. She had, it seems, been allotted accommodation alongside the Maharishi in the same bungalow before developing a yearning to visit other places of interest. She came and went at will, going for jaunts to a game reserve and hitch-hiking as far as Goa, a place made particularly famous for being a hippie resort. Finally she flew to London where she threw herself into a new film production. During her brief sojourns at the *ashram*, it had been observed that she received favoured treatment from the Maharishi, and her disappearance caused many a tongue to wag. Paul McCartney also left, returning to London sporting a full growth of facial hair (after prolonged electricity cuts at the *ashram*, many dispensed with shaving), rolls of 8mm home-movie footage and his actress girlfriend Jane Asher. Of the many songs he had composed in India were some directly inspired by the Maharishi, like 'Mother Nature's Son' and 'Cosmic Consciousness'. His reasons for leaving were not disclosed, hut Cynthia Lennon thought she understood:

> They had missed the early stages of the course, and the growing feelings of friendship that we had all gained, they were very much on the fringe of activities.[195]

The prolonged bouts of meditation took their toll on some of the course members, who found themselves suffering some unwelcome side effects, in particular the phenomenon of waking the 'sleeping elephants' of the mind. As the meditator became acclimatized to long periods of silence, there would be unexpected moments of distress, explained as being the unwinding of the accumulated deep stresses of life. Sometimes these were personal experiences and therefore fairly easily dealt with but at other times they were more difficult to isolate. One such instance, a sort of 'collective calamity', is worth noting. To deal with the situation the Maharishi convened a lecture in which he explained that what was disturbing their meditation was just the process of inner purification. Afterwards, he sent his followers back to their rooms so that they could see the process through. Soon after they had re-entered the silence, the sound of hammering rent the air. If anything was designed to upset the students, it was this! How could they be expected to attend to the absolute when the relative came incessantly battering at their senses? A delegation was dispatched to try to quell the noise. It seemed to come from the direction of the Maharishi's bungalow. Imagine their amazement when they saw the Master fiddling on the roof with hammer and tacks. They perceived that in some inexplicable way the Maharishi was passing on an esoteric message of life, so they went away laughing and contented.

The experience of unwinding continued, leaving many students temporarily oversensitive and potentially moody. Cynthia Lennon noticed these unwelcome effects.

> Meditation practised for long periods renders the meditator truly sensitive to any overt or strong vibrations.[196]

She mentioned this in order to convey the state of mind her husband slipped into in the latter weeks of the course. His mind was additionally strained by his attempts to conceal his clandestine relationship with Yoko Ono, which he continued by post whilst in India. He had even contemplated bringing Yoko on the course but had later thought better of it, for his real enthusiasm lay for the moment in meditation and nothing mattered to him more than the chance to become enlightened – to be bestowed with the vision of cosmic consciousness. He worked surprisingly hard for his merit badge but became increasingly frustrated in his ambition. He wanted more than just a handful of songs for the next Beatles album; he wanted nothing less than the spiritual equivalent of promotion.

> 'John thought there was some sort of secret the Maharishi had to give you, and then you could just go home,' Neil Aspinall says. 'He started to think the Maharishi was holding out on him. "Maybe if I go up with him in the helicopter," John said, "he may slip me the answer on me own." '[197]

John wanted some of the spiritual powers he had read about in the Swami Yogananda's book, and both he and Paul impressed upon the

Maharishi just how much they would like to see some transcendental magic, a bit of levitation perhaps. On this subject Paul McCartney points out:

> When we were out in Rishikesh, that was one of the things we were interested in ... We were almost throwing in the Indian rope trick too. It was all part of a new thing and we would ask him, 'Did they do that? Was that just a magic trick? Do they really levitate, Maharishi? What about levitation, is that actually possible?' and he said, 'Yes it is, there are people who do it,' but he took it as, 'Oh, you wanna see levitation, well there's a fellow down the road, he does it. We can have him up, he'll do a little bit for us if you like,' and we said, 'Great,' but he never actually showed. I say, 'Give me one photograph and I'll have you on *News at Ten* tonight and you'll be a major source of interest to the world and your organisation will swell its ranks.'[198]

The balmy days of what the press dubbed the 'love-in' wafted on. George continued to explore his passion for Indian music ever further, experimenting with a range of unusual instruments, whilst his wife toyed with her *dilruba* (a stringed instrument for accompaniment). He would also write down ideas, penning such lines as 'Looking for release from limitation? There's nothing much without illumination' for his song 'Sour Milk Sea'. Having found something to believe in, he and John were determined to succeed in it. There was even talk of putting on a concert in Delhi with the remaining Beatles, the Beach Boys, Donovan and Paul Horn. In this atmosphere of unreserved optimism, what they had not bargained on were the all-too-human weaknesses of greed and jealousy. These were marshalling their forces and finding embodiment in one particular individual among their entourage.

Midway through the course, Alexis Mardas had arrived, believing apparently that The Beatles needed him for stimulation, or stimulants, and smuggled in some rather vicious illegal alcohol. Quite why his presence was tolerated is hard to imagine, but John had the impression that this personable blond Greek was a magician of sorts and reserved a special respect for him. 'Magic Alex' was therefore free to air his views.

> 'An ashram with four-poster beds?' he demanded incredulously. 'Masseurs, and servants bringing water, houses with facilities, an accountant – I never saw a holy man with a book-keeper!'[199]

Neil Aspinall, another of The Beatles' associates, also voiced some criticisms of the Maharishi. He had been entrusted with the business end of a projected endeavour to produce a feature film on the life of 'Guru Dev', starring the Maharishi.

Neil expected to have a hard time explaining the business arrangements to the spiritual man, only to find the Maharishi employed a full-time accountant. For a long while Neil and the *guru* haggled over an additional 2½ per cent. 'Wait a minute,' Neil thought, 'this guy knows more about making deals than I do. He's really into scoring, the Maharishi.'[200]

The longer Mardas spent at the *ashram*, the more outspoken he became. He openly criticized the Maharishi for organizing the 'class photograph' in which The Beatles figured prominently. In fact he found fault in whatever way he could.

After a week he heard that the Maharishi expected The Beatles to donate 10 to 25 per cent of their annual income to a Swiss account in his name. He reproved the Maharishi for this, accusing him of having too many mercenary motives in his association with The Beatles. He claims the Maharishi tried to placate him by offering to pay Alex to build a high-powered radio station on the grounds of the ashram so that he could broadcast his holy message to India's masses.[201]

Such was the intensity of Mardas's desire to break the Maharishi's influence on The Beatles that he determined to bring about his downfall and proceeded to devise a simple plot in which his American girlfriend was to play the leading role. The headstrong conspirator had convinced himself that the old teacher would be unable to resist the temptation of the young blonde nurse. Mardas hid in undergrowth near the bungalow, hoping to catch the teacher in some compromising position with the girl. Fairly predictably, the scheme came to nought. Undeterred, however, the manipulative Mardas went hot-foot to John and George and confronted them with allegations about the Maharishi, in particular saying that he had tried to get fresh with the American nurse and various other female meditators. Mardas's intention had been to create a rift between The Beatles and their hero. Initially he met with little success, finding George stubbornly loyal. Cynthia Lennon recalls the night:

To me it was tragic – hearsay, an unproved action and unproved statements. The finger of suspicion was well and truly pointed at the man who had given us all so much in so many ways – the Maharishi. Alexis and a fellow female meditator began to sow seeds of doubt into very open minds.[202]

To resolve the matter, an all-night discussion was convened and only when George's steadfast convictions appeared to waver did John become confirmed in his doubts. At first light, he led a deputation down to the bungalow and announced their collective intention of leaving the *ashram*. When the Maharishi pressed him for a reason for this sudden decision, John responded somewhat petulantly by turning the question around saying:

'If you're so cosmic you'll know why,' because he was always intimating, and there were all these right-hand men intimating that he did miracles, you know. And I said 'You know why,' and he said 'I don't know why, you must tell me' and I kept just saying 'You ought to know.'[203]

At first sight, this attempt to assert himself appears somewhat childish, but on closer inspection it turns out to have been rather clever in the circumstances, for his real concern was not whether or not the Maharishi had succumbed to the pleasures of the flesh, but about how superhuman he really was. If the Maharishi could show himself capable of any higher power now was the time to signal it.

In the eleventh chapter of the *Bhagavad-Gita*, Vyasa through Sanjaya recounts that Arjuna, after hearing the elaborate philosophical arguments set out by 'Lord' Krishna, asks to witness his *swaroop* (divine form). It is recorded that he was rewarded with a vision so awesome as to leave him with hair standing on end. But the Maharishi was not the Lord and John Lennon was definitely not a confused launcher of arrows. Nevertheless, by John's account, it would appear he had a vision of sorts:

He gave me a look like 'I'll kill you, you bastard,' and he gave me such a look and I knew then, when he looked at me, you know, because I had called his bluff, because I said if you know all, you know. Cosmic consciousness, that's what we're all here for. I was a bit rough to him.[204]

The Maharishi evidently failed to demonstrate any particular superiority in matters of spiritual prowess and accordingly, disgruntled and disillusioned, the party returned to their rooms to pack. They were soon assembled and ready to depart. Cynthia Lennon recalls:

The real turning of the knife came as we were about to take our leave. While we were seated around the dining-tables waiting for the taxis and conversing in whispers, nerve ends showing, the Maharishi emerged from his quarters and seated himself not a hundred yards from our agitated group of dissidents. One of his ardent followers walked across to us and asked us to please talk things over properly with the Maharishi. He said he was very sad and wanted desperately to put things right and to convince us that we should stay.[205]

The Maharishi's request was ignored and the party filed past him without a sound. The tension and disquiet were too much for Cynthia.

I wanted to cry. It was so sad. The Maharishi was sitting alone in a small shelter made of wood with a dried grass roof. He looked very biblical and isolated in his faith.[206]

Peter Shotton, John's friend and confidant offers an alternative version of the incident:

According to John, the Maharishi – for just one instant – turned purple with rage, in effect blowing his cover. It was only then that John made his irrevocable decision to leave the ashram.

A few hours later, the Maharishi materialized in the distance as John and the others loaded into a couple of taxis that Alex had commandeered from the nearest village. 'John, John,' the *guru* called out mournfully. 'Please don't leave me! Come back, come back!'

'Even then,' John told me, 'he sent out so much power that he was like a magnet, drawing me back to him. Suddenly I didn't want to go at all, but I forced meself to carry on before it was too late.'[207]

13

— ★ —

THE COMEBACK TOUR

The Spiritual Guides' course had been in the process of winding down when John and George left, in preparation for a change of location. From Shankaracharya Nagar, a long straggling motorcade soon made its way to Palam Airport, New Delhi, and from there the Maharishi and his students flew to scenic Kashmir. For Westerners unacclimatized to the now soaring temperatures, the chill and drizzle of high-altitude Srinagar promised to be more conducive to study. The remaining weeks of the course were to be spent at Dal Lake, where both accommodation and shopping facilities bobbed and swayed upon the surface of the waters. The Maharishi made himself comfortable at the grand-sounding Green View Hotel but chose to hold court on an adjoining covered barge. As at Rishikesh, in addition to the lectures, occasional excursions were arranged. There were boat trips around the lake and surprisingly, a riding expedition where the Maharishi demonstrated his skill on horseback whilst clutching a bouquet of flowers and later allowed himself to be drawn across the snowy slopes of Gulmarg on a toboggan. These exploits were for the benefit of the attendant camera crew, who were collecting footage for the forthcoming documentary. But all was not well with the Maharishi. He was showing signs of strain. One evening he said to his followers:

> I am now a bad example to you. Because of too busy a schedule, I have not tended to my own body's strength. You must let nothing in life interfere with your meditation; there will always be a force trying to keep you from it.[208]

For him to make such an admission is some indication of the graveness of his condition. One of his aides insisted that a doctor check him over. The diagnosis was alarming:

> He has double pneumonia and should be in hospital. That man can't do anything for two weeks at least; it would kill him.[209]

In the event, he made a remarkably speedy recovery and was able to host the graduation frivolities, after which the course members returned to Delhi and, after bidding fond farewells to their teacher, departed for their various futures.

The Maharishi was now left alone to puzzle over the loss of his most famous pupils, The Beatles. He had hoped, no doubt, that the unpleasantness would blow over and that they could all be friends. What of all the plans, the movie, the all-star concert? The world at large was, as yet, still blissfully unaware of the rift and there was therefore still time, before the news broke, to reaffirm his standing in the world community. Inevitably, however, this would mean abandoning his stated resolve to remain in India.

> The venerable *guru* was distressed, but he didn't creep back into his expensive bungalow. Instead, he flew to New York, hired himself no less a public relations firm than Solters and Sabinson and installed himself at the Plaza, coincidentally the first New York hotel to accommodate The Beatles.[210]

At the invitation of Mike Love, he prepared himself to embark upon a venture of dubious promise, a seventeen-date tour of America as support act for the Beach Boys. After his requirement regarding the provision of appropriate diet and on-stage floral presentations had been met, the Maharishi accepted the invitation and on Friday, 3 May joined the group in their private plane. Unbeknown to him, the Beach Boys had passed the peak of their fame and were having problems attracting large audiences. In New York the show was promoted as 'the most exciting event of the decade', but the tour was not a success. Audiences stayed away in their droves and those who did turn up were, for the most part, not interested in hearing the Maharishi.

> There was a date at the Spectrum in Philadelphia where quite a few people showed up to see the Beach Boys, but when the Maharishi came on, they all left. No one cared, which is what everyone told Mike would happen. You can't slug your audience around like that and ask them to pay a high-priced ticket to hear this guy talk.[211]

Other reasons could be postulated for the public response to the Maharishi. Perhaps word had got round that the meditation was not quite what they thought, not as powerful as they had hoped. This was the time of the 'now' generation and things that required too much patience and commitment were definitely out. On the surface at least, however, the tour left Maharishi his normal bouncy self.

'The Maharishi laughed,' said Duryea [the Beach Boys' road manager]. 'He was laughing all the time. He got his money.'[212]

Whatever the case, the Maharishi had sampled the unwelcome taste of mass rejection. He high-tailed it back to his *ashram* in India to take stock of his situation where he allegedly declared: 'I know that I have failed. My mission is over.'[212]

It now looked as though the robed crusader was finished, the 'unlimited source of energy within' had run dry. But had the world really heard the last of his particular brand of optimism? This was a toughened, veteran campaigner who could take his fair share of brickbats and abuse. In his search to rediscover his 'bounce', he had only to reflect on the life story of his master Swami Brahmanand, for he too had not been a total stranger to the all-too-human conduct of mankind:

> Some inimical scandal-mongers, tasting blood, plotted a strategem to drag the saint into the mire. They got hold of a call-girl, bribed her heavily, dressed her up as a man and made her join the darshan-seeking throng. After the others left she was to keep Maharaj Shri's company on some pretext or the other and try to seduce him to a lustful night with her. When the time came for her to act, she lost her nerve, or God knows what happened, but she let out an eerie scream and ran down the steps. The conspirators waiting downstairs enquired what she was up to. 'Ooh! My body – it's aching all over. Ooh! Why did I ever listen to you? ... He's a saint. He's a saint.'[213]

On another occasion a 'sadhu-looking man was calling him names, loudly criticizing him, and uttering a lot of obscenities'. What should the *swami* do in order to uphold his reputation? Should he resort to retaliation and put the man in his place? He thought otherwise and told his disciples:

> 'I have given you many lessons on big and small matters, but so far I have not been able to give you a lesson in tolerating intolerance. God has today given me an opportunity to give you that lesson. Try to remain calm while this man hurls abuses at me.'[214]

A debate then ensued during which the Master observed:

> Many saints treat their most vociferous critics at par with their most devoted followers. The devotees serve and worship the Mahatmas but share with them their hoard of spiritual powers, but the critics take nothing for themselves, they just wash away their sins. We should indeed be very grateful for the beneficial service that they render and should in no case try to stifle their criticism.[215]

After a further hour of insult-slinging the intruder took a rest beneath a tree. At the Master's bidding he was served a good meal before being dispatched with two rupees for a *tanga* (horse-taxi). The following day he returned, not to continue his tirade of abuse, but to praise 'Maharaj Shri' chanting: 'Swamiji ki jai ho! Swamiji ki jai ho! Glory to the Master! Glory to the Master!'[216]

The continued clamour in the West for things Indian boded well for the sales of the Maharishi's books and records. The news that The Beatles no longer held him to be their *guru* had yet to become public. When interviewed they still upheld his practices, as such meditation was still in fashion. In May 1968, Bantam Books had published the very revealing *Meditations of Maharishi Mahesh Yogi*, containing reprints of three of his more compelling early lectures. And he received useful publicity from some of his celebrity fans. On Donovan's boxed set album *A Gift from a Flower to a Garden* was included a photograph of 'His Holiness Maharishi Mahesh Yogi and the Author'. Donovan had recently undertaken a tour in the company of Paul Horn, on which he had given an airing to songs written in Rishikesh before releasing a composition with an Indian feel about a 'hurdy gurdy man singing songs of love'. Paul Horn's plans for filming the Rishikesh course having been thwarted, he took his golden flute to one of India's most beautiful buildings, the Taj Mahal, whose inherent acoustics he used to dramatic effect on his *Inside* album. Meanwhile, The Bear, the hirsute, happy, generously proportioned singer of Los Angeles-based blues band Canned Heat, was commanding listeners to 'sit back and meditate as the Maharishi said'. With the 'love and peace' flag still waving freely amongst the young, there were few who absorbed the news which came out of The Beatles' New York press conference in mid-May, convened in order to announce the opening of their own corporation, Apple. John and Paul were asked questions about their association with the Maharishi:

> John: We made a mistake.
> Journalist: Do you think other people are making mistakes about TM now?
> John: That's up to them ...
> Journalist: (inaudible due to clatter of camera shutters)
> John: What ...? We're human, you know.
> Journalist: What do you mean by a mistake...?
> John: That's all, you know.
> Paul: We thought there was more to him than there was, you know, but he's human. And for a while we thought he wasn't, you know, we thought he was a ... (makes wide-eye movement from left to right).[217]

When Charlie Lutes told the Maharishi of the allegations that had precipitated John and George's decision to leave him, he responded: 'But, Charlie, I am a lifetime celibate, I don't know anything about sensual desires.'[218] In view of his position, it would surely have been reasonable to make a statement to this effect to quash the rumours that had now even spread as far as the American chat programme *The Johnny Carson Show*. But the Master thought otherwise:

> We do not recognize the negative. We just keep on working, putting one foot in front of the other. If we refuse to resist untruth, it will fall on its own. By resisting it, we give it support.[219]

A much-quoted maxim of the Maharishi was 'Pull back the bow to let the arrow flow.' Glossing over his losses, he now concentrated his attention on the next steps forward and by the end of the year had sufficiently recovered from his set-backs to announce his intention of having 1 per cent of the world's population meditating within three years.

PART II

—★—

Maharishi Upanishad

An Audience With The Maharishi

14

—★—

EVOLUTION TO IMMORTALITY

Of the sacred texts of India, the ones relating to the sharing of spiritual knowledge, the *Upanishads*, are the most cherished by teachers of *yoga* and meditation. The *Upanishads* are ancient records of the teachings of some of India's most famous wise men. It is recounted that in the past, men retreated to the forests and jungles in order to pursue a hermit life of contemplation, attempting to unravel the mysteries of life and discover its meaning. Stories abound of such *vanaprasthas* (forest dwellers) becoming absorbed in their meditations to such an extent that sufficient time elapsed for anthills to grow up and engulf them. It is said that many became imbued with a deep wisdom which they attempted to impart to sincere disciples and visitors. These wise men, known as *rishis* (seers) resided in hermitages situated in the midst of forests of bewildering natural beauty. Some dwelt alone whilst others lived their simple existences in the company of disciples and even, in rare cases, families. These forest dwellers were revered by all classes of society as knowers of reality, and the *rishi's* guidance was sought in matters both religious and secular. To these *ashrams* truth-seekers would journey in order to receive *darshan* and to hear tell of the higher truths of life.

The word *upanishad* means 'to sit down near', which is what those eager to improve themselves did. In their quest for liberation and enlightenment, the *rishis* not only took to meditation but also spent time in contemplation, attempting to formulate a scientific understanding of nature. As reference material they studied the four *Vedas*, and the *Upanishads* accordingly contain numerous references to epochs long since past. Attempts to pin down the age of extant *Upanishads* have divided scholars – some contend that the works are no older than about 2,000 years, others date them back as far as about 1,500 BC, and there are those who contend that they are far older even than that.

The contents of the *Upanishads* vary considerably, from complex theorizing to verses of devotional worship. The most accessible are those which give account of *rishis'* attempts to enlighten their students. In the following example, from *Chandoga Upanishad*, the disciple is Shvetaketu, the son of Rishi Uddalaka Aruna. After hearing from his father an account of the creation, he urges him to tell him more of his knowledge.

> Very well, my son. When the bees collect nectar from many different plants, blending them all into one honey, the individual nectars no longer think, 'I come from this plant', 'I come from this plant.' In the same way, my son, all creatures when they contact Being lose all awareness of their individual natures. But when they return from Being they regain their individuality. Whether tiger, or lion, or wolf, or boar, or worm, or fly, or gnat, or even mosquito, they become themselves again.
>
> And that Being which is the subtlest essence of everything, the supreme reality, the Self of all that exists, THAT THOU ART, Svetaketu.[220]

Rishi Aruna goes on to give many further colourful examples of his point, repeating time and again that all creatures are but emanations of one basic supreme reality, caught up in identity crises. In *Mundaka Upanishad* is to be found the clue to how one might conquer this inability to unite with 'That':

> Taking the great weapon of the Upanishad as your bow. Place upon it the arrow of the mind, made pure and sharp by meditation. Draw it back with a will made strong by contemplation of the Eternal. Then, my friend, release the mind, let it fly from the bow and swiftly find its target.
>
> Meditate with the *mantra* as your bow, consciousness the arrow, and Brahman still the target. Free from distractions of the senses, take aim, release the mind, let it fly with Brahman, and be oned with It as the arrow is oned with its target.[221]

The Maharishi had more than a passing acquaintance with these works and would sometimes quote verses of other *Upanishads* in support of his thoughts. If further proof were needed of his familiarity with these writings, we find in his descriptions of his master, the following lines:

> His Darshan made the people feel as if some ancient Maharishi of upanishadic fame had assumed human form again, and that it is worthwhile leading a good life and to strive for realization of the Divine.[222]

The 1969 teacher-training course in India was not like its predecessor, in that partying was quite definitely off the agenda. This time the accent was placed firmly on acquiring greater intellectual understanding of meditation and its attendant philosophy. Lined up for the course were

'I will fill the world with love.'

Swami Krishanand Saraswati, *guru* to the Maharishi's *guru*.

Shankaracharya Swami Brahmananda Saraswati of Jyotir Math, guru to the Maharishi.

The Maharishi in Sweden,
December 1960.

Addessing a capacity audience
at London's Royal Albert Hall,
13th March 1961.

In expansive mood at a press conference in September 1961.

Expounding his teaching to the press in London, September 1961.

The Maharishi in Paris,
October 1962.

A press conference to
inaugurate the establishment
of the International Meditation
Society as a registered charity

The Maharishi's mission was often misunderstood, he was even mistaken for a flower seller.

The Maharishi envisaged his message of meditation passing from generation to generation.

About to board the 'mystical Express' train to Bangor, Wales,
25th August 1967.

The Maharishi finds approval with the 'pop royalty'. Seen here with Beatles
John Lennon and George Harrison (in the background).

David Frost is presented with a flower after interviewing the Maharishi
at Heathrow Airport London, 29th September 1967.

Recieving devotees in New Delhi, India, November 1967.

It was Patti Harrison who first introduced the Beatles to Transcendental Meditation, seen here attending a concert in Paris, 18th December 1967.

According to the Maharishi, it is possible to become spiritually fulfilled
whilst living in the material world.

The Maharishi accompanying actress Mia Farrow en route to India, 24th January 1968.

To the right stand Charlie Lutes and Jerry Jarvis as the 'giggling guru' meets well-wishers in New York, 20th January 1968.

Everywhere thw Maharishi went followers would present him with flowers.

A walk in the grounds of his *ashram* at Shankaracharya Nagar near
Rishikesh in Northern India.

A lesson for his Indian students

Seated before a portrait of his master Shankaracharya Swami Brahmananda
Saraswati, the Maharishi presents a gift to Beatle George.

Giving a televised message to the Japanese before his 'retirement'

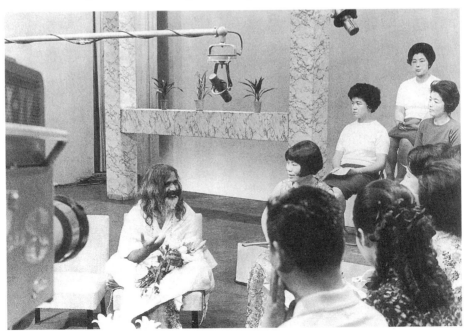

The master of meditation
taking a rare moment alone.

Back in the USA, pictured
in the company of mayor of
Los Angeles Sam Yorty,
May 1968.

On a comeback tour to promote his Science of Creative Intelligence,
the Maharishi is here pictured in London 1975.

some particularly enquiring minds, less interested in soaking up the good vibrations, much more intent on posing the questions that might define the very limits of the Maharishi's capacity to explain himself.

They knew little of the Indian tradition to which he laid claim. However, something of his gentle manner and appearance spoke quietly of a noble past. As they listened to the flow of their teacher's thoughts, the scents of the jungle would waft on the breeze with the scattered sounds of monkeys, peacocks, parrots, crows and stray dogs breaking their attention from time to time. In this setting, with time far from mind, notions of a bygone golden era were easy to contemplate. The sleepy whirring of tape recorders reassured that this *maharishi's* outpourings would be forever accessible and that these lectures would not become but scattered images across the fabric of memory.

The Maharishi's lectures were fairly informal affairs and being only loosely sequenced and structured, there were many chances for impromptu discussions. There was much ground to cover before the actual process of teacher-training could commence. One thing that he needed to impart to them was the importance of meditation in the quest for self-realization, so he provided his students with this thumbnail sketch:

> Every generation has realized people, lots of them here and there. Coming to realization by that 90 ... I ... 2 ... 3 ... 4... 99 and 100 per cent -gradual realization. Realized people are found everywhere in all the generations, but this wisdom of natural integration, this system, this completeness of wisdom of what we speak – this is not brought to light in such utter simplicity and natural level ... before.[223]

Here then was the basic claim – that the goal of realization was not in itself something new, but that his knowledge of 'natural integration' had not previously been available. If, as the Maharishi maintained, his teachings were ancient and to be found in the *Vedas* and *Bhagavad-Gita*, how had they become overlooked?

> What is lost is the correct expression. The correct expression of the wisdom gets lost. It's there in the scriptures, it's there. What gets lost is the meaning of the expression, that gets lost. And it is this meaning that gets revised, generation after generation, according to the current language.[224]

To his vision, each age has it's own language, whether religious, scientific, political, economic or of some other kind. Accordingly, if the prevalent feeling of an era was of a particular slant, a vocabulary would be espoused that clearly transmitted those ideas. But regardless of what vocabulary was adopted, the language must still be able to describe a path to realization. In the Maharishi's 'Beacon Light' lectures of 1955 he had chosen to strike a balance between the languages of religion, mysticism and science. Even after arriving in the West, he still sometimes referred to the goal of meditation in religious terms such as 'the Kingdom of Heaven within', but he generally preferred to describe his technique in broader terms, using words such as being and absolute. Such terminology, however, had an altogether less graphic quality about it.

The Maharishi raised this point about language changing over the millennia to support his argument that such changes accounted for periodic lapses in the understanding of realization. Perhaps this is a valid point, but it is interesting to note how well one can understand the words of a poet who lived in the Vedic era, in what is claimed to have been the dawn of time:

> Our thoughts wander in all directions
> And many are the ways of men;
> The cartwright hopes for accidents,
> The physician for the cripple,
> And the priest for a rich patron.
>   For the sake of Spirit, 0 Mind,
>   Let go of all these wandering thoughts!
>
> With his dry grass and feather fan
> And his tools of fashioned stone,
> The blacksmith seeks day after day
> The customer endowed with gold
>   For the sake of Spirit, 0 Mind,
>   Let go of all these wandering thoughts!
>
> I'm a singer, father's a doctor,
> Mother grinds flour with a millstone.
> Our thoughts all turn upon profit
> And cowlike we all plod along.
>   For the sake of Spirit, 0 Mind,
>   Let go of all these wandering thoughts!
>
> The horse would draw a swift carriage,
> The entertainer a good laugh,
> The penis seeks a hairy slot
> And the frog seeks a stagnant pond.
>   For the sake of Spirit, 0 Mind,
>   Let go of all these wandering thoughts![225]

Also contained within the *Rig Veda* are verses which suggest a procedure for obtaining the bliss of realization, made all the clearer by its devotional context:

> O God, do thou cut off all our shackles of mind and body and free us from worldly bondages! 0 Eternal Being, by faithfully obeying Thy commands, we shall be freed from all sins and thus enjoy eternal bliss.[226]

Notwithstanding these examples, the *Vedas* are on the whole, abstruse in the extreme, owing to the obscure nature of their content.

The hymns of the *Vedas* are more properly sung rather than spoken, the sound allegedly having the power to affect the listener in *a* profoundly positive way. The power and beauty of verse was not lost on the Maharishi. His lectures frequently found punctuation in poetic observation:

> Action is the language of nature. Through action nature manifests its desire. Nature of man manifests man's desire through action.
>
> Action speaks much louder than words and leaves its footprints on the sand of time much longer.[227]

This concern about the changing use of language is not enough to explain why he found it necessary to amend his vocabulary. This was obviously due in order to meet the differing persuasions of peoples in disparate parts of the world, thus facilitating the spread of his meditation. But behind the superficial changes in vocabulary lay the same age-old (Hindu) beliefs. A keen observer could detect, even in relatively innocuous statements, skeletal traces of traditional Indian wisdom, although they were usually stripped of references to faith and devotion. This is not to say that the Maharishi had no use for these aspects of spiritual unfoldment, only that he did not commend them to his students. However, many was the time he let his guard slip, coming out with veritable show-stoppers. In discussing the loss of wisdom over the ages, he mentioned in connection with the changing *yugas* (epochs), the presence of immortals! He named one immortal called Vashishta in the *Treta Yuga*, and when questioned as to whether an immortal might exist in the present *Kali Yuga* he answered: 'Vyasa is another immortal.' Vyasa, it will be recalled, was credited with the writing of *Bhagavad-Gita.* If what the Maharishi was saying were true, there was a man living somewhere (presumably in a Himalayan cave) who had been on this planet countless centuries. Did the Maharishi seriously expect his students, people of the modern age, to believe in immortals? One inspired questioner, accepting this proposition, asked why the spread of meditation was not being undertaken by such a soul. After a significant pause the Maharishi responded, his answer evasive but none the less revealing:

I think he must be whispering to me when I am commenting on *Brahma Sutras* or on *Gita* and things. He must be in the air ..., around.

According to the Maharishi, not only was it possible to postulate the existence of immortals, but also to recognize the presence of life in apparently inert material. Earlier in the same lecture he had expounded this theory, explaining that material substances were but lower life forms, of which sand and stone were the least evolved. On the premise that destruction of the least evolved living matter would result in the minimum upset to nature, he recommended to his pupils a vegetarian diet.

His students had primarily come to learn how to teach his meditation method and as such they must sometimes have wondered at his flagrant attempts to indoctrinate them into Hindu beliefs. When anyone was bold enough to probe or question their teacher's wisdom too deeply, a mocking murmur of disapproval would arise from the other devotees. Fortunately, this was not enough to deter the rare individual from breaking through with an awkward question or two.

Having placed rocks at the bottom of the evolutionary ladder, the Maharishi then pointed out that certain stones were exceptions. He held that precious stones – gems such as diamonds – are more evolved and that each has its own distinct vibration, the power of which can be harnessed to benefit an individual, adding that a competent jeweller would be needed to select the correct stone, and offered to bring one in on the course. One of his more questioning students sought to explore this issue further and chipped in:

> Certain stones that man can make in the laboratories now, like sapphires and diamonds and emeralds and things like that. Is man helping out somehow in the evolution from the rock material to the evolution of matter, through making precious stones, or do they have a different significance to the ones you find in the rocks and caves?

Had he found a flaw in the precious stone business? Apparently not, for the Master answered coolly: 'Depending on how near the truth is the imitation!'

A particular problem was how knowledge about meditation might disappear and yet from age to age find revival. How could it be that such information could have existed and yet go unrecorded? What of Prince Siddhartha, the Buddha, had he not taught a system of meditation? In acknowledging the greatness of past spiritual giants the Maharishi made particular mention of the Buddha:

> Somebody told me that during the lifetime of Buddha 500 people got

Nirvana, 500. So he must have made a great impact on the masses during his lifetime, otherwise he wouldn't survive till today. Must have made.

He appeared to be saying that the teachings of the Buddha have survived, but this would argue against his contention that the message had become lost. It is more likely that he was pointing out that the Buddha survives in name only, along with the legend of his greatness, and that this is not enough. If the Buddha's success in bringing 500 people to Nirvana were due to the use of a secret teaching, then it is easy to see how it might have become lost. By the same token, however, if the Maharishi's movement continued to keep the finer details of its teaching secret, fate would deal with it equally unkindly. The Maharishi thought otherwise:

> We are obliged to these jets flying twenty-four hours around the world. Jets – quick, quick. This was in favour of our movement, quick communication, quick.

But whatever the advantages of modern technology, they were surely as nothing in comparison to the living presence and example of an illumined master, seen by some to be prerequisite in acquiring any great success in *yoga* practices. The Maharishi himself freely acknowledged his debt to his own 'Guru Dev'. It might be wondered by what method old Swami Brahmanand had prepared his pupil for the world mission undertaken in his name.

> Oh he must have known. He never said to me, otherwise quite a long time would have been wasted in planning. He saved us from that waste, just of planning. It just blossomed and blossomed and blossomed and blossomed.

During the last years of the Shankaracharya's life, it appears that he initiated quite a number of people into the mysteries of spiritual development. One of the course participants became intrigued as to whether 'Guru Dev' had taught the same techniques of meditation as his disciple, such as the use of single-syllable *mantras*, or whether he deployed the use of long *mantras* of many syllables. The Maharishi replied a touch whimsically: 'Must be using better techniques than I am using!'

But this was not the time to be deflecting questions and he knew that. He tried a different tack:

> It's very difficult for me to find out what he was using, because initiation is all in private ... and I was never interested who was given what *mantra*. I was interested in myself...

This lack of knowledge had evidently not deterred the Maharishi from applying himself to the task of unravelling the mysteries of *mantra* selection in general and for householders in particular and then confidently offering them up for mass consumption. To the casual observer his remarks would seem to indicate a certain irreverence and lack of respect for his *guru*, but this was far from the truth. Speaking of his master he explained that he was:

> ... full of divine radiance. People don't have to do the *mantra* and meditation in his presence. The transformation was in his air, so full of life ... Out of that fullness I started to teach. At least by practice people could raise themselves up.

Whilst many of the Maharishi's followers must have wished that they too could have been disciples of 'Guru Dev', in his absence they put complete trust in the Maharishi, believing him to be capable of conferring a deeper understanding and experience of the union with being that he spoke of.

The Maharishi's students were on this course to learn how to teach others how to meditate and of the many things they had to learn, the complex ritual of initiation was not the least. All were eager to hear the Master's view of the subject as he pointed out to them that the 'body of the effect [of initiation] is from the sequence of instructions, but the sanctity of the whole situation is contributed by this [ceremony]'. The 'sequence' of the ceremony or *puja*, involves the offering of various items such as rice, water, cloth, fruit and flowers, and in addition requires the initiator's 'one-pointedness' of mind. The ritual offerings are accompanied by the singing of Sanskrit verses in praise of the 'Holy Tradition', former teachers of meditation.

> The growth of Being in the field of activity is the direct result of words being spoken, hands moving and the mind floating in meaning and getting serene and serene and serene and serene and serene. By the time we have done so many things, moving the hands and words coming out and mind on the meaning, item after item, there are about sixteen items. By the time the whole thing goes, the whole mind is settling down deep and by the time we just prostrate, the mind gets to that deep state of silence within and it sings ... 'Good initiators'.

The new initiate is only a witness to this ritual and is not asked to become involved. At the conclusion of the ceremony, the initiator becomes silent for some moments and then begins to intone the sound or *mantra* that is to be used by the initiate. The Maharishi tried to explain this process:

> Just in that one momentary bowing down, just sink into That. And the deeper

they are to pick up the *mantra*, more effective is the *mantra* and then they speak the *mantra* and then they lead that *mantra* back to the same situation, the same depth from where it was picked up and this circle being complete is called 'initiation'.

This last statement is very revealing in that it yields a deep insight into aspects of *mantra* theory. The Maharishi was contending that beyond the boundaries of our limited range of hearing there exist certain subtle sounds. These sounds are those which are given as *mantras*. They are perceived as somehow more blessed than ordinary sounds and are therefore highly effective at settling the human nervous system. The *puja* ceremony is conducted in order to attune the initiator's mind to 'pick up' these sounds. Having done so, clear and effective communication of the chosen sound or *mantra* to the new initiate is possible. This might lead one to infer that anybody whose mind is sufficiently purified would have the capacity to recognize these *mantras* and to impart them to others. In reality, however, initiators are not expected to hear the *mantras*, but are given a list of them along with formal instructions regarding their choice and pronunciation.

The Maharishi was ever eager to emphasize the benefits of performing the ritual *puja:*

This is the gain to the initiator: that he gains the value of cosmic consciousness, rising to cosmic consciousness when he is leading someone else to transcendental consciousness. It's very scientific! It's very great! It's very beautiful! It's beyond words!

15

——★——

CELESTIAL CONNECTIONS

I deally, in order to be really effective in teaching the Maharishi's technique of meditation, the initiator would have to be permanently in the state to which he or she was attempting to guide the initiate, that is cosmic consciousness. But the Maharishi had decided to press on with his initiative to spread the news of his meditation, and for this he would need many more trained teachers. According to him, all that was necessary was that the teacher's awareness become purified before starting to instruct anyone in a *mantra* or its usage. This purification of the initiator was to be achieved by the conducting of the *puja.*

Whatever the stated reasons he gave for the performance of this *puja*, some observers felt uncomfortable about its religious connotations, since *puja* is customarily regarded as a purely Hindu ritual, an act of worship to a Hindu god or gods and the Maharishi had deliberately attempted to liberate his meditation technique from its religious associations.

However, by presenting his beliefs without religious terminology, he was able to address a far wider audience that he might otherwise:

> It is I who gave it the present expression, but I learnt it from him (Guru Dev) in the traditional way … through very old expressions of religious order. Every religion has its own vocabulary; Hinduism has its own vocabulary; *yoga* has its own way of expression of the reality; Vedanta has its own approach. He taught me in the traditional way of *yoga* and Vedanta and Indian religious language. I gave it an expression in the universal way…[228]

Despite the *puja*, therefore, new initiates were therefore reassured that meditation would involve neither a change of religion nor conflict with any religious beliefs they might have.

That traditional methods of *yoga* should become so dramatically reappraised is at the very least, thought-provoking. But it is quite possible that even in prehistoric times, Indians were not superstitious idol worshippers, but that their religious rituals were based on some kind of logic and had developed methods of self-improvement. And if this is possible then there is no reason why the 'active ingredients' of their practices could not be isolated. Some believe that there is much knowledge of great value hidden beneath the supposed superstitions of indigenous peoples, as the following example from Africa shows:

> The Pedi, in South Africa, believe that infection can be cured by eating grain that has been chewed by a cross-eyed child and hung for three days in a gourd shaped like a snake that is suspended from a particular tree that grows near the water. And they are right, because under these conditions the grain grows a mould like *Penicillium*, with antibiotic properties, but the child's eyes and the gourd's shape and the species of tree do not necessarily have anything to do with the cure. In just this way, alchemy stumbled on some great truths but produced theoretical structures in which the line of reasoning between cause and effect was cluttered up with all sort of irrelevant mystical and magical red herrings. This has discouraged modern science from investigating the source material, which is a pity.[229]

Let us therefore assume that the Maharishi had been successful in prising a self-help technique from the inaccessibility of its custodians, the Order of the Shankaracharya Tradition. Having dropped the religious language that surrounded the teaching, was it also necessary that he should dispose of his own religious beliefs? Surely not, for if his followers were entitled to pursue their own faiths, so too was he. And from references (apparently poetic) to gods and angels in his works, it would appear that this was the case – he neither could nor wished to shake off his religious habits.

As **the** authority on his meditation technique, the Maharishi's word was frequently taken as definitive and his religious beliefs cannot therefore be ignored. There were instances in his conversations where these beliefs would predominate. It is quite likely that his unassailable faith in the meditation technique was in part due to a broader philosophical commitment. But where did his concepts of celestial beings fit into the scheme of things? In the following explanation, the Maharishi demonstrates his favourite style of oratory in the later years. He was given to repeating himself often – sometimes words, sometimes phrases, sometimes whole sentences. Although this clearly served to help his followers to catch his drift, it is probable that the main reason was merely to give himself time to think his subject matter through.

> The fine strata of creation is everywhere, underneath every existence uh? And taking this logic further on, the celestial strata of existence is everywhere, everywhere, everywhere, everywhere, everywhere ... uh?

Celestial strata of existence, everywhere. And ... now, there is also a range
in the region of the celestial – gross celestial and subtler celestial and subtler
celestial. Supreme, most supreme celestial, one with the Absolute, almost
one with the Absolute till eventually it ceases to he and gives way to absolute
Absolute alone. So this ... when the cognition of the celestial will become at
home with the celestial field of life, then this question of the details of the
field of the celestial brings to us all these which we may call 'presiding
deities', of different elements, of different gunas also.[230]

From this it appears that the Maharishi not only believed in the
existence of divine beings, but also considered that 'cognition of the
celestial' was also a real possibility. He seems to he indicating that those
who experience a finer objective reality are liable to chance upon
inhabitants of a celestial realm. But since there have as yet been no
public testimonies to this phenomenon, perhaps these presiding deities
are not objective realities, merely projections of wishful thinking.
Perhaps gods and goddesses are only as real as one wishes them to be.

There are two aspects to life, the objective aspect and the subjective aspect.
There are gross levels of objective aspect, there are gross levels of subjective
aspect. There are subtle levels of objective aspect, subtle levels of subjective
aspect. So in all these, both, two, both fields of life, subjective and objective
the creation runs parallel.

If the Maharishi was prepared to postulate the existence of celestials, did
he therefore rule out the presence of one absolute God, as worshipped
by the many faiths? From the following description of the initiate's
passage to inner realms, it would appear not:

Gross and subtle and subtler and subtlest and transcendental. Eventually in
the Absolute transcendental, both merge and the distinction of both is no
more found, It is one. There is a teaching in the Upanishads somewhere and
they say: 'God created the world and entered it' and therefore the world is
permeated with God. Creation, he created creation and then entered the
creation and it's not that the personal God is everywhere, it is that the
celestial field of life which is the field for gods to roam about is permeating
the whole creation, underneath creation all are running about here and there
and there and there.

He makes his heaven sound quite a busy place!

But the fact that the Maharishi himself believed in the existence and
activity of gods in no way impinges on the validity of his meditation
method. On the contrary, the significance of this explanation of his faith,
is that it shows how well he succeeded in stripping his relaxation
technique from the complexities of religious thinking. In his
explanations of the celestial he identified various personal deities by

name, but cautioned that the quality of the god was more important than the name. None the less his assertion that the 'cognition of gods, personal gods, transforms cosmic consciousness into God consciousness' sharply defines the higher goal of his meditation technique. Might it not therefore be handy to be forewarned about the identity of those whom one might come across?

On Saturday, 15 February 1969 a *pandit* visited Shankaracharya Nagar and explained to the Maharishi's students the significance of the festival of Shivaratri (Night of Shiva), which one the austere *yogi* identified with Being, the other, the irrepressible Nataraj (King of the dance). His consort, Mother Parvati, is worshipped as Shakti (spiritual energy). The Maharishi pointed out that 'during these four nights [of Shivaratri] inner awareness is maintained'. The reason given for this was that during these four nights a state of 'most intensified ignorance' is at play. During this same dissertation he also mentioned that:

> Even in the most intensified structure of ignorance, then one is awake, one is in union with Shiva, one is in union with Vishnu one is in union with the Mahashakti. A very great significance of a practical nature, in all this. And Shiva is supposed to be ... he is not supposed to he ... he is ...! He's so merciful

Later, speaking not so much from faith as from personal experience, he spoke of the places where the energy of Lord Shiva is most pronounced and easiest to contact, citing both Cape Comorin and Shankaracharya Nagar as examples.

His enthusiasm for discussion of the celestial had not lessened when he came to speak at an outdoor lecture the following day. According to him the principal Hindu deities can be identified with the elements. Obligingly he listed the following:

Space   – Vishnu
Air   – Surya, Sun god
Fire   – Devi, Mother Divine
Wisdom – Ganapati, Ganesha
Earth   – Lord Shiva

Whilst imparting this information he all but broke one of his self-imposed codes in allowing himself to be recorded singing, in this instance giving a melodious recitation of an excerpt from a *bhajan* (reverential or devotional song) to Ganesha (the god of wisdom depicted with the face and trunk of an elephant).

Apart from this self-conscious concern about his singing, he was not bothered that his lectures were being recorded. Only when something confidential was discussed would he request that the tape machines be switched off. Otherwise he was tolerant, probably flattered, that people would wish to record his lectures. When the courses were over, the tapes, often varying in speed and audibility would frequently become the focal point of meditation group meetings being conducted by the new teachers.

As his students had only a rudimentary academic grasp on matters celestial, they struggled hard to spell the names of these Hindu gods. The lecture, held as it was in the open air, was interrupted by crows loudly squawking their responses and local labourers continuing their work on the building programme. Apparently unmindful of the din, the Maharishi continued with his discourse on matters celestial:

> Between human species and these [gods] ... finest level of creation, the celestial level of life, gods. Huge number of angels and gods, and they are different species, that's all, different, different species.

At this point one of his devotees asked him to enumerate the celestials. Unsurprisingly he proved a touch evasive:

> Below man's species there are 8,400,000 species and then coming up to man ... and then between man and God there is no record. Because we don't have to keep the record of all that we are going to by-pass. That's the whole thing.

The crows, perhaps sensing the importance of this statement, screeched so loudly as to be almost deafening. The Maharishi paused a while and the crows quietened down considerably. Naturally, what he was telling his students would later be passed on to others. At a meeting of meditators in Philadelphia, Charlie Lutes, the Maharishi's representative in the USA, explained:

> Top of creation are five gods, Shiva, Vishnu, Mother Divine, Ganesha and Surya, Surya is the sun god. There are also five elements, earth, water, air, fire, space, which is *akasha*... Now each person on earth is a combination of these five elements. However, one of these five elements predominates in each and every individual. So there are five channels of creation – space, air, fire, water and earth in that order, each channel is a channel of creation. So you have at one end the unresolved creation and the other end you have perfect creation. At the top of creation are five gods all at the same level. Each individual is connected to one of these five gods according to which element predominates in that respective individual. The spirit of Mother Nature is always rising upwards. As human having free-will is free to act according to his own desires. You can rise upwards step-by-step or swiftly to the top by use of a *mantra*. *Mantras* are pertaining to the gods at the top of creation. Medium of the almighty has taken, each god has a thousand names. Now, a name now is not taken at random, a name is taken that has a special

meaning which again means has a very special vibration, the most useful vibration for us. The vibration that has a most specific effect that can take you from the grossest aspect of life to the finest subtle aspect of creation, and transcend it. This is why the effects are very rapid. So there is the devotion to the personal god as well as to the intellectual aspect. We have both the personal and the impersonal aspect together. Therefore we can by-pass the personal god and go to the impersonal.

According to the Maharishi there is literature which deals with the subject of communication with deities.

> *Karma Khand* that is the section on action. *Upasana Khand*, that section of activity which is devoted to the highest attainment in the relative; communication to these gods. When I say gods, goddesses are naturally included, gods and goddesses, because we can't ignore Mother Divine otherwise we will be in trouble. And the third section of the *Vedas* is called *Gyan Khand.* G-Y-A-N means knowledge. *Upanishads* are the expressions of *Gyan Khand* the knowledge section of the *Vedas.*

If one wished to gain a knowledge of the *Vedas*, would one therefore have to read and digest all the hundreds of thousands of words of these works? For those without the time for such a monumental task, the Maharishi had some good news, that the essence of the Vedic teaching was to be found in the relatively compact work of the *Bhagavad-Gita* (sometimes considered as an *Upanishad* – certainly, some verses recorded in the *Gita* bear an uncanny resemblance to verses of the *Upanishads*).

The Shivaratri festival proved a memorable occasion for all concerned and left the Maharishi's followers with a greater understanding of the remoter aspects of the master's thought. But with all this talk of celestial beings, there must have been those who ached for the simple truths of their own upbringing and for the reassuring comfort of familiarity.

One query that was persistently raised concerned the optimum period practitioners should sit in meditation. A common misunderstanding amongst new initiates was the belief that longer meditations would necessarily equate to increased bliss. Whereas at one time a stint of one hour had not been seen as excessive, the recommended periods became reduced to half an hour and then reduced further to just 15-20 minutes. The principal reason for reducing the recommended time for meditation was that experience had shown that meditators did not always derive increased benefit from longer sittings – indeed sometimes the contrary – thus providing support for the adage that sometimes less is more.

None the less, meditators attending residential courses were encouraged to spend long periods 'rounding', spending much of their time absorbed in inner meditation. The theory was that greater exposure to the pure consciousness or Being would accelerate the initiate's evolution towards higher states of awareness and consequently confer increased happiness. In reality, however, the increased time spent in meditation would often throw meditators into a state of confusion, occasionally causing depression and even temporary mental imbalance. The Maharishi explained that this was just the outward symptom of the nervous system becoming purified. For committed students, therefore, these experiences were to be expected and tolerated, even welcomed. In rare instances this 'purifying' process not only affected individuals but also occurred *en masse*. At such times, they sought out their leader in the hope that he might offer some explanation and reassurance.

> Where all the senses are witnessing that horrible scene, ears are hearing something horrible, eyes are seeing some horror. All the senses of perception, the whole field of experiencing machinery is being wound up, twisted up in great stress and strain and all that is happening at a time. And... huh? It took you so many days of constantly rounding, rounding – that means giving the system, giving the nervous system deeper and deeper rest every day through these rounds, through these rounds. So by tomorrow the system was rested deeply enough to give unwinding influence to all those deep-rooted stresses. And it's started. And as such are outbursts of these deposits of stresses. You are absolutely right to see clearly that at such a overwhelming and overpowering misery in such a collective way, nothing can help except love for God or love from God, some ... only God could help.

The Maharishi's hypothesis that anxiety experienced in meditation is not so much a result of incorrect technique as of numerous accumulated stresses becoming neutralized, is most interesting, if not convenient. By way of explanation he maintained that the release of stress was an indication that very real progress had been made, the nervous system being better able to support the experience of pure Being. The stresses the Maharishi spoke of referred to the accumulated impressions of past experiences, both good and bad, but most specifically physical shocks, jolts and the like. The argument was that if one were to narrowly miss being run over by a car, in all probability one would at least sustain shock to the nervous system if not prolonged tensing of the muscles. Multiple shocks could, in theory at least, accumulate and conspire to produce a condition whereby an individual was permanently stressed. Some might say that these stresses need not have a gross physical origin, that they are more frequently incurred by subduing feelings and responses as a result of the mind overriding automatic physical reactions. But there are times when stress is occasioned by less direct means, as for instance when one feels a sense of personal failure or rejection. It could be argued that all or any of these examples might contribute to the accumulation of 'knots' in the nervous system.

But even if we accept this theory of stress release, it would not excuse the Maharishi's failure to give advance warnings about these experiences of 'overwhelming and overpowering misery'. His students were there to experience the bliss of the 'Kingdom of Heaven within'; they were now discovering a new meaning to the old maxim about there being no gain without strain. Rather than perceive these upsetting experiences as situations to avoid, practitioners were encouraged to view them positively, as evidence of progress.

It is quite possible that accumulated tensions could hamper ones ability to be at peace with oneself – after all, the whole realm of psychoanalysis has its basis in this belief. Since the Maharishi held that meditation differed entirely from psychoanalysis, however, it is interesting to note how he distinguished between them. Unlike those involved in psychoanalysis, meditators are actively discouraged from analyzing past experiences which might be held responsible for discomforts suffered during rounding. This is because whilst some stress might be experienced during the meditation, the thoughts that accompany this 'unwinding' process are considered to be unworthy of consideration. Meditators are therefore counselled not to place particular importance on thoughts that might arise in meditation, for these are deemed merely as results of 'unstressing', not as causes. This theory has been taken so far as to suggest that if one experiences *any* thoughts in meditation it is evidence of the effectiveness of the technique – a frail and sophic argument!

Having expounded the basis of his theory of 'unstressing', the Maharishi further amplified the positive factors of this kind of experience within the context of his method of meditation:

> [It] depends on how much one is anchored to the eternal stable factor of life, the Being. How much one is anchored and what is the strength of the cyclone. How much one is anchored. If one is permanently established in the eternal Being, fine, any amount of gain in the relative, it will shake and it will just shake but it won't break it down. That is the reason why we are here, to get as deep contact with Being as possible, as soon as possible. And that's the reason why we are not doing anything other than digging deep into ourselves ... uh? And when we dig deep well, very deep, sometimes when the rocks come, we have to blow them out through dynamite. See there we have ... we are putting up dynamite against the rocks that are coming on our way to clear the whole situation – for full reflection of the omnipresent

Being. That's the idea.

So there appeared to be light at the end of the tunnel, but with one precondition – in order to ensure that no regression would occur, all must continue their practice of meditating twice a day without fail.

The fact that the Maharishi showed such understanding of and familiarity with problems of stress release leads one to wonder whether he had himself experienced this phenomenon of unwinding and had come through it unscathed. But whatever the reason for the phenomena of 'unstressing', was there nothing that could be done to minimize their impact? Fortunately for the meditators, there was something they could do and that was to 'feel the body'. This sounds like a physical exercise but is in fact a mental process whereby the meditator moves his or her attention from thoughts that provoke discomfort and instead focuses on the body. This technique is also advocated for those who are sick or ill, as a means of healing or at any rate subduing symptoms long enough for the meditator to continue with his or her practice. The Maharishi's views on 'unstressing' prompt one to ask whether he is not confusing cause with effect.

The subject of *karma*, the science of action, is central to Hindu philosophy, and it is not surprising to find the subject raised in connection with the Maharishi's meditation. This theory, that for every action there is a corresponding reaction, is a familiar one and, apparently, a scientific fact. Surprisingly, therefore, it has yet to find universal acceptance. Many people stand firmly by the belief that one may get away with all sorts of misdemeanours, but Hindu faith has no place for such concepts and actively promotes the understanding that the law of *karma* is irreversible (notwithstanding the aid of divine intercession). If the notion of *karma* is combined with another Hindu doctrine, that of reincarnation, then the subject shoots out of the bounds of methodical research and becomes merely a matter of faith.

When the Maharishi spoke of past actions, it is probable that he was alluding not merely to just one lifetime but to an immeasurable legacy built up through successive reincarnations. If it were true that human beings had 'previous form', how long would it take to remove the incalculable adverse effects of the past? Whilst addressing the topic of 'unstressing' the Maharishi touched on this complex topic:

> This line on the board, and it seems to be such a long line. We can make it short without touching it, by drawing a much bigger line along... uh?
>
> If we have done some ... we have taken some loan, some loan, some loan and we make a big, big income now. That loan becomes tiny, little, little, small, small ... uh? Whatever *karma* we have done, whatever action we have

performed, that is imprinted in nature, we can't reduce it or enhance it. What we can do now is, do a better *karma* than that and let that better *karma* dominate, so that that becomes small ... uh? A $500 loan now, next moment 5 million gained, and that 500 loan seemed to be tiny, if it doesn't seem to be at all. Like that, if some bad has been done, something has been done, it can't be undone. But it can be complicated by a bigger action of a good nature.

Two things can be said of this statement – one that the Maharishi had taken time to think out his beliefs, and that he was a very forceful and persuasive salesman!

Practitioners of the Maharishi's style of meditation are asked merely to witness the thoughts and sensations experienced in meditation, but it is contended that meditation is not a state of passivity but an action, albeit an inner one, which can dispel or neutralize the results of stored *karma* in the individual. It is believed that meditation can not only ward off illness but sometimes even cure it. Strangely, not only is 'unstressing' seen to be beneficial in terms of personal evolution, but to some extent so too is illness. The manifestation of disease is said to be related to the phenomenon of 'unstressing', as both are perceived to be due to the expulsion of foreign matter from within the body. It is said that the origins of all medical complaints can be explained in terms of personal *karma*. It begins to appear that *karma* is therefore a byword for disaster! But there is another side to consider, made easier by first establishing the quality of the *karma*. Bad *karma* is perceived as that which causes difficulties, complications and even regression, whereas good *karma* is life-supporting action, which assists evolution. The complexity of calculating the possibilities of causes and their effects is enormous not to say unending, and potentially brings into question the act of breathing, one's very existence in fact. But fear not, help is at hand. The Maharishi's answer is that an intellectual appreciation of the laws of cause and effect is not necessary, only the ability to take one's mind to a level of such deep rest that transcendental consciousness becomes established. Having first attained this stage of restful alertness, one would be able to emerge imbued with the capacity to act in accordance with nature. Quite automatically, quite spontaneously, by virtue of a simple natural innocent process, meditators would be able to act rightly and enjoy life to the full. To gain this control over *karma* the practice he recommended was, as ever, Transcendental Meditation. But how innocent a process was it, when its practitioners were so full and overfull of exalted exhalted expectations?

16

---★---

THOSE WHO SPEAK DON'T KNOW

For those attending courses with the Maharishi, the major objective was, naturally enough, to achieve experiences of states of higher consciousness and thereby hope to enjoy the delights of increased happiness, greater appreciation of life and perhaps even greater personal freedom. But they had first to pass through the inner turmoil frequently associated with longer periods of meditation. Those present on the spring 1969 teacher-training course at Shankaracharya Nagar also had to come to terms with dimensions of the Maharishi's philosophy that they had hitherto been only dimly aware of.

One of the chief gains claimed for the Maharishi's method of meditation is the experience of 'unboundedness' and to a backdrop of steady chirruping from the jungle blending with the ticking of a clockwork timepiece, the Master braced himself before divulging a fuller understanding of the term:

> Now, from our own experience we know that we have to go beyond the finest activity and then that ... awareness which even for myself is without any boundaries, unbounded. Now, this unboundedness with reference to myself, how can I attribute that this is here also? That is the question. No? But because this experience of unboundedness with reference to myself has been gained by going beyond the finest experience. And there what we conclude is, beyond the finest strata of material existence is the non-material unboundedness which is myself. And because the entire manifest or material universe has layers of existence, layer after layer, layer within the layer, layer within the layer, from gross to the subtle layers ... uh? And therefore, every little bit of material universe deep within is nothing but unmanifest awareness which is this, what I myself am.
>
> And therefore I am all that I am without a second. Huh? I am the monarch of all I survey and more than that![231]

This declaration of the identification of the individual with the universe is therefore unboundedness, the establishment of individual awareness of the upanishadic wisdom that 'I am That, Thou art That, All this is That'. Is this state of unboundedness really a state of enlightenment or an intellectual condition brought about by autosuggestion? The words enlightenment and illumination both suggest an increased presence of light. Coincidentally, in order to shed light on the difficulties likely to be encountered on the way to an unbounded state of awareness, the Maharishi chose to use an analogy focused on light. It went something like this: a mirror's ability to reflect is largely dependent on available light and as such would easily reflect the sun, which is a source of light in itself. However, any dust or dirt on its surface would impede the mirror's capacity to reflect the image of the sun. Similarly, according to the Maharishi, an individual's ability to reflect the light of the Supreme is considerably lessened by his or her impurities.

> Sun ... water ... reflection, which is a combination of the two. Reflection, and that is small self, self is the reflection on this nervous system and the reflection of omnipresent Being. So the original thing is Being, but when it is reflected, then full value of Being is not reflected, it is small self. Now this self lingers on three relative states of consciousness, waking, dreaming, sleeping, waking, dreaming, sleeping, waking, dreaming, sleeping. But with the modification of the reflector nervous system the quality of the small self begins to shine more and more in the value of the big self the cosmic. And eventually the value of the reflection the small self gains the value of Being, then we write it with big S ... the Self. So it's just the transformation of the self small into Self big, by virtue of the modification of the nervous system from its stressed and strained condition to its normal functioning level.

Continuing this contemplation of reflections he noted that in the process of reflecting the sun, the colour of the water would inevitably affect the quality of the reflection. A green hue to the water would tinge the clear light of the sun and would colour the reflection green, giving an image of a green sun. His message was clear: those who still had karmic impurities would be inadequate conductors of the light of the Supreme.

The word evolution was often used by the Maharishi, but seldom if ever defined. The evolution to which he referred was applied to progressive levels of personal consciousness, and accordingly it has little or nothing to do with Darwin's evolution of the species. The Maharishi did not support the notion that the human structure is in a state of evolutionary flux, that one day it might give rise to another species. His vision of evolution was very different in that he saw man as having an incomplete awareness but believed that by guidance this incompleteness could be addressed. Those who acknowledged and rectified these shortcomings could hope some day to achieve optimum consciousness and in so doing become normal. Those who aspired to reach the goals of meditation were to become normal and any great difficulties impeding their progress on the 'pathless path' were to be put down only to physical or psychological abnormalities. But there was a let-out clause. To those who perceived his philosophy to be only catering for the physically and mentally fit, he said that his practice could be undertaken by anyone, just as long as they could think. In fact no-one would be likely to embark on a time-consuming practice like meditation if they believed themselves to be totally devoid of problems or impurities. Abnormalities were not so much a bar to progress as a prerequisite, for how can one become normal without first being less than normal?

These concepts, along with many others which he offered, defy ready explanation, and the Maharishi often had to repeat himself. Lecture after lecture found him covering the same ground from different directions, restating his points again and again, hoping to make himself understood. Many of his philosophies were made more difficult to grasp by virtue of their abstract content, and he frequently resorted to the use of analogies in order to offer a clearer understanding. Still speaking about the distinction between self and Self he further explained:

> I don't see any damage of logic in presenting this explanation of Being and transformation of the quality of the nervous system in order to live full Being. I think this reflection analogy is most accurate and it explains the whole idea in a very concrete and picturesque way ...
>
> Because the Absolute is attributeless we cannot explain it through language or remaining in the field of the attribute. What we say is, because the absolute Being is attributeless therefore it is not possible to speak the language of that field and if it is to be explained it can only be explained from the field of the attribute and therefore we say and we explain it. Because it in itself is attributeless and in that sphere of the no attributes the language, the speech is mute ... uh? The words don't come out and that is why from its own level it cannot be spoken of. From its own level it cannot be explained. Therefore we explain it from the level it can be explained. And that's why we are talking about it. We are talking, not because we can't talk about it, but because we can talk about it. We can't talk about it because it can only be talked about on the level of speech. It in its own level cannot be talked about. We don't have a language of the Absolute value but we have a language that can enumerate the Absolute value and therefore we are open to talking about.

Surely this was the real reason that the message had become blurred with the passing years. The problem was less that language was by its nature fluid, much more that the message was in itself exceedingly difficult to convey. Ancient texts can still readily offer up their descriptions of lives and events of the past; it is in the province of matters metaphysical that the power of words becomes strained. If the topic of emotions has placed enormous demands on the skills of lovers who wish to communicate their feelings, is it likely that it will be easier to speak of subtle spiritual realms? The Maharishi demonstrated the difficulty well:

> Once we start living the Absolute and therefore the speech is running through the Absolute, the sight is running through the Absolute and in this case we can really speak of the Absolute from the level of living it. In [the] other case – from the level of guessing it, guessing about it. But from this level by living it. Huh …?

Whilst many mystics of the past signalled their faith through poetry, others chose the language of silence, communicating only by their presence. A criticism commonly applied to those attempting to elucidate the nature of God is the oft-quoted sentence 'Those who speak don't know.' Thus it seems that the ones who speak out on matters of extreme depth are destined to be dismissed as frauds. This no-win situation would be an unenviable position to find oneself in and it is clear, from the following remarks, that the Maharishi had given the subject very serious consideration, enabling him to raise some significant questions and offer some novel insights into this predicament:

> Those who *know* it, they only can talk about it and it's … it's … it's … it's wild to say that those who know don't talk about it. Then who brings the knowledge from generation to generation… uh… if the talking is to be only in the field of ignorance? Then we say just 'Those who … those … they don't know about it.

> Now, there are some such passages in the *Upanishads* somewhere, that 'those who know it don't talk it'… beautiful passage. It means that those who know it have realised cosmic consciousness … huh? By being it and those and those who live it in life, whatever they speak, they are only a witness to their speech and they are not speaking that. They are only a witness to whatever they are speaking, So if they are speaking 'God', they are not speaking not speaking 'God', they are just witness to that speech. So those who know it, those who live it, don't speak it. But speaking, they don't speak it. Speaking they don't speak it. Huh? Not speaking, they don't speak it, but not speaking they don't speak it. So it is also right that they don't speak it because not only it they don't speak but the fact is that they don't speak anything. Because, just because by their own status they are a witness to things, whatever they are speaking they are a witness to it.

His torrential outpourings and his outbursts of laughter when pausing to witness to the words, left his devotees in no doubt that he understood his subject. Certainly, if he could not confer the immediate exaltation of an expanded consciousness, he could certainly stimulate his students' intellects. The belief that words could provide a pathway to understanding the inexplicable led him to add:

> So the knowers of reality don't speak it, but certainly they speak it. Otherwise how will this wisdom be transferred from generation to generation? It would have ended long ago if they had not spoken it. But because established in that reality they are a witness to whatever they are speaking, so speaking they don't speak, in this sense knowers of reality don't speak about it otherwise they do.

> Supreme knowledge speaks. It speaks. It speaks. When a knower-man in supreme knowledge speaks, it speaks, the Absolute speaks, and that's it. And no matter about what it speaks, but it is its speech. *Shruttis* are speech, and any man in supreme knowledge is it personified. It personified. All this perception, experience, activity are the activity of it, and therefore, it's not that the knowers of reality don't speak about it or don't speak it. But the fact is that only they can speak it out or only they can speak about it. It is only the knowers of reality that can speak, the ignorant can make gestures about it.

But who were these ignorant people who could only make gestures about it? Were there no other teachers that could point a way to inner peace and greater health and prosperity? For the most part his disciples convinced themselves that their way was the best, they were not interested in the rest. It is alleged that the Maharishi had offered a means by which any other method of meditation might be measured and that was to ask whether its technique became transcended by its practice. If the vehicle of meditation diminished to a point where it disappeared and yet the practitioner was found wide awake and in a state of fullness and bliss, then that meditation also qualified as Transcendental Meditation. Of the other forms of *yoga* available in India, many promoted the use of *mantras:*

> The state of *yoga* brought about by a *mantra* – this is *Mantra Yoga*. The state of *yoga* brought about by a *mantra* – *Mantra Yoga*. But we refrain from using that term because so much wrong understanding about that science of *Mantra Yoga*, very very deeply mixed up and therefore we don't categorize our system of meditation in any systems of *yoga*.

The most popular *mantra* adopted by those desirous of spiritual awakening is the use of *om*. Much favoured by *bhakti* (devotional) groups are *mantras* in praise of the gods or their *avataars*. The chant of 'Hare Rama, Hare Krishna' is claimed by their exponents to be transcendental, but is it really? Since devotees of this *mantra* often sing or dance while chanting, one wonders what would happen should they indeed transcend. Frequently, those practising *japa* (repetition of *mantras*) make use of *mala* (rosaries sometimes known as *rudraksha*, with twenty-seven, fifty-four or 108 beads) to establish a 'count' of the chants. The Maharishi asserted that not only does this system of meditation tire the mind, but the real gain in its practice lies in the silence that follows the chanting. The instructions given in teaching his forms of meditation are in stark contrast to the 'chant and chant and chant' method of the *bhaktis*.

It would be interesting to know what *yoga* teachings the Maharishi's *guru* embraced. Swami Rama is of assistance here, for in recalling his meeting with Swami Brahmanand, he remembered the swami showing him a Sri Yantra (the visual equivalent of a *mantra*), its geometric design of superimposed triangles made entirely of rubies.

Of the other organizations which also teach *mantra* meditation, there is evidence that a few are extremely similar but are taught within a specifically religious framework. Some people, after being initiated into the Maharishi's system of meditation, have gone on to wonder whether the more 'difficult' practices might not yield greater satisfaction. The Maharishi is adamant in his claims:

> A system which produces the synthesis of benefits gained by all the systems of *yoga*, collective benefits of all the systems of *yoga*. Uh? The spontaneous purity of the system is the achievement aimed by the *Hatha Yoga*, so many systems of purification, so many systems of purification of the body, bring about all kinds of purification which are contained in, in the purification brought about through Transcendental Meditation on both levels, material and structural. Huh?
>
> Experiments have been performed by German meditating medical people to show that the chemistry of the system changes. And naturally these stresses and strains are released. So structural and material changes brought about by Transcendental Meditation are aimed through these various practices of *Hatha Yoga*.

Many spiritual aspirants see the exercises of *Hatha Yoga*, the *asanas* (*yoga* postures), as preparation for a more 'serious' spiritual discipline. Many teachers advise that a seeker with an out-of-condition body, with bad habits of diet and habits of 'unspiritual' behaviour, is impure and therefore unable to attain higher experiences. Having established a more wholesome body and mind by exercises, spiritual tuition and so forth, the advanced student may only then perform techniques of *kundalini*, the raising of *shakti* (serpentine energy). Predictably the Maharishi saw the situation rather differently, citing that the various forms of *yoga* are not to be seen as steps to progress, rather as 'limbs' or branches of *yoga* philosophy, and further contended that all the advantages claimed by the different schools of *yoga* are gained by the practice of his techniques, quite automatically and without further study.

It is difficult to understand how the practitioner of his system, sitting virtually motionless, could hope to derive the muscular strength and flexibility gained by those practising *yoga assanas*. Indeed, a common experience amongst meditators is a temporary stiffness of the body, presumably brought about by their inactivity. Like so many claims for his system, this one is difficult, but not impossible, to verify.

If the system of meditation is so complete within itself, why was it necessary to employ Professor Han Krishna to prepare a course of *yoga* postures and *pranayama* (systematic breathing exercises)? It seems to be a confession of his system's shortcomings. None the less, the inclusion of *asanas* in rounding makes a lot of sense, for these exercises provide the much-needed 'outward stroke' of meditation, the chance for the mind and body to resume contact with external reality before continuing further inner meditation. One of the Maharishi's favourite analogies illustrates concepts of the inner and outward strokes of meditation. It is of a cloth being placed in dye (meditation) and then hung in the sun to dry (outward stroke), and this process being repeated until the dye is fixed. According to him, it is the repetition of the process that makes both dyeing and meditation successful.

Another 'limb' of *yoga* is that of *kundalini* or *Laya Yoga*, defined as the raising of serpentine spiritual energy, which is supposed to reside in a dormant state at the base of the spine. It is held that through proper guidance this energy can be awakened and distributed through to the various spiritual centres or *chakras* of the body. This is a highly esoteric subject, the practice of which should only be undertaken under expert supervision, and then only by advanced adepts. Those who are not ready are warned about the irreparable damage that may result from use of such techniques whilst the mind and body are as yet unprepared. The Maharishi, on the other hand, suggested that this raising of the *kundalini* is but another by-product of his meditation and appeared to believe that all his students had experience of it:

> *Laya Yoga* which deals with *kundalini*. We are experienced, everyone experiences the rising of *kundalini*. So all the effects desired through the practice of *Laya Yoga* are naturally gained without bothering about any one of them.
>
> The practice of *Raj Yoga* aims at making permanent the state of transcendental awareness. The range of *Raj Yoga* is from the level of

transcendental consciousness to the level of cosmic consciousness. This thing naturally results through Transcendental Meditation without taking into account any aspects of the practice of *Raj Yoga.*

It must surely have appeared unbelievable to his devotees that the Maharishi could teach them a system that could rival the most venerated schools of practice. But this was the Maharishi's claim, and certainly whilst they were in his company it appeared to them possible, even likely, that this was so. They were insufficiently knowledgeable in these matters to challenge his generalizations and they most certainly did not wish to engage in confrontations. There was not a Malcolm Muggeridge or Allen Ginsberg amongst them and perhaps this is unfortunate, for a greater depth of discussion might have resulted.

The Maharishi's basic criticism of other *yoga* systems was that they had been misinterpreted in that they advocated the use of 'control' instead of utilizing the 'wandering nature of the mind'. One thing that was evident to all was that before them sat a master, at least of himself. He never appeared angry, never resorted to shouting, seldom made dismissive remarks and seemed to hold fast to a strict moral code. In short, he seemed to be the personification, the definition of self-control. All those years of obedience had certainly left their mark on his character.

After lecturing on the classic schools of *yoga* the Maharishi found the wandering nature of the mind all too evident in his students. Apparently unprovoked, one of his devotees asked about the presence of life in human form on other planets. After some preamble the Maharishi dealt with the question evasively:

> Life in other planets? We would say nothing can be useless in creation. If something is created it must have some use. There may be planets without life but the majority of planets should have life in it. Lots of planets may be without life but the very existence shows that they can't be without life. Must be some life.

This answer elicited a certain amount of amusement from those gathered around him, but the question remained unanswered.

Time was getting on and even those who practised meditation found that their energy sometimes waned. After working through several more topics the Master then delivered his views on sleep, for many the closest they ever came to the deep rest and freedom of which the Maharishi spoke.

> Due to habit the fatigue overtakes and one has to sleep. But the time comes when one doesn't much sleep. Sleep is a nuisance to life but it is inevitable

nuisance, a waste of life. But it is inevitable waste. We can't say it.

The nights and days of the three-month course continued, spent alternately meditating and listening to lectures. For some, the course was their only opportunity of getting close to the Maharishi and hearing his teaching at first hand. In addition to understanding the way their enigmatic Master thought, they also had the task of learning how to teach his method of meditation. This entailed not only learning the instructions to be given at initiation but also developing the ability to engage in public speaking. Not everyone was taken with the notion of becoming teachers, but they all did their best to absorb their lessons.

Those who succeeded in all aspects of their training would also be expected to perform the function of salesmen for the organization. It was this 'business' side of their responsibilities that posed particular difficulties for new recruits, for how could they ever equal the Maharishi's talent for presenting his teachings to new audiences? Like all those new to the field of selling, they needed a pep talk. The 'sales manager' obliged, outlining the role of those who were to take the news of his technique to the masses.

> This is the purpose of the Movement; we take delight in bringing the light to the other people, making them happy. That is our joy, which lies at the basis of our participation in the Spiritual Regeneration Movement. It's very simple. We are very selfish people, we don't want to see anyone unhappy and therefore for our joy for not seeing any unhappy face around us, we are busily engaged in teaching meditation. It's for our joy.

And how should they best deliver this message so that it would inspire people and make them want to take up this meditation? 'Tell the people that they are born with that ocean of happiness – come on take a dive!'

Having found fresh converts to whom the technique of meditation could be taught, new teachers should know how to deal with the overwhelming gratitude they were likely to encounter from new initiates!

> The teacher of Transcendental Meditation flows in all love and happiness for everything everywhere around him. And in order to set much higher and tidal waves of love in his heart, he is entertaining other people and giving them meditation. If a man says 'I am very thankful to you and you have done so much to me', say: 'Ah, you have brought me such great joy with these experiences, and you deserve more happiness, you deserve more thanks. Because all these expressions of yours bring to me such great joy in my heart and that is the reward that you have given me so I must thank you for that.' And then he feels more and then you feel more.

It appeared that henceforth all new meditators would have to content themselves with hearing about the Maharishi's teaching from his representatives. Once the course was over it was believed that he would retreat from the limelight and disappear from sight, possibly returning to his cave in Uttar Kashi. It appears that this was still his intention.

> And then when I go in silence, then our activity will have much more far-reaching effects. Then I'll be with the root and watering the fruit. That also for greater success to all the coming generations. These are the two reasons, basically two reasons.
>
> Once I have successfully established this training of teachers programme in all the countries then the work is done, then it will continue and continue and continue and continue.

He shared with his students his delight that, even if he had not yet achieved all his objectives, he had been reasonably successful at communicating his basic philosophy – that there are two aspects to life – inner and outer, spiritual and material. He had spoken of this concept in terms of a life where 200 per cent of life could be lived, 100 per cent inner and 100 per cent outer, and believed that this philosophy had gained considerable acceptance, promising a very real chance for the success of his movement, which now had centres dotted right across the free world, where people could avail themselves of his teaching. Also available through his movement were publications, records, tape recordings and films of his lectures and discourses, not to mention the opportunity to attend further courses to gain a better intellectual understanding of his philosophy. But although he had gained much ground he had yet to establish a teaching force sufficient to fulfil his ambitions. Part of the problem was that he demanded a strict uniformity in the pattern of teaching methods, hence the need to school his students personally. The *ashram* at Shankaracharya Nagar was sufficient only for the training of a few dozen or so at a time and advances were therefore painfully slow. To make matters worse, only a percentage of the course participants were destined to be invested with the power to teach, and fewer still became active on behalf of his mission. The situation he most deeply desired was to be able to sit back in the certain knowledge that his chosen devotees continued his work. He certainly saw his organization in terms of a product and his teachers as a sales force with a strong marketing strategy.

> So having manufactured the ice-cream, ice-cream, and having found a beautiful label and then advertised and accepted its value in the market, now I have to see that every generation receives those beautiful packets in their purity.

All in all it looked as though he were creating a business empire, with him as the sleeping partner. Rather than argue against this perception he seems rather to have endorsed it.

The Maharishi's long-term goal was to develop an organization which would outlive him. In this there is strong evidence that his intention was not merely to gratify his own desire to see the spread of all the benefits of his methods, but to secure the possibility of those as yet unborn being offered these 'packets in their purity': 'Our efforts in this generation may go on for thousands of generations and all the world will enjoy.'

But how could he fulfil his stated commitment to retire and yet also train enough new teachers to fulfil his grand plan for getting 1 per cent of the world's population meditating within three years? He appears to have been unable to acknowledge the impossible dilemma.

> So now whereas you are taking upon yourself to spread, I am taking upon myself more to consolidate. So the consolidation at the root and spreading on the level of the branches and leaves, both will simultaneously go on...
>
> It's such a joy to have so many many good people to just spread and spread and ... take care of expansion, expansion. Then the root should be secured and I must keep it secured.

17

—★—

WATER THE ROOT AND ENJOY THE FRUIT

As a preparation for the time when some of his students would be speaking out as authorities on his meditation method, the Maharishi paid close attention to the topic of public speaking. To pave the way, he chose to address the several issues that had consistently created controversy amongst his audiences. Concern was voiced that his teaching might be a form of self-hypnosis or worse, self-worship. Others feared that the Maharishi was engaged in an operation of Hindu missionary work. But by far the most common criticism concerned the fees levied for the teaching of meditation, for few but the very wealthy could feel comfortable about parting with a week's wages on a whim.

It was time for the Maharishi to volunteer answers to these problems. His response to the concerns that his organization was a new religion was to deny it categorically. He was emphatic that his student teachers should adopt a similar attitude. He restated and reinforced this position whenever the subject arose.

> Religion is a big thing! Very huge ... big! It covers all phases of life and leads all the phases towards highest attainment, that is a religion. Religion covers the individual, family, nation, international, world, God, Creator, Almighty, Omnipresent. All these things are covered by religion.[232]

In fact these phases are covered by Hindu religious thought, but not by all religions. For example the concept of an omnipresent God is not common to all faiths; some believe that God in his heaven has little or no contact with the mundane. If the truth be acknowledged, the Maharishi's definition of religion might equally well be applied to his form of *Mantra Yoga*, for he claimed that its practice brings fulfilment to all these phases. Where then is the distinction between meditation and religion? He seemed to be saying that religion, in addition to providing a place for worship and ritual, deals only with the development of attitudes, offering such things as moral guidance – this might account, in part, for his reluctance to offer firm guidelines of conduct to his devotees. His view of religion might well find strong opposition amongst those who feel they have much more to offer than ritual and morality.

There must also be some doubt as to whether the teaching of his meditation is free from any form of indoctrination that could be interpreted as religious. Consider for a moment the view that the goal of meditation is to contact the Being, otherwise known as God. It might seem to be an invitation to participate in prayer. It is worth noting that some years earlier, when the Maharishi had been asked whether his meditation was in fact prayer, he answered that it was indeed a 'most refined' and 'powerful' prayer.[233]

The assertion that his meditation is not a religion seems to be rooted in the conviction that even the Maharishi's own religion, Hinduism, had failed to lead people to a normal life. So his claims that meditation could lead to fulfilment even for the non-religious is encouraging. It is particularly reassuring to note that he specifically advocates the cultivation of individuality, a peculiarly liberal approach if he were bent on mass conversion to a particular style of religious thought.

> So this [meditation] is useful to man to develop his individuality and then the fully developed man will find his God through his religion. Christians will realize God through Christianity, Muslims will realize God through Islam. But they will become fully developed Christians and fully developed Muslims and fully developed Hindus. So this we say is a technique and not a religion. Useful to the people of all religions.[234]

By tradition Hinduism is perceived to be all-embracing in that it makes no firm distinctions about what and what is not religious. Attendance at the temple is not a prerequisite for performing worship; any action can serve the purpose. However, the Maharishi wished his followers to recognize the distinctions between the various aspects of their lives. He cited the responsibility for earning a living and the role of making purchases as quite distinct from the responsibilities of either churchgoer or meditator. Even at home the separation of activities could not be overlooked:

> When I go to the kitchen, then I look for some delicious dishes and this ... then I don't think of Shakespeare in the library. Then I have some good food before me and when I go to my library I don't think of sweet dishes in the kitchen. Then the Shakespeare and the Milton and Wordsworth and this is my concern in the library.

Established religions have a recognized tendency to create a degree of exclusivity for their adherents, leading followers to become prejudiced against the beliefs of other faiths. Disarmingly, the Maharishi made light of these potential antagonisms:

> And just as when we feel headache we go to the doctor and then we don't see whether the doctor comes from my church or not. He is a doctor and he gives us aspirin and then we don't see whether this has the label of my church or not.

However, in order to determine whether or not his meditation could be classified as a religion, one would have to take many other factors into consideration, and this would require open access to the method of its teaching, the surrounding philosophy and the attendant belief system.

Much easier to counter was the charge that the Maharishi's meditation was self-hypnosis. His commonly-used defence was that self-hypnosis is the result of introducing an idea and maintaining it even in the face of its absurdity, as in the example of a poor man proclaiming 'I am a king, I am a king.' The teaching of his meditation requires that one focus on a sound 'without meaning for us' and let other thoughts slip away. In a state of 'no thought', there is obviously no room for thoughts of ownership, status or anything else and one could conclude that there is also no room for self-hypnosis. Commentators have presumed that because his basic philosophy could be used as a tool for self-hypnosis, the practice of his meditation must necessarily employ such a strategy, but the Maharishi reassured his devotees:

> Self-hypnosis means self-delusion, hypnosis – putting oneself into the unrealistic state. But in Transcendental Meditation the effects that we gain, in the process of gaining those effects, we don't think of those effects. We get peace without thinking of peace. We get happiness without thinking of happiness. We get energy without thinking of energy.
>
> So here we enjoy the state of more energy, more intelligence, more happiness. And in hypnosis we place ourself deeply sunk in the thought of these things and that is why Transcendental Meditation is completely opposed to what self-hypnosis is.

Never one to miss an opportunity to promote his teachings, he went on to condemn hypnosis for its role in breaking the co-ordination between mind and body, pointing out that in his meditation co-ordination was improved.

The task of convincing his students of the merits of charging for initiation was another matter entirely. It might be remembered that before the decision to fix the fee (euphemistically referred to as a 'donation'), contributions were made voluntarily. As if it was not difficulty enough to go out as envoys of the Maharishi, the newly trained teachers had also to cope with the embarrassment of asking for money. Their teacher advised them how to tackle this issue:

> We want to announce the charge but we want to announce these words also: 'We are a charitable organization... SIMS is a charitable organization'

His devotees sensed his apparent hesitation and sought to assist their Master in his explanation. They suggested words and phrases that might be of use to him and gradually a statement was prepared:

prepared:

> 'Non-profit is the word. Non-profit char- Non-profit education corp- organization.'

Having honed the party line, the Maharishi took time to soften his audience with some anecdotes taken from the early years of the Movement. He recalled that it was in Los Angeles that the decision to standardize 'donations' came to be made:

> People had made a rule, that they put some basket there so that people when they come and when they go, they put something in the basket. And I felt very ashamed with that basket on the door and people coming and I said 'It is like begging on the door', because it was too odd to me to put a basket in front of my room.

Another, more obvious, answer would have been to move the basket elsewhere and stay with the voluntary contributions. However, the Maharishi had many prosperous visitors and therefore wondered whether a regulated pattern of financial support could not be made available. It was his suggestion that a move be made towards a fixed 'donation', a proposal that was discussed and agreed. Initially the figure had been set at a week's wages per family, and later, in certain countries, it had become modified, with fixed individual rates being introduced.

Certainly money was needed. How else were his followers to book halls, print leaflets and publish books? But the insistence on compulsory 'donations' ran contrary to his professed doctrine. He appears to have forgotten his message to the people of Kerala, that the 'path is straight and entry is free', for he now said:

> We are not ashamed to talk of money, to ask money or to accept money and to spend money. Because more money we have, more quickly we will spread this meditation. Money is needed for quick expansion of the ideology and if we can afford to be very slow then we don't need anything.

Recognizing that his students needed help in coming to terms with this extra responsibility, he offered to make their task easier by teaching them a selection of his winning one-liners:

> Say, 'This is such a great gift to life that it can't be evaluated in terms of some dollars or what or what', like that. That is a good expression to it.
>
> We can always say, 'It can't be repaid, the teaching of Transcendental Meditation can't be repaid, but this is how the organization runs and money is needed more and more' and ... like that.

But no amount of explanation could conceal the fact that the 'donation' was in fact a fee. Traditionally, spiritual organizations have relied on the goodwill of their supporters for funds. The Maharishi angered many of his countrymen, who felt that spiritual teaching should always be free of charge. His own *guru*, the Shankaracharya, had demonstrated his views on the subject quite unambiguously, having gone so far as to prohibit people from making any material offerings to him whatsoever. The tale is told that on one occasion a follower sought to share some new-found wealth and concealed a few gold coins amongst some flowers close to the Shankaracharya. He received an unexpected response in that he found himself temporarily banned from access to the old *swami*. According to the Hindu belief system, all objects have their own *karma* and evidently he who was hailed as 'infinitely bestowed' had no wish to share the influence of this man's *karma*, golden or otherwise. It is surprising that the Maharishi should have taken such an apparently opposite view. He tried to explain:

> The organization needs money, but the method of receiving money has been so constructed, the style of accepting money and giving money. The word donation provides that structure, the man feels contented in his heart: 'I am giving a donation for some pious work, for some good work.' Now he can give money in this way, feeling good about giving, or he can give money feeling that 'it were better if I had not to give' and yet giving it. Now the money is received by the organization but in one way, as far as the receiving is concerned, the value is the same for both .

One might say that to feel 'contented in his heart' the new initiate would probably prefer to retain control over his or her money. After all, if the meditation were that wonderful, surely the new meditator would wish to help defray the costs incurred in its teaching.

> That element of the heart and of this ... it's completely missing, it's a matter of the cashier recording it and finished. There is no pious or holiness attributed to it to culture the heart in the act of giving.

So how should the student teachers deal with their mixed feelings about demanding and taking money, about having to be not only teachers but salesmen and cashiers? The Maharishi could see no problem:

> [the donations] which we have fixed for ourselves in all these countries, international standards. We just follow that, easily and comfortably.

Before someone could be taught the method of Transcendental Meditation, they had first to follow a sequence of mental preparations. The first step was to attend an introductory talk, the second a follow-up preparatory talk, and the third a personal interview. The object of the introductory lecture was to outline the Maharishi's basic philosophy and to indicate in general terms what the practice of meditation entails. Having won the confidence and interest of the audience, the second lecture could be mentioned. The need to make a decision whether to attend the second lecture filtered out anyone who had no real desire to further their knowledge of the subject. Only after attending the second lecture would members of the audience be invited to make arrangements for private discussion and then be considered for initiation.

The success of the introductory talk was considered crucial if the Movement was to be successful in gaining fresh converts. In the early years, the Maharishi had taken responsibility for all the introductory, preparatory and private talks and had expert experience in this field that he was determined to pass on to his task force. Since so much hung on this initial contact, nothing was to be left to chance. Not only were the lecture topics carefully prepared beforehand, so too were the answers to the questions most frequently posed. It was perceived that greater gains were to be made by the use of more than one speaker.

> That three, four speakers appeal to the people more, someone is charmed by someone, someone is charmed by someone, someone is charmed by someone ... something like that.

What he meant of course was that if one speaker failed to appeal, for whatever reason, another might come over better. At any rate, the goal was to persuade the highest proportion of the audience to attend the preparatory lecture: 'Maximum initiations have come from many speaking in one lecture, many.'

Those who embarked on the teaching-training programme were encouraged to note any topics, phrases or anecdotes that they might find useful when lecturing. Students were to make sure that they could speak on issues such as education, health, religion and world peace. The mainstay of the introductory talk was the preamble outlining the

Maharishi's basic philosophy. Although this could be presented in diverse ways it could be effectively stated in just one sentence. 'Water the root to enjoy the fruit.' On this basis it was suggested that society could be likened to a forest in which all the trees had to gain nourishment. In order to stay healthy and fruitful, each tree would need to be watered separately, so by supplying the needs of all the individual trees, the needs of the whole forest would be taken care of. Having placed this simplistic but irrefutable logic before the audience, suggestions could then be offered as to how this ideology might be applied to human society.

> Meditation is like watering the root and supplying nourishment to all the aspects of the tree. 'Watering the root' can be defined in terms of the growth of leaf, also 'watering the root' can be defined in terms of the growth of the branches, also in terms of the growth of the flower, also in terms in the growth of the fruit. So 'watering the root' can be defined in numberless ways with respect to the effects it produces in all parts of the tree. Now, like that Transcendental Meditation can have innumerable definitions because it produces effects in all the phases of life.

But no matter how much work had been put into planning the introductory lecture, there might still be difficulties in getting the message across.

> Only speaking is not the responsibility of the speaker. He should see that whatever he is speaking reaches the ears first and then the mind and also pierces through the heart.

A pretty tall order! But what could be done to ensure that the speakers were not only heard, but also properly understood?

> There could also be a technique of capturing the attention of the people and that is, raise a question sometime. Some question. Maybe you don't wait for the answer from the audience and you answer it yourself, but raise the question and wait ... Five seconds waiting and your silence will awaken the minds and make them all alert.

But why go to such lengths? Could the speakers not just take it as it came? Besides, what if only a handful of people had turned up to listen? Presumably (at least in terms of profitability) it would be a complete waste of time to make such elaborate preparations. The Maharishi begged to differ:

> Even if one man comes we want to inform him all these four points, so that at least he, who had time to receive the message, could get the benefit of our presence. Because if we have gained one man, through him, his friends, their friends, it progresses like snowballs.

He gave an indication of his fascination with numbers by asserting that four speakers would have sixteen times the impact of a solo appearance. He argued, fairly persuasively, that the presence of a diverse panel of individuals, differing in age and drawn from both sexes, would enhance the chances of successfully imparting the message. One of the Maharishi's students was perplexed that it might also be necessary to have as many speakers at the preparatory talk. He was reassured:

> That could be given by single individual, once the man has come for the second time, he is more or less drawn to the thing. Then you could breathe a little easier.

Having elucidated the means of gaining success in public speaking the Maharishi issued a salutary warning to his followers. Of paramount importance to the success of his Movement, he insisted, was solidarity amongst the ranks, and he cautioned his students against indulging in any open contradiction of each other. He explained that any evidence of a lack of mutual respect amongst his initiators would only serve to detract from their status and in turn spread confusion about the meditation:

> Initiator carries an aura of all-knowingness around. The aura of all-knowingness. People like to believe an initiator because they hear that they have been trained.

> We never in our thought or speech or action ever depreciate the value of another initiator. Absolutely, we always hold him high in our mind, in our heart and ... in public. Very very very important, it's absolutely important.

He could have left the subject there, but he also had the responsibility to 'reach the ears first and then the mind and also pierce through the heart' of his students. He chose to entertain them into submission.

> What happened once upon a time.., two *pandits* started from home and they went into a new village and then they were entertained by a very hospitable host. And he went to one and wanted the introduction of the other and then he said, 'Oh, he's just a bull, no intellect, just a bull.' And he went with all respect to the other one and he wanted the other wise man, *pandit.* So he said, 'Oh, he's just a horse, absolutely idiotic, nothing.'
>   When the dinner time came, he prepared the dish for a bull and he prepared some good grass, very nicely cut, for the horse. And when the two dishes came each started to look to each other – 'Now what to do?' And then he requested them to start on their delicious dish and they would not eat. They just looked at each other.
>   He said, 'I asked you about him, so you said "He is a bull", and you said, "he is a horse" and this is the food beautiful, delicious food for the bull and

for the horse.'

Seemingly the problem of integrity was not restricted to that of his teachers; the Maharishi made it clear that he was also concerned with his own reputation:

> One initiator holds the other initiator down, either in his thought or speech or action, in public or in private, then what he is doing openly is misjudging the value of the founder who had trained him.

Not only was there to be no antagonism between initiators but they were also expected to live up to pretty high standards generally. Here was an area in which 'watering the root' was apparently not enough to ensure success. The Maharishi felt inspired to list the qualities that initiators should possess, what the 'man in the street' might expect from them:

> He expects from the initiator something more laudable, more remarkable, more ideal than he would expect from any other man, naturally.
>   Friendly and loving and appreciative of each other is ordinary human value, the members of the same club at least.

> People feel that a man who has the ability to give peace to the people and some spiritual experience and raise the level of consciousness, his level of consciousness would naturally be, if not much, at least a little higher than the normal and he would behave a little more humanly at least, if not divinely than other people.

But in order to cover the subject completely, he also offered guidance as to what should be done if differences of opinion occurred which created ill-feeling. One recommendation was to 'feel the body', the mental exercise of sensing an area of anxiety within the body and neutralizing it with calmness and patience. He further explained that by the contemplation of wrong thoughts or actions, the same erroneous behaviour is inculcated in the beholder. This advice gives an insight into the Maharishi's own behaviour. It explains the method by which he avoided confrontations and prevented discord. In an interview in 1967 he had been asked whether or not he ever became angry. His answer seemed almost too saintly to be believed but, seen in the light of the above, it becomes easier to comprehend. He said:

> I am concerned with the suffering of the world, but I don't become angry with those who are suffering (laughter – shrieks) because I know through love I could make them happy. I could make them meditate and love. And if I feel angry with them then they are suffering – they will suffer out of my anger more. So there is no reason for me to be angry on any account.[235]

The Maharishi had now to devise ways in which he might prevent his initiators from becoming angry, or at the least from expressing their anger. Although this might give them a reputation for equanimity it might also repress a fundamental need for self-expression and hence redouble the power of ill-feeling stored within. Rather than concern himself with the possibility of such accumulated stress, which might at some time find release in a torrent of uncontrolled rantings, he chose to confine his remarks to making the situation sound very simple and called the aid of an old Indian proverb:

> The sword will fail to serve where the needle will accomplish the goal. A big sword will prove to be useless and the needle will do the trick.[236]

One cannot but recognize the wisdom embodied in this saying, but the need to 'let off steam' seems to be an unavoidable fact of life.

In order to protect the teaching of his system of meditation from distortion, the Maharishi had devised a set of instructions to be learned 'parrot fashion' by his students. It was believed that this pre-formulated approach to instruction and checking would bring about the correct experience of meditation. These instructions are known as the 'checking notes', and have a series of numbered points which are supposed to cover every contingency that might arise. The initiator or checker, by memorizing the points, could then use them as a method for fault-finding. If the answer to a point was 'yes' then the checker could proceed to another numbered point. If the answer was 'no' then a different point would be used. In this way a universal procedure was instituted which would, at least theoretically, prevent any personal variations finding their way into the teaching of meditation: 'With all these thirty-eight, thirty-nine points of checking, training of checkers has become very easy and mechanical.'

In this attempt to keep his system of teaching free from impurities, the main aim was to prevent his students 'getting ideas' about themselves.

After the cloning process had been successfully completed, the Maharishi would then decide who most closely resembled the original. To these chosen students he would disclose the vehicles of meditation (the *mantras*) and the means of their selection. It might be presumed that possession of this knowledge of the *mantras* would in itself be enough to instruct someone in the method of his meditation, and since there are many who are deeply curious about the *mantras* and the method of their selection, why should they not have their curiosity satisfied? This would surely be a very direct method of fulfilling the Maharishi's desire to produce a significant increase in those who knew how to meditate. But the Maharishi looked at the situation from the completely opposite viewpoint. His concern was to ensure that the new initiate would know how to use the technique he or she was given: 'Use of the *mantra* is one technical thing which is the central core to the whole training programme.'

Accordingly, the ability to train someone in the correct use of the *mantra* is acquired before the specific details of the *mantras* are given. Another reason for confining information about the *mantras* to trained teachers was that if they were communicated in any way other than orally, mispronunciation would be likely to result.

Even this precaution, however did not totally prevent misunderstandings, for even amongst those who were taught under the auspices of the Movement, there was some confusion. The Maharishi guardedly acknowledged this situation:

> With experience it was found that some steps which were thought to be useful were no more useful, better they leave them. So some little change in the expression of instructions but that does not change the basic thing.

As an example of this confusion, he cited an occasion when an initiate asked to have her *mantra* checked by a novice initiator. Later, the matter came to the Maharishi's attention.

> Her *mantra* became very subtle, then it expanded, naturally it become lonnngggg… like that. And experiencing that long drawn *mantra* of two or three syllables, she thought that her *mantra* is changed and she took her *mantra* to be that lengthened state of the *mantra* which naturally was more charming. *Mantra* in its finer state – much more charming, and it came out to be two or three syllables, whereas her *mantra* was one syllable and because it happened to be more charming she picked it up.

The novice teacher had been unable to offer such a clear explanation, which all added credence to the Maharishi's claim that in order to teach meditation, it was necessary to become thoroughly familiar with both the practical and the theoretical aspects of his teaching. It is not necessarily a reflection on his sincerity or motives to observe that he had no intention whatever of loosening his hold over his system, and that come what may he would guard his secrets jealously. This knowledge of the *mantras* was the vital information that would turn his initiators into *bona fide* teachers of his brand of meditation and he saw to it that every precaution was taken to keep them in line.

18

———★———

FREE WILL OVER DESTINY

Although the Maharishi's training courses conformed to a structure of sorts, this did not inhibit his tendency to follow his own inimitable and spontaneous flow of ideas. Having proposed the basic topics, lectures would usually develop a life of their own. Sometimes he would tell a story, share an anecdote or quote from Indian scriptures, but mainly he would focus on the fundamental issues of meditation and its teaching. Themes would be examined and repeatedly re-examined, and through this process, a thorough revision of vocabulary resulted. The students attending the three months of lectures were eager to remember all that they had heard. Not all could afford the luxury of a tape recorder, and even those who had brought one had not foreseen the need to bring many dozens of blank tapes with them. The problem was remedied in an old-fashioned way, by taking written notes. The *ashram* had thoughtfully provided hard-back exercise books for the purpose, with a picture of the Maharishi on the front cover and the course date and location shown. There was so much to write about, including the theory of *mantras*, information regarding the Holy Tradition and 'Guru Dev', the celestial connection and philosophical concepts such as free will and destiny, not to mention the basic techniques of lecturing and teaching.

Each time any subject was discussed, different facets of the Maharishi's thinking would emerge. Of the broad array of topics, by far the most intriguing was that of the mysterious and seemingly magical *mantras*. These were the vital ingredients that set the Maharishi's method of meditation apart from other mental exercises. Continuously dwelling on a particular sight, smell or sound would seem like an act of concentration, but the Maharishi steadfastly maintained that concentration was not a part of his method. This leads one to suppose that the benefits of meditation are to be achieved by first saturating one's mind in the sound of the given *mantra* and then slipping into a state of blissful ease, devoid of thought. The poet Tennyson is said to have discovered a similar phenomenon. He found that if he repeated his own name sufficient times he would be transported into a beatific state of mind and freed from all anxiety.

The Maharishi trained his teachers to believe that only those personally trained by him could have the ability to teach this method of meditation. But on what basis did he make this assertion? Why use 'meaningless sounds' taken from Hinduism rather than some from any other religion. Come to that, why not choose *any* sound one preferred? One reason he gave was that his *mantras* had been passed from teacher to teacher over many thousands of years, that they sprang from an unbroken tradition of masters who possessed the correct knowledge concerning their selection:

> They are passed on from the master to the disciple in every generation and this is the teaching that concerns very fine levels of the whole creation. The theory of the *mantras* is the theory of creation. As from the unmanifest, manifest comes. So the basic structure of individual life is considered as a whole and the vibrations or the sound waves which would create soothing influence on the existing vibrations of the individual. A *mantra* may be just a word or a sound for one man, and that sound may become the *mantra* of another man. So the sound becomes a *mantra* by virtue of its quality to resonate with the existing impulse of the individual.[237]

So, not just any sound would serve as a vehicle for meditation; it would appear that an individual would resonate better with one particular sound than with another.

> Physics tells us everything is nothing but vibration, bundles of vibrations, specific permutations and combinations of the impulses ... That is what makes the individual life. A sound that will resonate with some other sound. See, if we play a tuning fork and a wire is strung on a particular tension starts ... huuuummmm. So this quality of resonance makes a sound, a suitable *mantra* for the individual.

But this statement assumes that the human form has the capacity to resonate. How could a solid body be made to resonate merely by the inaudible inner chanting of a *mantra* other than at a level of internal existence far too subtle to be appreciated in ordinary existence?

Taking the Maharishi's theory a step further, it must be assumed that a different *mantra* could be specified for each individual. But this would presume the existence and knowledge of an incalculable number of different *mantras*. If this were the case, in order to make a confident selection it would be necessary to make a very close examination of the subject. With what technology could such an examination be undertaken? The Maharishi provided a convenient and even plausible answer to this seemingly impossible conundrum. He taught his students that humanity could be grouped into categories and that one could with confidence specify the same *mantra* for anyone within each category. He illustrated this principle with an analogy:

> When the doctors infuse blood, transfusion of blood, they tally the sample with the specimen of the body. If the two samples match or correspond with each other, then that is the blood that will be transfused in that body, that's it. So the harmony between the vibrations of the body and the vibrations of the *mantra*, the harmony between them decides the suitability of the *mantra* to the individual.
>
> Through long practice of usages of these *mantras* for different types of people, certain universal formulae have been obtained and using those formulae of judgement the selection of a proper *mantra* is brought about on a very mass production level. Everything has been made easy, nothing is so much difficult.

As with most analogies, this one is useful only to a limited extent and cannot provide a complete understanding of the point. It overlooks, possibly deliberately, the question of why the individual should need to be given an infusion of something that he or she has not lost. It might also be argued that with so many references to the development of higher consciousness, it could be reasoned that the selection of *mantras* should be based upon the level of consciousness of the aspirant.

It is commonly held that whilst some words could reasonably be described as meaningless, the same is not true of thoughts. This did not stop the Maharishi from referring to a *mantra* (which he had defined as meaningless) as a 'thought':

> And when we have to experience the subtle states of a thought, then we must consider what quality of a thought we should take, what kind of thought we should take. And then we are very careful to select the suitable thought, suitable thought.
>
> The suitability of the thought lies not so much in the meaning of it, but more in its physical quality. And therefore the knowledge of the suitability of a thought for an individual is a very expert knowledge for which we depend on the tradition of our masters. What thought will suit what man? The tradition of masters is the most authentic place to take these suitable thoughts from. Authenticity from the tradition is the only measure which will give us some confidence about the absolute suitability of the *mantra*, of the thought.

This raises a matter of possible concern, for although the Maharishi had repeatedly reassured his audiences that his meditation was not a matter of faith, one finds that the crux of his teaching is that faith in the 'tradition of masters' is actually vital.

Should anyone be tempted to doubt his authority and decide to go their own way, he issued warnings which might unsettle even the most determined of dissenters. He claimed that the formula for selection of the 'thought' should to be foolproof, that using an incorrect *mantra* could result in disastrous consequences.

> If the *mantra* is right it means 100 per cent favourable effects will be multiplied millionfold as the *mantra* becomes finer and finer. If the *mantra* is not proper, not proper means maybe 5 per cent less than suitable, 10 per cent less than suitable, 50 per cent less than suitable, 1 per cent less than suitable and when *mantra* becomes very fine then 99 per cent suitable effect will become million times great. At the same time 1 per cent unsuitable effect will become million times great. That effect we certainly don't want.

By reinforcing time and again how highly technical and scientific this process was, he was gradually preparing his students for the time when they might understand the selection criteria. When in due course they became authorities on the subject, how were they to deal with people bent on finding out about this knowledge. The Master had a lot of experience in dealing with awkward situations and was in the position to share a few tips:

> We don't mention it from our side, but if asked, we ... are not in a position to say, 'We are not going to speak', so we speak about it and this is the point that we speak. It is in our favour to say, 'The correct choice of the *mantra* is highly necessary.'

The Maharishi explained that in the 'subtle regions of creation' the power of the *mantra* is tremendously increased:

> And then we say, 'For this reason we must have 100 per cent suitability of the word that we want to use during meditation.'
>
> We can also say one more thing: 'The value of gaining the contact with the Absolute is one value and until the mind has transcended the increasing power of the *mantra* to produce all good effect is another value.'

Stated more directly, the Maharishi was telling them not to disclose the method of *mantra* selection but to blind the enquirer with scientific-sounding pronouncements. If the criterion used for selection was consciousness, then why not say so openly? After all, every new initiate was also a potential candidate for becoming a teacher of meditation. Would it therefore not make sense to sow the seeds of knowledge as early as possible?

The assertion that the Shankaracharya tradition were the custodians of the *mantras* sounded remarkably plausible. It is highly probable that a monastic community would have amassed a number of secret disciplines and passed them on from successive teachers to disciples. However, since the post of Northern Shankaracharya had been vacant for some one and a half centuries, a break in continuity might well have occurred. Swami Brahmanand, the Maharishi's 'Guru Dev', had studied, not under a Shankaracharya, but under Swami Krishnanand Saraswati a *swami* of Shringeri Math. One could reasonably infer from this that it was he who passed on the knowledge of the *mantras* to Swami Brahmanand.

Along with the parrot-fashion learning of the checking points, students training to be teachers also had to learn a set of Sanskrit verses commonly referred to as the Holy Tradition. The intoning of these verses is an integral part of the initiation rites of Transcendental Meditation. If the new initiate asks about this ingredient of the initiation, he or she is likely to be reassured that it is only a list of previous masters of this meditation. It is curious that in all the available transcripts and translations of this *puja*, the name of Swami Krishnanand is not listed. On closer inspection the Holy Tradition is less a list of former teachers than a prayer to the Maharishi's 'Guru Dev'. Certainly, the names of others are recited, but they do not form anything like a complete record of a lineage of teachers.

An extract from the Holy Tradition is given in the Appendix to the Maharishi's commentary on the *Bhagavad-Gita*, Chapters 1-6. The verses listed form an invocatory prayer addressing both Hindu divinities and celebrated spiritual teachers of antiquity: Lord Narayana, Brahma (the creator God), Vaishistha, Shakti, Parashar (son of Shakti), Vyasa, Shukadeva, Gaudapada, Govinda, Shri Shankaracharya (disciple of Govinda) and Shankara's disciples (Padma-Padam, Hasta-Malakam, Trotakacharya and Vartikkar). To bridge the gulf of the innumerable centuries, reference is made to 'others' and to 'the Tradition of our Masters', and bringing the list almost up-to-date, the name of Brahmanand Saraswati is included. As a part of the *puja* ritual, the initiator bows to all of them.

To confirm the suspicion that the Holy Tradition is not just a listing of spiritual teachers but a devotional prayer, one need only take a ferry ride across the River Ganges from Shankaracharya Nagar to Swami Sivananda's Divine Life Society *ashram*, complete with *ayurvedic* dispensary. In his lifetime Swami Sivananda, a retired doctor, was highly regarded for his many good works and his writings, including a commentary on the *Bhagavad-Gita* and the *Brahma Sutras*. His devotional sect worship the *gurus* of their tradition and in their *Guru Vandana*, several verses are similar if not identical to those that were being memorized by students at Dhyan Vidhya Peeth, the Maharishi's *ashram*. These are quoted below:

I prostrate myself to Lord Narayana, Brahma, Vasishtha, Shakti, his son Parashara, Vyasa, Shuka, Gaudapada, Govindapada, his disciple Sri Shankaracharya, his disciples Padmapadacharya, Hastamalaka, Trotaka, Sureshwaracharya, the commentator, and all other Brahmavidya *Gurus*.

I salute Sri Shankara Bhagavatpada, the bestower of peace and auspiciousness to the world at large, the ocean of mercy, and the seat of all learning inculcated in the Shruti, Smriti and Puranas.

I adore, again and again, the Lord Siva who is Shankaracharya and the Lord Vishnu who is Badarayana [Bhagavan Vyasa], who wrote the Sutras [Vedanta] and the commentaries.[238]

One wonders just how many different communities lay claim to belonging to the Shankaracharya tradition.

The absence of The Beatles and other famous musicians on the 1969 course did not deter the Maharishi's devotees from occasionally lifting their voices in song. Accompanied by some tidy strumming on a guitar, a group of students performed devotional songs of their own composition (mainly in praise of the Maharishi and his teaching), and with zealous fervour they recited chosen verses of the Holy Tradition. Amongst the verses offered up, the name of one individual predominated, that of the Maharishi's 'Guru Dev'. Excitement ran high when it was learned that a film of the former Shankaracharya had come to light:

Jerry got Guru Deva's very deteriorated film renewed and revitalized. Yes, it has come and we will see it some day. It's very beautiful. It's just five or ten minutes film but it gives some shots of 'Guru Dev', so beautiful. Something very precious, beautiful, that you feel like it was yesterday.[239]

The subject of destiny loomed large in the teachings of Swami Brahmanand. How did his disciple translate this aspect of traditional Hindu thinking? How could this doctrine ever find itself in harmony with a belief in free will? Some years earlier the Maharishi had deliberated on this very subject, suggesting that unlike other species, man has freedom of action. But how could he reconcile this view with the apparently opposite view of man bound by destiny, a slave to fatalism? What was it to be, free will or destiny? His students awaited his verdict:

Actually these are the two names for the same thing. Two names for the same thing and what lies between the two names is some time distance. Some difference of time, some distance of time. With the time difference taken off, destiny and free will are the same thing.

Expanding this statement, he said that destiny is the direct result of actions taken in the past, actions undertaken in a state of free will, and that the influence of those past actions create circumstances in which further action is to be undertaken, also in a state of free will. He summarized this philosophy and at the same time offered his students a little Sanskrit tuition using a verse from Patanjali's *Yoga Sutras*:

Destiny may influence, but we are not compelled to be overthrown by the force of destiny. *Heyam dukham anagatam* – it will be good to remember this in the original Sanskrit.
    It means: Avert the danger that has not yet come.

To reinforce the meaning of this saying, the Maharishi pointed out that it adequately portrayed 'the play of free will against the force of destiny'. Evidently, by carefully predicting the effects of past actions, one could better assess what action to perform in the present, thus ensuring that potentially negative effects are minimized and positive effects maximized. If before deciding a course of action, sufficient thought is given to its likely outcome, one might free oneself from any unexpected reactions and, in consequence, be prepared.

As with any topic to which he referred, some mention of his meditation was never very far away. In this case he framed the practice of his meditation as an action that could avert the unwelcome dangers that had not yet come:

TM is absolutely conducted by cosmic intelligence, by the nature of life. Nature of life is to move more and more towards infinite. This nature of life pushes the mind on and on to the infinite. So most spontaneous action of minimizing activity which is Transcendental Meditation is the technique of living. That means, now here is the technique of living which is capable of raising man above the influence of his own doings of the past. Most spontaneous, most natural action of Transcendental Meditation which puts an end to activity, is the technique of action which cuts asunder the bondage of action in the past for the doer and establishes him high above the reach of his own doings of the past. This is free will over destiny. That's it!

With respect to past actions, his meditation technique was being prescribed as some kind of 'karma-buster'. But how could this be? If action always engenders reaction how could a simple relaxation method act as a buffer or shield to protect an individual from his or her just desserts? This appears to argue against the very fundamentals of the law of *karma*. Could someone escape the consequences of a criminal act just by sitting down to meditate? If this were so, might one also fail to derive rewards of past labours? According to his theory, not only is past *karma* destroyed, but also any need to mention destiny: 'Only those who do not meditate complain against destiny in their laziness to rise.'

The Maharishi had often said that by repeatedly gaining transcendental or pure awareness, a state of cosmic consciousness is developed. He postulated that if this higher state of consciousness could be brought about by the individual mind repeatedly submerging its identity within the cosmic mind, then one could naturally arrive at a state in which the heart becomes sufficiently expanded to give rise to a condition where cognition of the celestial can be achieved. One assumes that he was not speaking of an increase of the heart's actual physical size but of the capacity for love. This suggestion, that a person both hearty and loving has the innate ability to comprehend a world of angels and gods is a revelation indeed. But can his words be taken literally? Is this cognition of the celestial anything more than a grand intellectual play? Surely it needed more than a feeling or belief for him to be able to tell his students:

> The atmosphere about angels is so pretty that even though they have principally, and practically also, greater ability of performance and action, but their free will is hampered by the great prettiness of the atmosphere. Here in man the atmosphere is just enough to keep him hoping for more and more and more.
>
> Greater free will in the life of the angels is hampered by the much more valuable and more fulfilling environment of the angel world.

This suggestion of a heaven inhabited by angelic forms immediately raises questions concerning entrance to such a sphere. Those whose belief system encompasses the doctrine of reincarnation are likely to hope that at some time they too might enter such a divine world. How did the Maharishi feel about such ideas? What news had he from the 'great beyond'?

> The suffering at the time of birth and death is tremendous. That suffering is great, that's why there is no fun in getting to the pool of suffering over and over again. Very great suffering at the time of death and at the time of birth. And therefore even though the life of angels seems to be very alluring, but this is path to the angelic life, through so many births and deaths, simply horrible. It's just unbelievably horrible.

From these and the following remarks it appears that the Maharishi had vivid memories of a life before his birth in Jabalpur:

> Now imagine a house in darkness and you have to feel around every door
> and every bedroom and bathroom and everything and everything and just all
> in darkness, darkness. That is how terribly miserable will that state be, until
> you have located everything that there may be, and then you start living it.
> All that period of tremendous ignorance and trying to establish in that
> darkness, this is what happens when one enters the body.
>
> Then the faint fragile almost incomplete structure is there, the eyes are
> there but they don't open, the ears are there but they don't ... nothing. And
> then the sense of sight has to enter this dwelling house and then it has to find
> its place and proper ... sense of hearing and sense of smell and then the
> breath begins to flow and the lungs and all. Every aspect of the subjective
> personality has to feel its way and establish its new home in that lump of
> flesh.

It would be useful to know whether the Maharishi was indeed speaking
from experience or handing out second-hand concepts. The intimacy
with which he described the period before birth would lead one to think
that he was drawing on personal recollections, but in an interview some
two years previously, he had been most unforthcoming when asked
whether he could remember anything before his present birth. The
interviewer was rewarded with this cryptic remark: 'I can find out if I
want ...'[240]

On many a sensitive issue he would avoid offering a direct response,
apparently preferring to retain an air of mystery about himself. This
practised art of evasion could be interpreted in two ways; first, that since
his goal was to promote greater understanding about his meditation he
chose not to confuse the issue by being drawn into a discussion of
personal matters. The second option is less attractive: that by creating a
reputation of a man of mystery, he would draw greater attention to
himself, leaving his audience to speculate on what possible status and
powers he might possess.

Having warned his students of the suffering involved in birth and
death, he had partially quelled their eagerness for knowledge of
reincarnation. Nevertheless, the inevitability of death had to be faced
and his students wanted to know whether he believed that by meditating
one was better prepared for the 'very great suffering' of death? In
Sanskrit and in Hindi a word most closely connected with death is
prana. Although it has other, finer, definitions, this word is commonly
used to mean 'breath'. The Maharishi had this to say about it:

> *Prana* ceasing to function! Now, disease here and there is a grosser
> explanation, but *prana* ceasing to function is the phenomenon of death.[241]

He has claimed that in meditation the rate of breathing becomes shallower and upon entering the state of transcendental consciousness breath becomes minimized, and, very occasionally, suspended. He thus contends that by habituating the body to entertain states of little or no *prana* the experience of giving up one's life breath would be made that much easier. This sounds reminiscent of the Christian thought that one should 'die daily', although a different mode of action or prayer is advocated.

It has been seen that the Maharishi's prime task lay in his training of teachers of meditation. Every new topic raised should therefore have some relevance to this practice and he therefore showed his disciples how to harness his perception of death to their teaching practice. He chose to share another anecdote. Several years before, at a three-three-day camp in Benares, an elderly physician had come to him. In the course of his work the doctor had witnessed the deaths of many people and through their pulse he had sensed the great agony that their deaths apparently entailed. The Maharishi recalled the elderly doctor saying to him:

'Now it is my time, very near. I have come to you because you are the disciple of a very great master. Can you help me in dying in such a way that I don't suffer death?'

I said, 'It's very simple.'

He said, 'What?'

Just this one thing I said. 'If your body is habituated to maintain itself, even for a moment, without *prana*, and if this maintenance of the moment is a pleasant, blissful state of experience, then when your mind will go, when your body will start going out of the influence of *prana*, then you will really enjoy. It's only a matter of giving the body a habit of maintaining itself without *prana*, and this will happen if you can gradually minimize *prana*, if you can minimize *prana*, minimize *prana*, minimize *prana* and then come to a normal state of *prana* and minimize *prana*. This habit will give you the stand in that state where the *prana* is completely gone and the body is surviving.'

This description conjures up images of 'suspended animation', an idea beloved by science-fiction buffs. The tools of modern science would have no difficulty measuring such a state, so was the Maharishi suggesting that the physician go into a state of suspended animation? Almost! Whatever the dilemma, the answer was seemingly always the same. This man wanted to know how to die without suffering.

That was the question of him and I gave him Transcendental Meditation, but, on the level of his demand. Where is this question of death and where is

Transcendental Meditation? But in five minutes I connected him with his needs, which is the fulfilment of his needs. That's all!

This is what a teacher has to do, just the salesmanship. You sell your product to someone who needs it or to someone who doesn't need it. An intelligent businessman gains profit whether the rates go low or high in the market. He wins, whether the market is rising high or falling low. It doesn't matter, but he makes a profit.

So the Spiritual Regeneration Movement was really 'selling' spirituality to the people whether or not the need was there. This surprising assertion was probably a shock to his devotees, but few of whom had any use for doubts or divided loyalties, which would only led to discontentment. The measure of their future achievements would lie in how many people they brought to the practice of meditation.

Since lecturing was the key element in the sales strategy, it was of the utmost importance that all course participants derived sufficient inspiration and drive to go out and convince their audiences. For future reference trainee teachers were to keep copious notes on all aspects of lecturing and to record any useful points made by their fellow students:

> This is the time to be bee. We have been talking of being Being, now we are talking of being bees. One flower and pick up something nice, and the other flower and pick up something nice, and the other and pick up something nice.

By sharing their material the Maharishi felt that his students would find the responsibility of lecturing easier. The main role of lecturer was simply to make the audience crave the chance to be taught the Maharishi's system of meditation:

> We don't have even to create hunger, the man is hungry already. We just let him know that he is really hungry. Just information that there is Being and then information that it is possible to experience. Everyone knows the Being is there. Fine. But only he doesn't know how to get on to it. But just this one information that it is available by nothing else other than its own nature. Nature of the mind and nature of the Being, one glides into that, and this is enough.
>
> You can't imagine what a shock he gets. In all that you speak for ten minutes, you have been giving him ten shocks. Every information that you relay is a flash of knowledge to him.

PART III

The Enlightenment Business

19

NOTHING BUT THE SWEET TRUTH

As the spring 1969 Spiritual Guides' training course drew to a close, the Maharishi's students looked forward to a brief holiday in Kashmir. As if the shocks they had received during the course were not enough, their *guru* now announced that he wished to see them at their best. They took him at his word and dozens of bemused devotees cast off their jeans, sweatshirts and tennis shoes, and scrabbled through their luggage to find the most formal articles of clothing they could. Consciousness of the Self lost ground to self-consciousness as the race to outsmart each other took hold. This seemed to be the total antithesis of the Maharishi's philosophy, but he was determined that the 'class photograph', in contrast to one The Beatles appeared in with its hippie overtones, should this time depict his students as clean-cut academic types, conformist, conventional and thoroughly normal. Evidently he wished to distance himself from the contemporary trend towards individualism and free expression, and so regain the respectability his Movement had lost by his free association with the celebrities who contributed to his rise to fame.

Speculation over his retirement into a life of silence was refuelled by the announcement that one of his *brahmacharin*, Swami Satyanand, was to undertake a world lecture tour in his place. It looked to all concerned as though the present crop of students might well be the last the Maharishi would instruct, for it seemed that he had nominated his successor and could now disappear from sight.

In August 1969 a hirsute and denim-clad George Harrison gave an interview in which it sounded as though he still very much supported meditation.[242] It appeared that the feud that had erupted between The Beatles and the Maharishi might yet be overcome, but George stressed that having once involved himself in giving publicity to meditation, he now preferred to stay out of the limelight:

You can't say that going on the television and speaking to the press and doing things like that is a bad way to tell people about meditation. On the other hand, after being through all that, it was part of our everyday life. I wanted it to be quieter, much quieter. Anyway, the main thing was you asked whether it had ended or not – it's just that we physically left Maharishi's camp – but spiritually never moved an inch. In fact, probably I've got even closer now.

Not only was he still meditating but he was also still very active in his advocacy of its attendant philosophies. However, his style of presentation might have raised some eyebrows amongst the Maharishi's henchmen:

Well, again I'll quote Maharishi, which is as good as quoting anybody else, and he says 'For a forest to be green, each tree must be green', and so if people want revolutions, and you want to change the world and you want to make it better, it's the same. They can only make it good if they themselves have made it – and if each individual makes it himself then automatically everything's alright. There is no problem if each individual doesn't have any problems. 'Cause we create the problems – Christ said 'Put your own house in order', and Elvis said 'Clean up your own backyard', so that's the thing. If everybody just fixes themselves up first, instead of everybody going around trying to fix everybody else up like the Lone Ranger, then there isn't any problem.

According to Harrison, the Christian Church had failed to provide him with Christ consciousness and that only through his contacts with Indian thinking had he gained a proper understanding, a spiritual awareness:

Donovan said a great thing a while back, he said 'I never went to church much, but since I found the temple in my own mind I visit it very often.' Which is great. That's what all the meditation thing is about.

But what about those who might be sceptical about his unreserved recommendation of Hinduism and its by-product, meditation?

Vivekananda, who was one of the first swamis who came to the West, said 'Don't believe in anything, if there's a God we must see him, if there's a soul we must perceive it – it's better to be an outspoken atheist than a hypocrite.'

He was evidently up to his eyes in Indian philosophy and happy with it. But why had he opted to take a lower profile on the subject, when he obviously had so much to say?

The more I know about it, the more pointless it is to say anything because I realise how ignorant I am about the whole thing. There's so much there to know that it's ridiculous.

The youth culture, oblivious of the image changes occurring in the far-off Himalayan foothills, still perceived meditation to be a part of the hippie culture and was happy to accept advertising copy from the Maharishi's movement. Over the page from George Harrison's interview, sandwiched between advertisements for sex magazines, films and toys, appeared the following small ad:

Transcendental Meditation

Transcendental Meditation is a simple technique which takes the attention naturally from the ordinary thinking level to the source of thought, the Inner Being. This automatically results in the expansion of the conscious mind.
STUDENTS INTERNATIONAL MEDITATION SOCIETY
Founder MAHARISHI MAHESH YOGI
for information write to SIMS ... London SW6[243]

With the Maharishi no longer the subject of media attention, his disappearance into silence would have gone virtually unnoticed. His meditation technique was already being dismissed as yesterday's fad and had it not been for certain developments, his organization might soon have fallen into disarray. Whatever plans the Maharishi entertained for his retirement, they were soon to evaporate. Whether it is true, as rumours circulated by his detractors had it, that he fled from India to evade inspection of his tax returns, or whether he merely wished to revitalize his ambitious teacher-training programme, plans were being made for his return to the West. This bold U-turn provoked a degree of gossip, for how could he say one thing and do another? One possible answer comes from his perception of non-attachment:

> The art of gaining self-consciousness and rising to the state of cosmic consciousness is the art of remaining free from the binding influence of speech.[244]

With the announcement of his re-emergence came news that there was to be a change in the presentation of his teaching; a strenuous overhaul of the vocabulary was to be effected. Henceforth his students would have to familiarize themselves with radically revised terms of reference. The scene was being prepared for the introduction of the Master's new brain-child, the restructuring of his philosophies under the banner of 'The Science of Creative Intelligence (SCI)'. The idea was, that by de-emphasizing the religious connotations of his teaching, it would gain greater acceptance and an increase in initiations would follow.

In February 1970, at Stanford University in the United States, the very first SCI course was held, not by the Maharishi, who was holding another teaching-training course at Shankaracharya Nagar, but by his deputy, SIMS boss Jerry Jarvis.

In an age increasingly dependent on the opinions of 'experts', major companies frequently enlisted the support of a white-coated scientist to endorse their products. The Maharishi, with his degree in physics, hoped to highlight the demonstrable aspects of his teaching and slowly but surely he was gaining ground. In March 1970 a scientific paper on the effects of the practice of Transcendental Meditation had been published in the journal *Science*. Scientists had long been at loggerheads with unproven systems of belief, so the Maharishi had to make sure that his teaching was purged of any allusions to topics of a mystical nature. This was almost impossible, for how could he even begin to prove his claims about reincarnation, the existence of celestial beings and magic powers? Nevertheless, the belief that the Maharishi's meditation might yet receive scientific verification and acceptance contributed a new impetus to his mission.

In June 1970, a summer course was convened at a hotel in the wooded location of Poland Springs, Maine. To their surprise, students discovered that in order to meet with the Maharishi, they had first to dress in their best evening wear! As with previous camps, the emphasis of the programme was on gaining increased familiarity with longer periods of meditation, and an extensive programme of rounding was therefore commenced. Lectures again found the Maharishi offering reasoned explanations for experiences of 'unstressing', along with tasters of his new Science of Creative Intelligence. He declared that henceforth expressions of a religious or spiritual nature should be set aside in favour of scientific terminology. To some his attitude might have appeared somewhat dictatorial, but for many of his American students the news of an academic bias was not at all unwelcome.

After Poland Springs, he moved on to Humboldt State College in Arcata, California. The desire to focus his followers' attention on his new approach resulted in the Maharishi's involvement in a succession of advanced meditators' and teacher-training courses. Since plans to present his ideology in exclusively scientific terms were not yet firmed up, it was difficult for the Maharishi to resist the temptation to revert to past patterns of speech. Though God now became renamed as 'the source of creative intelligence' and the state of supreme knowledge had become 'unity consciousness', God consciousness and the celestial still received the occasional mention. Those attending these formative 'scientific' lectures at Humboldt participated in an uneven struggle to forge links between the old SRM style of presentation and the new, streamlined 'science'.

Towards the end of the 1960s the interest in things Eastern had stimulated a brisk trade in Indian artifacts and also created openings for purveyors of rival forms of *yoga* and meditation. The Maharishi found himself under ever greater pressure to explain why his followers should accept only his interpretations of *yoga* philosophy. In order to keep ahead of the competition, he sought to dissuade any of his students from taking to Hindu devotional teachings.

It would be useful to acquaint oneself with a reliable definition of the word '*yoga*', since in these days it is so frequently used merely to describe a particular branch of *yoga* dealing with physical exercises. The earliest known definition of the word *yoga* is to be found in a Sanskrit work of some antiquity entitled '*Yogadarshanam*' and commonly referred to as the '*Yoga Sutras* of Pajanjali'. The second verse reads: '*yogash chitta-vritti-nirodhah*' '*yoga* [is] mind-activity-restraint'. Since sutras are statements made with least words, a clearer reading could be '*Yoga* is the state of consciousness brought about by choosing to slow the mind's thinking process and bring it to a halt'.

Citing the *Yoga Sutras* as the authoritative text on *yoga*, the Maharishi put forward the view that the 'eight limbs' (*ashtanga*) of *yoga* referred to in the *Yoga Sutras* need not be understood as steps as has been commonly suggested, but as different systems. By the practice of his meditation he claimed that the benefits of all the different systems could be derived simultaneously:

> With all these experiences on our personal level we understand Patanjali to have advocated only Transcendental Meditation, the soul of all the *yogas*. This is *yoga* philosophy. We are not responsible for the misinterpretations of *samadhi*, and if misinterpretations have become common everywhere, we can deplore the whole situation and start refreshing the whole atmosphere. If everything has gone wrong ... Someone in India said to me, in open lecture like this, and he said 'You mean to say that all these saints who have gone by were wrong and you only are right?' I said, 'When I see your life, I am only concluding that this new voice only is right and all the old voices from wherever they came, they must have come from the field of ignorance!'[245]

But the man referred to was justified in his question. It is true to say that many highly-regarded individuals have advocated detachment and surrender as the path to liberation. The Maharishi, however, was in no mood to surrender his control:

> Whosoever advocated concentration, control, the need of detachment, renunciation for enlightenment, whosoever he was, he didn't know what he

was talking about. Whosoever he may be, he may be God, he may be God's incarnation speaking from heaven, but we'll say 'Please stop! Let us hear the voice of the earth.'[246]

Having stated his position unambiguously, he was obviously prepared to stand alone in his interpretation of the words of the wise. Yet his own fellow disciple, His Holiness Shankaracharya Shantanand Saraswati, was one of those who commended the role of renunciation stating:

Whatever one sees in creation, all that lives and moves – one should use it fully and enjoy the Absolute in everything, but one should enjoy it with renunciation.[247]

In the same lecture, the Shankaracharya shed further light on the topic:

The creation is such that everything has a purpose and must fulfil its function; so it must keep circulating, it must be used. Use everything, and give up the idea that you are renouncing. Don't hold on to anything in this creation; that can only be done by this final renunciation of giving up the idea that you have anything.[248]

In spite of the popularity of other *yoga* teachings, the Maharishi resolutely stood by his claim that they were all based upon misunderstandings. Most of the rival Indian teachers who had aroused the interest of Westerners, were predisposed in favour of *mantra japa*, the chanting of auspicious *mantras*. The differences between the Maharishi's teaching and the other systems were such that the subject was destined to become contentious. The predicament was increased by George Harrison's decision to make public his association with the Radha Krishna Temple, a devotional cult which promoted the repetition of their free 'transcendental *mantra*', '*Hare Rama, Hare Krishna*'.

In a bid to reaffirm his position and make his opinions abundantly clear to his followers, the Maharishi restated his views on this particular practice:

The principle of these chantings, long hours in continuous chanting, the principle of this is that the mind is wandering by nature. It is like a monkey jumping from branch to branch all the time. When we want to control the monkey it's very difficult to control the monkey because it always jumps off, always jumping on. If there could be a way to get the monkey tired very much, give him such fast running that he gets tired and then he sits in one place ... Mind is a monkey, we want the mind to be not wandering, mind wants steady. What we do, give it such heavy work, one word keep on repeating, '*duun, duun, duun, duun*', all the time all the time all the time. The tongue becomes tired, the lungs become tired, the mind becomes tired, the whole thing collapses.[249]

His explanation greatly amused his followers and provided them with much-needed ammunition with which to launch a broadside at anyone daring to suggest that their way was better than the Maharishi's. According to their teacher, not only were these other paths relatively ineffective but they also spread confusion. The Maharishi suggested to his Humboldt audience that as a result of an incorrect understanding of spiritual existence, his countrymen in India had fallen prey to a philosophy which opposed material advancement:

> Such a beautiful country, the source of all knowledge, where the *Vedas*, the truths of existence, are preserved. But look at that country, what has become of it? All lethargy and this and this and this. It's waking up now, but it should have not fallen into that tragedy of ignorance.[250]

These were harsh words from a man of love, peace and flowers. Perhaps this foray into the arena of mud-slinging had unsettled him, for he then softened, adding in the sweetest of tones that the chanting of the 'Hare Krishna' *mantra*, whilst having 'good meaning', was 'not very comfortable'. Meanwhile the 'Krishnas' and their elderly leader Swami A.C. Bhaktivedanta were, for their part, busy running down the Maharishi and his claims. The matter was additionally complicated in that they too laid claim to a tradition of masters going back to Lord Krishna and claimed that their *mantra* could bring the initiate to higher states of consciousness.

The Maharishi had the habit of illustrating his ideas by reference to nearby objects, such as the microphone or a particular flower. In his explanations concerning differing states of consciousness, many a bloom had been toyed with, scrutinized and dismembered before being scattered about. Using the anatomy of a flower he postulated, in the language of his Science of Creative Intelligence, the difference between outer and inner reality:

> Beautiful golden flower, but if we put it to analysis what we find is every fibre of this is nothing but colourless sap. Beautiful light green stem, if we put to analysis, every fibre of this will be nothing but colourless sap. All the various things will be found, nothing but colourless sap, all the various colours. Now, on the surface it is beautiful golden colour, underneath, colourless sap. This we say when we don't appreciate the colourless on the colour, we only see yellow, [we don't] see the colourless on the surface, but because every fibre of this is nothing but the colourless sap, therefore the colourless sap is even on the surface. It's not only at the depth, it is also on the surface. This is the reality of this, that even though we don't see the colourless sap we see only the golden colour, but the reality of all the golden colour is that even when we see it's golden, the colourless is there even on

the surface and even at the depth. When our vision is dominated by the golden then we don't comprehend the colourless, but if our vision is cultured enough or refined enough to cognize the reality of this golden colour, it will cognize golden colour and colourless sap, both on the surface of this. Because that is the reality.[251]

Continuing this tireless, timeless explanation, he asked concerning the colourless sap: 'Where do we find it?' Those who had been paying proper attention should have immediately answered: 'On the surface and at the depth!' But this would be to assume that they already enjoyed familiarity with the state of unity consciousness. The master knew otherwise and counselled them accordingly:

> We go to the root and there is a root and then the finer root and finer root and finer root and finer root. At end of the finest hair of the root there is that drop of pearl, a pearl, a dewdrop-like colourless sap, a crystal colourless sap which has not yet become the root, but is now ready to become transformed into a root. It has separated itself from the soil it has not yet become the root.

In introducing the idea of 'the colourless sap' as a metaphor for divinity, the Maharishi was setting the stage for a future discourse on the abstract. He wished to communicate exactly what it was like to be established in the state of consciousness beyond God consciousness, that which he had dubbed 'unity'. The capacity to live this state of consciousness would come, he promised, when meditators' nervous systems became 'modified', a condition brought about by the removal of 'impurities'.

Amongst many earnest established meditators, competition to be first to exhibit signs of cosmic consciousness had become rife. The race was on to see the sap on the surface, and to this end they closely scrutinized the master's daily routine in the hope of finding clues to help them accelerate their evolution. Those who had not already taken to a strict vegetarian diet, now thought again. Those who smoked tobacco, drank alcohol or used non-prescribed drugs, now had a good incentive to clean up their systems. But in this desperate bid to root out impurities, hidden dangers lurked, for in trying too hard they might lose interest in the material charm of life and themselves become colourless, sapped of individuality and personal initiative.

The Maharishi had previously made the road to illumination sound so much easier to comprehend and had used the analogy of a darkened room being lit by the mere flick of a switch (the practice of his meditation) and in the 'light' (of higher consciousness) the entire realm of forms and phenomena being made clear. In his use of this analogy he was following a time-honoured method of teaching, as demonstrated in this venerated analogy: in a darkened place, fear could well ensue from the belief that a snake has been seen in the grass, but with light the snake may well be found to have been nothing but a stick. The Maharishi wanted his students to realize that the material world can only be fully understood when spiritual illumination is gained and that the diversity of creation is then found to be just the emanations of the eternal Absolute (the source of creative intelligence). His contemporary, His Holiness Shankaracharya Shantanand Saraswati also used this light and dark analogy to convey his essentially religious message:

> If a coiled piece of rope is lying where there is not enough light, one may think it is a snake. Then with the thought that it is a snake there comes a fear of death, but that can be removed by a flood of light – this knowledge that it is not a snake.
>
> When by the light of discrimination one understands that this is not real, and that it is all a manifestation of God himself – the Lord Almighty – then one knows that everything is God himself. All that we can see is not the world but God himself.[252]

The Maharishi had frequently described truth as like an iceberg, with only a small fraction of the whole visible. He himself adhered to a policy of using 'iceberg' truth in being fairly selective about what he made public. For this attitude he most certainly had scriptural support, for in the *Bhagavad-Gita* lies the message:

> Those deluded by the qualities of Nature are attached to the functions of the qualities. The man of perfect knowledge should not unsettle the foolish one who is of imperfect knowledge.[253]

It would be reasonable to assume that information one might receive from someone in a higher state of consciousness would only be as useful as one's ability to utilize it fully. The sentiment embodied in this verse of *Gita* is not without parallels; the same principles seem to be embodied in the Bible's 'Cast ye not your pearls before swine.' But since truthfulness is one of three prerequisites for becoming or remaining a Hindu (the other two being harmlessness and a sincere desire to know God), it is unthinkable that Lord Krishna was offering a defence for dishonesty.

At Humboldt the Maharishi offered his followers a formula by which they might better understand truth:

> Many people say, 'I am truthful and that's why people dislike me because I say something on their face.' Truth is not characterized by whips. If you say a truth, fine that the truth is there, but it should have some sweetness to it.

Manu said – Manu, the first law-giver to human race – Manu he said, about speech he said '*Satyam bruyaat, priyam bruyat, na bruyat satyam apriyam*' – 'Speak the truth, speak that is sweet, don't speak the truth that is not sweet.' Not that you can take liberty with truth and massacre the whole field of behaviour. The truth, simple, natural which is supporting life, which is nourishing life. Truth is always life-supporting if it is really truth but it must come from a melted heart and not from a very unconcerned mind.[254]

This statement is dynamite! Certainly it would not go down in the courts of justice where truths are frequently revealed which are far from sweet. Strangely enough, the Maharishi, had himself told only half the truth about this very verse for it continues with the words:

'*Priyam cha na anritam bruuyaat esah dharmah sanatanah.*' In the Penguin Classic version of *The Laws of Manu* the verse (in its entirety) is translated with an altogether different emphasis:

A man should tell the truth and speak with kindness; he should not tell the truth unkindly nor utter lies out of kindness. This is a constant duty.[255]

Furthermore the translators ascribe this work (known variously as *Manu*, *Manusmriti* or *Manu Samhita*) to no one author:

The Laws of Manu, like all other works we have from the ancient period of India, was composed by members of the social class (*varna*) called Brahmins or 'Priests'. Indeed, the text is not only *by* priests but to a large extent *for* priests.[256]

Central to any attempt to understand the Maharishi is the need to identify his definition of truth. It is evident from his remarks about the need to speak only 'sweet truth' that he himself practised a form of self-censorship, but just how far this process impeded his message is less clear. The demand that truth should always be 'sweet' could present some very real barriers to effective communication. For instance, how could one relate news of a misdemeanour so as to prevent its recurrence?

If the wrongs of some other people come out, that means the wrong was stored inside. It just tells the structure of the heart, what is contained inside there. So if someone never speaks ill of others, that means he has a pure heart, doesn't have the wrong.[257]

It might, of course, also indicate someone's wish to project an image of purity! The Maharishi continued:

Someone does some wrong, something wrong was done by some man…Why should I bring that wrong through thinking or remembering and try to keep it in my heart? And if I speak, that means I had stored something of that and if wrong is stored then the heart is not pure. It just indicates what kind of storage is there, whether purity is stored or impurity is stored or what is there. Speaking ill of others means first, transplant the wrong of his heart in our heart, transplant the wrong of his mind to our mind and then let that plant grow into a tree till it comes out, manifold it comes out.

The whole process is dragging to evolution, it drags us down. That's why amongst all the things Lord Krishna said to Arjuna is 'I know you are a good recipient or deservant of this knowledge, because I haven't known from you any wrong of anyone.'[258]

The philosophy of speaking sweetly and never doing anyone down has a certain appeal, but it presumes that the individual concerned is already living an exhalted state of consciousness where others' wrong-doings do not impact on him. Or were his students to take his ideas on truth as implicit spiritual instruction, and believe that by speaking nicely they would quicker evolve? That one of his audience explicitly stated that he had never experienced bliss, seems to indicate that not all his followers were yet able to follow the Master's dictum without strain.

20

— ★ —

RESEARCH AND DEVELOPMENTS

But for the shortage of trained teachers of his Transcendental
Meditation, the Maharishi might well by 1970 have been passing
his time in the seclusion of some silent cave in Himalayas of northern
India. His *ashram*, a symbol of his success, had been left in the hands of
his closest devotees and *brahmacharin*. One young Western student, an
Australian named Bevan Morris, had taken the unprecedented step of
requesting the Maharishi to accept him formally as a *chela*. In
preparation for the time when his master might have specific tasks for
him, Bevan was to remain at the *ashram* and become acquainted with
the rigours of his vocation. Custom decreed that as a *brahmachari* he
must take on the traditional garb and habits of a monk and in addition to
wearing ankle-length robes he also grew his beard and hair long. Since
courses had been temporarily suspended at Shankaracharya Nagar, only
the occasional visitor came to trespass on the solitude of the *ashram*.
Those wanting an interview with the Maharishi were advised that he
was presently in the United States of America, and in the absence of the
Master it fell to those who served him to undertake the duties of
lecturing and teaching meditation.

In late October 1970, a two-and-a-half-month teacher-training camp
was to be held at Estes Park, Colorado. The basic components of the
teacher's kit remained largely unaltered: checking points to memorize,
familiarization with material for lectures, learning the *puja* ceremony,
and of course receiving knowledge of the magic *mantras*. Course
participants were presented with copies of the *Orange Book* containing
not only a full rendering of the Holy Tradition (in Sanskrit and English)
but also the bonus of a commentary on its content. Having perfected
their pronunciation and presentation of the *puja*, trainee teachers hoped
to receive instruction about the *mantras* from the Master himself. But
before that they had first to complete one last piece of outstanding
business, the signing of a pledge. The pledge amounted to an oath of

silence concerning the hidden aspects of the Maharishi's teaching, and since the pledge was couched in legal phraseology, the commitment had, in addition to moral overtones, perhaps even legal implications too.

Although the Maharishi was said to be working on the remaining chapters of the *Bhagavad-Gita*, rumour had it that he had already started work on a commentary of another Hindu scripture, the *Brahma Sutras*. It had been some years since the publication of his last book and speculation was rife as to when a new one would be launched. While he was spending time on these projects his national leaders directed the administration of his organizations, dealing with publicity, the co-ordination of courses and the routine task of running the numerous national centres. As supplies of his commercially-released lectures dwindled, followers had no choice but to attend meditation meetings in order to hear the Master's voice on coveted audio tapes of uneven sound quality. But so long as it was the Maharishi talking, nobody was likely to protest about the quality or content.

Information regarding the Maharishi's whereabouts and plans were becoming increasingly hard to come by, and they were only communicated in hushed whispers amongst the privileged *cognoscenti*. This situation happened to coincide with news that John Lennon had been speaking out against him in an interview with *Rolling Stone* magazine.

> There was a big hullabaloo about him trying to rape Mia Farrow and trying to get off with Mia Farrow and a few other women and things like that.[259]

It was these allegations that had provoked John to write a song disparaging his former teacher, entitled 'Sexy Sadie'.

> That's about the Maharishi, yes. I copped out and I wouldn't write 'Maharishi what have you done, you made a fool of everyone,' but now it can be told, Fab Listeners.[260]

Lennon still had a lot of influence on public opinion, and those of his fans who had become meditators were caught in a confusion of loyalties which a timely denial by the Maharishi might well have averted. But instead of tackling the rumours head-on, the Maharishi's supporters, at least in private, attempted to discredit Lennon's position, pointing out his much-publicized use of drugs and his discontent with life in general. It was easy for them to put such outbursts down to severe 'unstressing'. John complicated the situation further by readily admitting that he still, albeit infrequently, practised meditation.

Now that the Maharishi seldom made public appearances, his organizations were taking ever greater responsibility for the spread of his meditation technique. Within the Movement, the pyramid of power that had begun with the training of teachers and checkers, was by now spreading to encompass the ranks of volunteers who manned the typewriters and telephones. The emerging hierarchy was based roughly on two criteria – how long a person had meditated and their age – whilst additional merit points were awarded to those who had received personal instruction from the Master and to those in possession of the rare advanced techniques.

As the months passed, it soon became clear that the Master had more important things to do than involve himself in the day-to-day business of his centres. For those with no inclination to become teachers of meditation, the way to his presence seemed to be permanently barred. If one had the time and the money, the most likely way to meet him was to apply for a place on a teacher-training course. But these might be anywhere, for the Maharishi was always on the move; sometimes he was in the USA, sometimes in Europe. It was difficult to guess where he would be next.

With the decision to press on with the SCI initiative, those meditators with scientific backgrounds suddenly found themselves very much in demand and given ready access to the Maharishi. But their job was not easy, for no objective criteria had been established by which the various states of higher consciousness could be distinguished from each other. His scientists were therefore in the unenviable position of looking for quantifiable effects of meditation. Westerners had long been intrigued by stories of the feats of *yogis* from the East: tales of mystics lying on beds of nails, of *yogis* with the ability to suspend their breath and being buried alive for days at a time. And there was a rumour that the Maharishi had himself at least once offered to demonstrate the skill of walking on water. It seems he had a change of mind, but the idea that he had miraculous powers had students looking for evidence of his abilities. One student reported to me their conviction that he had 'vanished', only to reappear moments later. Could the scientists prove these powers, however?

At the Guru Purnima celebrations at Amherst, USA, on the night of the full moon, Friday, 9 July 1971 the Maharishi narrated a short tale about his master. Whilst talking about him, he assured the assembled disciples that his 'Guru Dev' had lived a 'life in unity' (the highest state of consciousness of the seven referred to by the Maharishi). He then confided that it was he who had coined the expression 'His Divinity' in favour of 'His Holiness' as a means of glorifying his master. At the appropriate time, those attending the celebrations were invited to make offerings to the departed master, in the belief that they might share something of his rare state of purity. Attempting to explain how it was possible to derive such a blessing from one who had cast off his body, the Maharishi asserted: 'Exceptional is always to any rule.'

At the First Symposium on the Science of Creative Intelligence, conducted at the University of Massachusetts in Amherst towards the end of July, scientist R. Buckminster-Fuller proclaimed:

> Our young world at first manifested great abhorrence for the non-truth, the superficial misleading information about customs, and now that young world has gone beyond just being dismayed and being disapproving of the non-truth, but is demonstrating in this wave of inspiration by Maharishi, demonstrating its yearning and its determination for humanity to survive on this planet. Very deep forces are operative here, the forces of the great intellect of the universe itself. This is the news. It's not easy to report in the newspaper this kind of news, but this is the news![261]

In addition to being the creator of the geodesic dome, Buckminster-Fuller was also well known as a scientist, architect, mathematician and philosopher. It was a great coup for the Movement to have him on stage for two whole days. The Maharishi gave the following response: 'You are a great inspiration…. The message Mr Fuller brings is the message of fuller life.'[262]

Buckminster-Fuller declared:

> What makes Maharishi beloved and understood is that he has manifest love. You could not meet with Maharishi without recognizing instantly his integrity. You look in his eyes and there it is.[263]

At a second symposium on SCI a month later, this time held at Humboldt State College, an example of how closely the Maharishi's followers were in tune with his ideas came in his response to Nobel Prize-winning chemist Melvin Calvin's dissertation on atoms and his explanation that 'stereospecific autocatalysis means that molecules are capable of inducing their own generation in highly geometrically specific fashion'. The Maharishi proclaimed with some enthusiasm:

> It's so beautiful. One expression of an outstanding scientist innocently reveals the essential nature of creative intelligence … The functioning of creative intelligence is such that under similar circumstances, similar results occur. Just this phenomenon explains why there is harmony in creation, not

chaos. The apple tree grows only into apple fruit; it doesn't produce guavas. But if the circumstances changed, grafting could produce guavas. The infinite flexibility of creative intelligence maintains its stereo-specific quality.

There is something definite; nothing is random, and it is this specific value of creative intelligence which automatically carries out evolution everywhere.[264]

As part of the renewed thrust for credibility, moves were being made to institutionalize the Science of Creative Intelligence and in September 1971 the Maharishi International University was founded in Goleta, California. The writing was on the wall that the spiritual orientation of the movement was fast being superseded by a drier, altogether more intellectual approach. A polarization of attitudes ensued with some members sensing that a great loss would result from the changing ethos, whilst others, who had formerly felt a little uncomfortable with the Maharishi's mystical leanings, allowed themselves a sigh of relief. The revised vision of possibilities contained no hint of esotericism (a word frequently used by his meditators as a term of derision).

> Although there are certainly many things in the world to be put right, we shall not be able to accomplish this humane ideal by merely reshuffling the environment. It will never humanly succeed until we can see and appreciate that environment at its full value, until we can envision all its possibilities with expanded mind and heart so that they may be actualized to the advantage of everyone and everything in nature.[265]

The publication in Britain of Anthony Campbell's scientifically oriented perspectives on TM reaffirmed the new direction and alerted those outside the organization to the change in emphasis.

Meanwhile, the Maharishi's followers were facing a common objection to the idea of meditation – that it appeared to be a selfish activity centred solely on personal gain. Jokingly the Maharishi would agree with this view, but contended that only by first taking care of the self could one attend to others. Notwithstanding this rationalization, his students still found themselves targeted for criticism. At a European course held at Kössen, Austria, in the autumn of 1971, the Maharishi is said to have offered the following observations:

> Naturalness is the basis of effectiveness. If one poses to be something else, one loses the charm of naturalness. The result is .that one accumulates stress. We do not think of life ... we live it. We do not think of others too much. We do not think of ourselves too much. We just behave in a natural way. Don't make moods ... wondering what anyone thinks of us.[266]

But what of criticism, how were meditators to respond to possibly well-intentioned attempts to offer advice?

> We do not live life on the remarks of others. It is enough that we are naturally helpful to others. What others think of us is not our concern... it is their concern. If we are weak, we will always put ourselves at the whim of others. We do not base our lives on the opinions of others. But if we are not clear in our conscience then we will always be weak and will always mind the looks and remarks of other people. It is the weakness of individuality if it always looks to others. It is important only that we radiate life. Every individual must be a joy to himself, to his family and to his society.[267]

On 8 January 1972 the Maharishi proclaimed the new year as the Year of the World Plan and at his new base in Mallorca, Spain, dedicated his efforts to instructing a new breed of initiators to oversee the plan's implementation. At this time there were no more than 1000 people trained to teach his meditation, but with an estimated world population of approximately 3.6 billion, it was calculated that he needed to train 3.6 million teachers and to create a total of 3000 'World Plan Centres' for them to use.

The World Plan had seven major objectives:

1. To develop the full potential of the individual
2. To improve governmental achievements
3. To realize the highest ideal of education
4. To eliminate the age-old problems of crime and all behaviour that brings unhappiness to the family of man
5. To maximize the intelligent use of the environment
6. To bring fulfilment to the economic aspirations of individuals and society
7. To achieve the spiritual goals of mankind in this generation[268]

These objectives, though laudable enough, begged the question of how they could possibly be fulfilled. Predictably enough, the practice of Transcendental Meditation was central to the proposed solution, but the Maharishi had another card up his sleeve, an adjunct to meditation, a prerecorded lecture course in his new Science of Creative Intelligence.

In early 1972 he spent a fairly long time in Italy at the resort of Fiuggi Fonte. Although the world's press continued to give coverage to the claims of his disciples, the Maharishi himself had, to all intents and purposes, gone underground. In the company of highly protective devotees, he contemplated ways by which he could gain greater popularity for his teaching. In the USA, a move to introduce the practice of Transcendental Meditation into a number of schools found little resistance. This led to a multi-pronged approach towards educationalists, politicians and the military, who all evinced progressively greater interest.

The SCI symposia continued, with the Maharishi flanked by an impressive array of speakers eminent in their respective fields, in addition to Buckminster-Fuller and Melvin Calvin, they included Marshall Macluhan, Nobel Prize-winner Donald Glaser, an Apollo 9 astronaut, Rusty Schweikart, and many others. Those who attended the symposia could hardly have failed to notice the onset of age in the face of the Maharishi. Some even suggested that he was beginning to resemble his aged master. Whether or not he was losing any personal vitality, his proven ability to sustain a torrents of words and ideas remained largely undiminished. The fact that his lectures were becoming increasingly abstract in content was generally regarded as evidence of his ability to present his 'Vedic knowledge' in a scientific manner.

The symposia attracted considerable interest and support. Coupled with the introduction of the teaching of SCI came a resurgence of interest in his stated belief that if a small percentage (as little as 1 per cent) of the world's population took to practising his system of meditation, crime would decrease and world peace would result – a notion that had by now found a label, the Maharishi Effect. Even though the investigation of the Maharishi Effect could not hope to quantify states of higher consciousness, it did provide his scientists with a concept that they felt *could* be measured. To start the ball rolling, researchers set about gathering data related to physiological changes perceived in meditators. They reported their observations: decreased respiration leading to decreased consumption of oxygen, lowering of the metabolic rate, reduction in cardiac output, decrease in the arterial concentration of sodium lactate, specific EEG changes, increased skin resistance to electricity and faster reaction time, all of which were seen as indicators of greater relaxation. Although these findings led to much rejoicing amongst his followers, they were not exactly earth-shaking, and were a long way from establishing evidence that meditators experienced any altered state of perception. Nevertheless the Maharishi and his movement, eager to capitalize on the findings, interpreted them as conclusive scientific evidence that TM worked.

Of the researchers into the effects of TM, not all were committed followers, and few, even of those who were dedicated to the Maharishi, wished to see their findings misrepresented. The research which was most quoted by the Movement had been undertaken by Dr Keith Wallace and Dr Herbert Benson, and the latter was quick to dissociate himself from some of the extravagant claims. His research had shown him that the benefits gained through the practice of TM might well be gained by the use of a word other than a TM *mantra.* He was not alone in feeling that the preliminary findings were far from conclusive. But the 'science' was in its infancy and steps were still being taken to accumulate supportive data, so there were few bold enough, as yet, to scorn the Maharishi's claims to scientific verification publicly.

Although the movement's attempts at scientific validation stimulated a new interest in meditation, the introduction of TM into schools was another matter entirely. Opposition to the Movement was mounting. Some people were openly hostile to the scheme, fearful that the TM technique and the teaching of SCI were back-door attempts at conversion to Hinduism. In the Year of the World Plan came the first published condemnation of the Maharishi, his meditation and his movement. Although sometimes ill-informed and frequently disjointed, it did make its point if only to a very narrow audience.

The year 1973 was hailed as the 'Year of Action for the World Plan'. Certainly, it looked like being a bumper year for the promotion of meditation, with General Franklin Davis, Commandant of the US Army War College, and his successor Brigadier-General Robert Gard advocating the introduction of TM into the army and insisting that the force should also pay for the privilege. Other prominent dignitaries were also found supporting the Maharishi's cause. The State of Illinois even passed a resolution encouraging a feasibility study on courses in TM and SCI. The list of those eager to spread the word appeared endless. The Maharishi, never tiring of his mission and with a distinct flair for originality, even held a World Conference of Mayors in Switzerland.

In May 1973, from a course in La Antilla on the southern coast of Spain came the latest batch of 1500 teachers, whose job was not only to promote knowledge of his World Plan but also to improve his public image. Their first task was to ensure that the Movement's centres were kept abreast of the changing approach. A disturbing aspect of their activities was the attempt to call in all private recordings of the Maharishi's lectures in order to 'fill in the gaps in the archives', to ensure that new initiates only heard the new 'expression of knowledge'. Early IMS and SRM publications were soon to share a similar fate: they became 'unavailable'. Elsa Dragemark's book *The Way to Maharishi's*

Himalayas, an account of the Master's teachings which was rumoured to have met with his disapproval, was not made available within the Movement and had to be sought from sellers of esoteric books. Notwithstanding the difficulties involved in locating the book, there were few teachers who did not buy or borrow a copy!

The World Plan tour-de-force was its masterful harnessing of emerging technology. The prohibitive costs of producing and copying film stock had previously placed severe restraints on mass dissemination of audiovisual material. Innovations in the realm of magnetic media had now produced a system that overcame these problems and was becoming increasingly compact and affordable. Scores of video machines were purchased by the Movement and courses were arranged for those wishing to become tutored in SCI. For those prepared to pay the not inconsiderable course fee, a total of thirty-three specially-prepared lectures were made available. For many this was their first chance to see the great man in action, and was preferable to committing themselves to a six-month residential course in some distant location. To complement the video lectures, recommended readings were chosen from the Maharishi's two available works, *Science of Being and Art of Living* and his commentary on the opening chapters of the *Bhagavad-Gita.* These publications enjoyed a massive, if temporary, sales boost.

Held in various local centres, the SCI courses were overseen by teachers of meditation who would take each video cassette from a secure hiding place, insert it in the machine and let the Master do the rest. Sitting locked in the crossed-legged lotus position the Maharishi would rock gently to and fro, in his hand a fresh bloom which he waved this way and that. Sometimes the coral necklace he wore would click against the microphone:

> Proceeding toward the subtler layers of the expression of creative intelligence within the mind, we experience a tender field of feeling. Deep within the tenderness of feeling we experience the 'Myness' of feeling. We say, 'I feel like this.' 'I feel.' 'I feel *my* feelings.' So the I in the seat of all my myness is more tenderly located within the feeling. Deep within the I is a more tender level of creative intelligence which is 'I-ness'. The 'I-ness' is almost the abstract value of individual existence, intelligence. And deep within, that individual 'I-ness' is boundless – the unmanifest, non-changing, immortal, eternal reality.[269]

The camera would remain locked on to his features for almost the entire duration of the lecture, wandering only to home in on the portrait of his master or on the freshly cut flowers surrounding the dais. The Maharishi clearly relished the opportunity of presenting these video lectures. It appeared that he followed no prearranged script but would speak off the cuff, effortlessly and spontaneously. At the conclusion of each lecture, the precious videotape was returned to its hiding place and the teacher would then offer his or her explanations and commentary on the lecture. For those who had studied mysticism before taking up with the Maharishi, the prime motive for attending the SCI course was to gain a deeper understanding of higher metaphysical states. They were to be disappointed in this regard, for by and large the Maharishi contented himself with working with fairly lightweight material:

> What is the nature of life? When we look around, we find that everything is growing, evolving, progressing. Progress, evolution, and growth are the nature of life.... This same tendency can be found in man's life. It is our experience that the natural tendency of the mind is to go to a field of greater happiness. Everyone wants more power, more happiness, and this desire expresses the tendency of life.[270]

One problem with the SCI courses was that no one had a proper chance to thrash out any of the points the lectures raised. There was no one to handle any objections to the sweeping generalizations the Maharishi was prone to indulging in. Theoretically one could take such matters up with the attendant teacher, but in reality they performed the function of host to the event. They could and did participate in discussions, but being His Holiness's representatives they were not prepared to dig too deep; certainly they would not tolerate anything that might be considered mutinous behaviour.

> Because the play of creative intelligence is in the direction of greater happiness, greater knowledge and greater achievement, it becomes obvious that life desires to be lived in the state of fulfillment, where everything would be of maximum value: maximum knowledge ... achievement.., strength ... power.., fulfillment. Life aspires to be lived on the level of abundance, on the level of affluence. To live infinity of life – that is life's natural tendency, and if the infinite value of life would become a living reality, that natural tendency would be satisfied.[271]

Unconditional approval for unbridled self-indulgence, self-interest, self-achievement and self-satisfaction is rarely found in one who proclaims to follow a spiritual existence. It is likely that many of the Maharishi's students came away from these sessions sensing that they had been brainwashed, feeling that they must always strive for more and more success in their lives.

Of the higher states of consciousness that had been postulated, the sixth, known as God consciousness, would surely confound any attempts at scientific explanation. There was a simple answer to this dilemma, which was addressed in the course, and that was to refer to this state as 'refined cosmic consciousness' and to sidestep any mention of such awkward expressions as 'cognition of the celestial':

> In this further development, the liveliness of the infinite is cognized on the bed of the finite. This is only possible when the conscious mind has become vibrant with the infinite value and the perception has become so refined as to spontaneously cognize the finest relative values. In this situation, the finest relative perception rises to the level of the infinite value of perception.[272]

With such nebulous descriptions, his scientists would find it extremely difficult to prove their case. But what of the seventh state, the state of unity? Had he come up with any clearer definitions of this highest platform of consciousness, formerly referred to as the state of supreme knowledge?

> In this unified state of consciousness, the experiencer and the object of experience have both been brought to the same level of infinite value, and this encompasses the entire phenomenon of perception and action as well. The gulf between the knower and the object of his knowing has been bridged.[273]

The SCI course was, in terms of numbers, hugely successful. Not only did it have appeal to existing converts, but by its new terms and packaging the Movement enjoyed a perceptible rise in clientele. In addition to gaining familiarity with the Science of Creative Intelligence, those who completed the course of videotaped lectures received a diploma, the acquisition of which became prerequisite for obtaining instruction in teacher-training.

There was also a certain amount of anxiety in the Movement that others might cash in on the teaching of TM. To the horror of rival organizations, a bid to register Transcendental Meditation and TM as trade marks proved successful. The Maharishi seemed set to establish a monopoly not only over his own TM technique but also over the terms of reference by which people understood other *yoga* practices.

A new optimism set in in 1974, dubbed as the 'Year of Achievement for the World Plan'. The Maharishi seemed intent on raising his public profile. He had not been seen in Britain since his ill-fated dalliance with The Beatles and it was a great relief to his followers that an appearance was announced at the Royal Albert Hall. In the event, however, his entourage did most of the speaking, with the Maharishi seated amidst a vast array of flowers sitting impassively, listening to their flow. Perhaps he believed that they would present his message better than he, but the occasion lacked the warmth and spontaneity that had characterized his former appearances. It might be speculated that perhaps after all those years on the road, the Maharishi had lost the will to meet his public. Before making his exit he paused a while, a diminutive, fragile-looking man, beloved of so many, and stood searching the eyes of his followers with an apparent sense of caution and restraint. There was no sign of the bubbling, mirthful man the press had dubbed 'the giggling *guru*'. Perhaps the move towards scientific recognition had forced upon him a need for a more dignified image, but if so it was flawed a little by his being driven away in an open-topped sports car by a devotee, Vesey Crichton.

A rare appearance on British television showed him again smiling and laughing as of old, but the mood did not last. The interviewer asked what became of the money derived from initiations and was given a particularly woeful look from the Maharishi. Instead of answering the question directly he became strangely distant as he hesitantly pointed at his robe and murmured, 'I have no pockets!' In a different context the comment might have provoked sympathy, even laughter. His expression put one in mind of a schoolboy being taken to task by someone in authority. This was not the kind of response one would expect from one who had established the Science of Creative Intelligence and had a university named after him.

Some years before, Bevan Morris had been recalled from *ashram* life in India, in order to continue his education. Conventionally attired and with his locks severely shorn, he had flown not to Australia but to Britain, securing himself a place at Gonville and Caius College, Cambridge, to study comparative religion. In his spare time Morris took part-time work to support himself. The local press, keen for a human-interest story, carried a profile of this struggling Australian and his consuming interest with meditation. But it seems that Morris had not informed them of his *brahmacharya* status, for the newspaper published a follow-up story, warning that a possible side-effect of meditation, might be a resistance towards the opposite sex. But he could handle himself well enough – after all he was the disciple of a master who was himself no stranger to uneven press coverage.

Attention to the role of education was by now a very big issue within the Movement and by September 1974, the Maharishi International University found itself a new home at the former site of Parsons College, Fairfield, Iowa, and installed as its president Dr Bevan Morris.

In his bid to re-educate the world, the Maharishi wanted to make an impact not only on the West but also on anyone prepared to listen to him. It seems that the government of Nepal was interested and the Maharishi quickly responded by supplying videoed transmissions of his teachings. No doubt the message they received was similar to that which he was promoting elsewhere:

> The solutions to the pressing problems that concern our world can be found quickly and easily when every man is living the full potential of life. The knowledge is available to unfold the complete glory of humanity. The validation of the effectiveness of that knowledge has been sufficiently established for everyone to see its truly unlimited capacity to universally raise the quality of life on this planet. All that remains is for every responsible and interested citizen to lead or follow in this challenge – to bring lasting fulfillment to the highest aspirations of civilisation in our generation.[274]

21

──── ★ ────

DAWNING OF A NEW AGE

The suggestion had been made that by practising the Maharishi's meditation one was contributing to world peace. To substantiate this claim, help was still required from the scientists. Essentially the premise of the Maharishi Effect lay in the belief that each and every individual meditator could spontaneously radiate waves of peace to his or her environment. Unfortunately, there was as yet no known device which could measure such radiations. In the absence of positive proof the Maharishi decided to bring the third law of thermodynamics into service:

> This law, the third law of thermodynamics, states that entropy (disorder) decreases when temperature (activity) decreases and that the condition of zero entropy, perfect orderliness, coincides with a temperature of absolute zero (absolutely no activity). In fact, the region near absolute zero temperature in physical systems is closely connected with a strong tendency towards wave coherence and synchrony and is exemplified in the onset of superfluidity and superconductivity near absolute zero temperature when activity is minimum.[275]

One can almost detect a 'reversion to type'. All those years spent in pondering spirituality with his master seem to have been swept aside in a bid to rediscover the thrill of mastering the physics of the material world. There is no sign here of the unquestioning simplicity of monkhood, the flow of worship between God, *guru*, and devotee. Nevertheless, the sheer weight of his vocabulary demanded attention:

> This suggests a striking analogy to the synchrony of brain waves induced by the very deep rest of TM. If we define for the purpose of comparison a 'mental temperature', corresponding to the level of mental and neurophysiological activity, and systematically reduce this through the technique of TM, we perceive a class of tendencies in the human mind that reminds us of the third law as seen in the realm of basic physics. This quantum mechanical analogy suggests that orderliness in the brain and in

thinking is natural to man. TM accomplishes this orderliness by providing an opportunity for the mind to follow the natural tendency of the most general patterns of nature.[276]

When all was said and done, there can be few who would not have been satisfied with a simpler explanation. Nevertheless, it is interesting to reflect on the Maharishi's linkage of these two concepts of inactivity and orderliness. Not everyone would agree that science's relentless search for order will necessarily result in an improved or more peaceful world. Surely one should be wary of ascribing too much importance to orderliness lest one lose touch with reality and become overly obsessive, for in deifying order one runs the risk of self-deification (by the worship of the capacity to perceive order). The fear that science might eventually place undue constraint on freedom of perception once prompted Pre-Raphaelite painter Sir Edward Burne-Jones to protest, 'The more materialistic Science becomes, the more angels I shall paint.'[277]

In truth, the Maharishi with his background in spiritual discipline, might have better served his purpose by displaying greater knowledge about what he termed 'the celestials'. Perhaps this was his ultimate aim. A contemporary rumour told of a visit the Maharishi made to a laboratory investigating genetics throughout which he maintained an expressionless stoic silence. When asked for an opinion of their work, he is said to have suggested, 'Why don't you investigate re-incarnation?'

It was 12 January 1975, and the Maharishi's birthday celebrations were in full swing aboard the Flagship *Gotthard* on the still waters of Lake Lucerne. As usual, the Maharishi was to name the year and make his customary speech, but this year a special surprise was in store. After 'coming out of silence' he announced the 'Dawn of the Age of Enlightenment' and 1975 as the 'Year of Fulfilment of the World Plan'. On hearing his speech, there could have been few present who did not believe that they would soon see an end to world strife and disorder. Although the Maharishi had made many grand pronouncements, the advent of an enlightened age was, even for him, an exceptional prediction. He explained his reasons for such optimism during his inaugural address:

> Jai Guru Dev. It is a very great and joyful time for us all today to be recognizing the dawn of the full potential of the human race on earth. We are recognizing, we are realizing today the full potential of the human race on earth, and that is in terms of unbounded happiness, harmony, peace,

fulfilment.

This we are recognizing on the basis of scientific verification, scientific validation of our teaching in the world for the last seventeen years. We have been teaching the knowledge that we received from Guru Dev, our Master, His Divinity – we like to adore him as His Divinity.[278]

It is worth noting that few of the Maharishi's disciples were particularly well informed about the life or thoughts of the famed 'Guru Dev'. Most knew only what they had heard through the Maharishi, and they must therefore have conceived a vision of this celebrated figure as a superior version of him. Some may even have wondered whether, since the former Shankaracharya was never directly quoted, the Maharishi was perhaps a greater teacher even than his master. Greater or not he was their teacher and he was telling them that the beginning of an enlightened age was at hand; it was a message they wanted to believe in.

A prayer was said to bring forth support from the beyond for their activities for the coming year and more. This was a rare opportunity to see the devotional side of the Maharishi's thinking. The following is an extract of the prayer he offered up:

I bow down to him who breathes out the Veda and creates the universe from it, remaining uninvolved, and who is the cherished shrine of pilgrimage for all the streams of knowledge.

Mother divine! Now on thine own, think of bringing the dawn of enlightenment to the whole world and destroying the fear of all that is not good. Do not wait for our prayers to reach thine altar, Ma! Thine immeasurable influence and strength is beyond the reach of prayers even from the Lord Almighty, the Lord of Creation, and the Lord of Dissolution.

I bow down to Shri Guru Dev, at whose door the impulses of creative intelligence assemble to pray for perfection day and night.[279]

In his announcement about this Dawn of Enlightenment, he was, in fact, only placing new clothes on his old ideas. Beneath the new declarations there still lay the notion that by the practice of TM (and the study of SCI), bliss would become an experience common to everyone. The novel twist came in the news that everyone would benefit, even those who did not meditate, a result of the Maharishi Effect. He had by now become familiar with the objections to his theories, and used this knowledge for his own ends:

It was a surprise to the people all over the world how we could dare to say, 'Life is bliss' when everywhere life was a struggle. Everywhere it is said, 'To err is human', as if man is born to make mistakes. When this has been the experience of life on earth, how could we dare to say 'Life is bliss'?[280]

Clearly he was building up to something, but what was it going to be this time – more promises? No. This time he really seemed to have something to crow about. The scientists who had been doing research for him had produced reams of charts and reports in support of TM. If one did not delve too deeply, the data looked very convincing indeed. It was not the Maharishi's style to probe the weaknesses of his evidence; he wanted only good news.

> About two weeks ago I heard that there was large number of cities in the world where the crime rate had gone down. When the statistics were researched, we found that when the number in the city practising Transcendental Meditation reached one per cent then the crime rate went down. So if one per cent of the people with a little more orderly minds than others moving around on the streets could change the tendencies of the people, then we have just to give an expression that it's possible now to create a new world; its possible now to create a society free from problems; it's possible now to eliminate suffering from society, it's possible. Inauguration of the dawn of a new age is just declaring the possibility on the basis of scientific validation.[281]

The claim was that, courtesy of the Maharishi, a situation had been arrived at where meditation could be scientifically assessed. Unfortunately for him this was not the case. Various objections were being raised regarding the lack of a blind control group (the inclusion of participants unaware of the nature of the experiments). But more fundamental even than that was the omission of any specific information on the basis of the technique of meditation, namely the *mantras*. If this were not enough to raise doubts over the findings, where was the proof that those involved in the experiments were actually practising TM? Nevertheless who could doubt the Maharishi's sincerity as he continued:

> We are in a scientific age. We have developed an age of science for us. Anything we want to do, anything we want to work on, we want to feel confident that we are not on false grounds. So on the basis of scientific experiments, on the basis of the scientific research carried out in different parts of the world during the last five years – we have confidence on the basis of what has been demonstrated in the lives of the individuals and in the lives of the cities as a whole.

There were other inherent weaknesses in the research. After all, what was to stop him now ascribing *any* improvement, personal, communal, national or international, to be effects of his work?

The goals of the World Plan had yet to be achieved to any perceptible degree. None the less, it had served its purpose as a rallying point, and had not been totally forgotten:

> When we designed the seven goals of the World Plan in 1972 we made one

of the goals 'to enrich governmental achievements' based on our thought that the knowledge was so beautiful, the practice was so simple and natural, that once we called the attention of any government to it they would pick it up, We approached some governments. Through our feelers there we found that either the letter didn't reach the head of state or he knew of the letter, knew that such a letter was there, but he didn't have time to know it. He was so sunk in problems, so preoccupied, that he didn't have time to look to a call of solution. Now, when we are inaugurating the dawn of the Age of Enlightenment, we have a strength in ourselves. No matter what the governments want to do, or do, or don't do, irrespective of the attitudes of the governments towards themselves or towards us, the world is going to be a better world. Because to make the world better, now, does not depend on anything.[282]

The Maharishi's desire to spread his message had escalated to a point approaching desperation. Not only was he determined to achieve his goal of teaching his meditation technique to 1 per cent of the world's population but he also wished to determine how the resultant society would function:

There has not been and there will not be a place for the unfit. The fit will lead, and if the unfit are not coming along there is no place for them. In the place where light dominates there is no place for darkness. In the Age of Enlightenment there is no place for ignorant people. The ignorant will be made enlightened by a few orderly, enlightened people moving around. Nature will not allow ignorance to prevail. It just can't. Non-existence of the unfit has been the law of nature.[283]

It would be hard to believe that the Maharishi meant this statement to sound ominous or sinister in any way. However, although his remarks may have been innocent enough, it is sobering to reflect on what measures he envisaged taking to ensure that everyone towed his party line. Could people be forced to co-operate? Meditators themselves might even pose a problem, owing to the phenomenon of 'unstressing', which could result in scoring 'own goals'. But how could meditators be prevented from causing upsets, intentional or otherwise? One possible solution lay in threatening to take away the *mantras* of the wayward. This unlikely suggestion was actually proposed in response to a residential course participant who felt disinclined to spend time rounding.

The message of the Dawn of the Age of Enlightenment was taken on tour. Inaugurations were held in Britain, India, Canada, Argentina and the Ivory Coast during March and April 1975. When the Maharishi returned to Switzerland, to Lake Lucerne, he was just in time to join up with a celebration in nearby Seelisberg. Two lakeside hotels had been

purchased and renovated for use by a newly founded organization, the
Maharishi European Research University, MERU for short. Those
familiar with Indian mythology might feel a twinge of recollection at the
name, for it is on the fabled Mount Meru that the god Brahma is
believed to reside and from its summit the river Ganges is said to flow
to earth. Mount Meru is even conceived of as the heart of the cosmos.
But this MERU was neither the residence of the god of creation nor the
centre of the universe. The Maharishi defined its aims thus:

> The first goal of Maharishi European Research University is to realize the
> ultimate goal of all scientific research by developing complete knowledge of
> the growth of human consciousness on the theoretical, experimental and
> experiential levels, and by then applying this knowledge so as to eliminate
> the causes of pain and suffering in all areas of human life, to render society
> free from problems, and to contribute maximum to progress and fulfilment –
> thereby creating an ideal society and ushering in the Age of
> Enlightenment.[284]

The basic role of MERU was to research the effects of TM and
determine the existence of higher states of consciousness. In addition to
its laboratory work, it was envisaged that it would also be responsible
for promoting its findings and to that end it would organize occasional
conferences. Two such events took place in the latter part of the year,
both in Switzerland and both attended by the Maharishi. The first was
promoted as the International Symposium on the Absolute Theory of
Management and the other more simply as 'Evolutionary Models in
Nature'.

According to reports, the Maharishi also found time to visit his other
university, the MIU, in Fairfield, Iowa, and hosted a press conference
there. The logo of the MIU used the image of a tree and surrounding it
was the legend 'Knowledge is Structured in Consciousness'. The
ancient symbol of the tree not only served to emphasize his message –
the need to attend to both outer and inner needs – it was also an
unintentional echo of the Maharishi's avowed intention to retire from
the field of action and spend his energy 'watering the root'. With the
advent of video technology, the work of training new teachers could
henceforth be undertaken without his direct participation, but he seemed
to have no desire to hand over the reins of his organizations just yet.
Excluding his cameo public appearances and his annual
pronouncements, however, he spent most of his time with his devotees.
Sometimes he would emerge to confer with some prominent dignitary,
but generally he confined himself to the company of those he knew to
be committed to his dreams. Tales abounded of his ability to function on

just a few hours of sleep and a minimal intake of food and drink. From India *gangajal* (water from the River Ganges) was transported to Europe. It seemed to his devotees that he was no longer eating his meals of *urud dal*, *basmati* rice and vegetables, preferring to eat only the occasional *barfi* (an Indian sweetmeat not unlike milk fudge).

Disloyalty was not a characteristic common to his devotees; adoration, adulation and awe were the norm, and he seldom encountered opposition or open confrontation. Although this could be perceived as evidence of the Maharishi's personal integrity, it may well have been the result of peer pressure, with a fear of the isolation which might follow any opposition. But of course there were those who quietly nursed feelings of disaffection until they could either resolve them or give up and jump ship. Inevitably, there were departures, and occasionally even defections to other movements, but it appeared that no one was found disclosing the secrets of the Master's *mantras*, at least not publicly.

After a year spent searching for signs of a new enlightened age, the time came again for the Maharishi to take stock and deliver his annual report. He had also to give the unborn year a name by which it could be distinguished. So 1976 was to be the 'Year of Government', which did not quite have the ring of hope that marked out the previous year as special. Again he chose the waters of Lake Lucerne and the trusty Flagship *Gotthard* from which to deliver his new-year greetings. In the previous year's speech, he had let slip that he had been less than overwhelmed by the response from heads of government to his letters of hope. This year he had something rather more impressive lined up; he was planning to form his *own* government, a World Government.

Was he really being serious? Was he really making a bid at world domination?

It is a very great joy to inaugurate the World Government for the Age of Enlightenment. Last year we inaugurated the dawn of the Age of Enlightenment. Now the continued evidence of a better time dawning for the world has awakened our interest in establishing an organization suitable for administering the sunshine of the Age of Enlightenment. The World Government will be a global organization for administering the wellbeing and progress of society throughout the world. Already national, provincial, state, country, and city governments exist for maintaining well-being and progress on their respective levels, but despite all the power and resources at their disposal and despite all the intelligent people serving their cause, all governments throughout the ages have been submerged in problems. No government has succeeded in creating an ideal society. Something has been universally lacking and this has paralysed the capabilities of all governments throughout time.[285]

He was not speaking figuratively, either. Ministers were soon chosen to oversee the new operation. The Maharishi had surrounded himself with an inner circle comprising at least 100, some say 108, devotees (108 being a number cherished by Indian numerologists). Since all of them had private incomes, he found no shortage of willing candidates. When it came to sharing out the ministerial posts, Sanskrit scholar Vernon Katz, Brahmachari Nandikishore and Vesey Crichton were amongst those entitled to be addressed as 'Right Honorable'. The functions of the various ministries were to be as follows:

1. Development of Consciousness
2. Natural Law and Order
3. Cultural Integrity, Invincibility and World Harmony
4. Education and Enlightenment
5. Celebrations and Fulfilment
6. Prosperity and Progress
7. Information and Inspiration
8. All Possibilities: Research and Development
9. Capitals of the Age of Enlightenment
10. Health and Immortality

In addition to these posts, the Maharishi envisaged his government as being supported by governors, whose role he defined in the following statement:

> To administer the Age of Enlightenment, Teachers and Governors of the Age of Enlightenment will be trained. A Governor of the Age of Enlightenment will be one who is spontaneously able to fulfil his desires.[286]

The pyramid of power was growing fast, with the simple meditators relegated to the ranks. Over and above them lay a whole network of bureaucracy, checkers, teachers, course coordinators, national leaders, trustees, governors and ministers of their World Government. As a result of this structure, the Maharishi became increasingly inaccessible to 'ordinary' people. Anyone wishing to meet him would first have to dig deep, very deep in his or her pockets. Even after having attended all the videotaped lectures they might still be thwarted in their desires, that is unless of course they happened to be extremely wealthy or politically powerful, hold a masters degree in science or be a Nobel prize-winner.

Of the spiritual missions targeting the West in the wake of the

Maharishi's lead, those which promoted devotional practices dominated. More often than not such missions were led by charismatic *guru* figures, often the object of worship by their followers. The Maharishi discouraged his disciples from becoming consumed with adoration for him, constantly redirecting their attention to his teaching and to the meditation. It was therefore something of a surprise when he agreed to meet Swami Muktananda, the middle-aged and eccentric leader of a mission expounding the practice of *Siddha Yoga*. Unlike the Maharishi's movement, Swami Muktananda's organization was close-knit and small, and all devotees had easy access to their teacher. His system of *yoga* centred on the ability of the master to awaken the spiritual energy of his disciples. Taking his *darshan* frequently triggered off reactions resembling alternative practices of *yoga*: breathing exercise, meditation, devotion etc. For some reason, the Maharishi felt a kinship with this woolly-hatted *swami* with the sunglasses. The feeling appeared to be mutual and following the conference between the two leaders in Switzerland, students of *Siddha Yoga* claimed that not only had their teacher been accorded the title of Advisor to the Dawn of the Age of Enlightenment, but had gained the Maharishi's endorsement that he enjoyed the highest state of consciousness possible. It appeared that the Maharishi was becoming broader in his vision and he was now open to the suggestion that other contemporary teachers might have something to offer. But it was not to last. It is alleged that soon after the meeting, the Maharishi requested that recordings made of conversations between the *swami* and himself be erased.

The 'Year of Government' saw the continuation of the scientific conferences held under the umbrella of MERU. The Maharishi attended at least some of them, in particular those convened in Switzerland. In March the theme was 'A New Awakening of Knowledge: All Possibilities in the Field of Consciousness'. This could not mean that *nothing* was impossible, for the Maharishi himself had declared as impossible the idea of altering the past. However from as early as May 1959 he had upheld the possibility of acquiring *yogic* powers, the *siddhis* mentioned in Patanjali's *Yoga Sutras:*

> All the great powers, all the mystic powers, all the powers that you read in the *Yoga* of Patanjali and all that thing the *yogis* do could be done through this meditation.[287]

He gave a clue as to how this might be achieved:

> If the mind is always on the surface level of the ocean of mind then the thought force is weak. And if the mind fathoms the deeper levels of

consciousness, deeper levels of the ocean of mind and stirs all levels there, coming out it brings all the latent faculties up on the surface of the ocean of mind and then – one thought, and it is realised.[288]

In the third chapter of the *Yoga Sutras* are listed the many powers that can be attained through *yogic* discipline. Of the more astonishing are the abilities to remember past lives, know another's mind, become invisible, become strong as an elephant, hear the divine message, enter another's body (astral travel), and the power of aerial travel:

> By concentrating on the relation between air and body, and identifying himself with light things like cotton wool, the *yogi* moves in the sky.[289]

Levitation, as this latter power is generally called, has stirred the imagination of visitors to India since time immemorial, even though the consensus of opinion can be summed up as: 'If man were meant to fly he would have been given wings.' When the Maharishi set out to break the code of these *Yoga Sutras*, there was no lack of volunteers hoping to fly.

Starting with a small group of long-term meditators the Maharishi put Patanjali's formulae to the test. These pioneers of his experiments began to train others and by December almost 1000 had signed up for instruction in the art of the impossible. The grapevine became alive with audacious claims of meditators disappearing and reappearing, materializing objects such as fruit out of nowhere, walking through walls and sailing through the air. The only catch was that no demonstrations of these powers were forthcoming. The most evident power was that the claims, unproven as they were, still ensured an enormous interest in the Maharishi's new 'technology'. If the promised ability to perform magic were not enough, there was always the lure of promotion, for graduation from the *siddhi* course conferred the exalted status of 'executive governor of consciousness'.

On hearing about the new developments, Charlie Lutes, the Maharishi's friend from way back, confided in another former light of the movement, Nancy Cooke de Herrara. 'Just when he gets respectable, he comes out with something like this. The press will eat him up.'[290]

With a 'parliament' and meditators claiming *yogic* powers, the Maharishi was in serious danger of losing some of the ground gained by previous efforts to reform his image. Perhaps when he saw the proof copies of the lavishly-produced bulletins and ostentatious commemorative publications his organizations were issuing, he realized that things were going too far, for in his next new-year pronouncements, instead of placing focus on the recent experiments, he chose the relatively safe domain of social ideals, announcing that 1977 would be the 'Year of Ideal Society':

> The time is right and the knowledge is available. It is my great joy to invite the responsible individuals, organisations, and governments of every country in the world to join in this global undertaking to create an ideal society.[291]

But opposition to the Maharishi's ideas and the activities of his organizations was in the air. Although the seventies witnessed a sustained flow of books advocating Transcendental Meditation, a few emerged with a rather different point of view. These came mainly from fundamentalist Christian communities, and forthrightly condemned the Maharishi and his ideas, even going so far as to suggest that Satanic forces were at work. In the early 1960s the Maharishi had believed that the lack of open opposition to his message was reasonable proof of his success. Now that the opposition forces were beginning to position themselves, was a change of fortune imminent? The anti-TM lobby in the USA was so alarmed that the teaching of the techniques had spread to high schools that in the state of New Jersey legal proceedings were instituted against the Movement. The Movement showed no signs of concern about this setback, however, and following the Maharishi's mood of confident optimism, meditators went about their business, blissfully ignoring the critics.

22

★

SUPERPOWERS

As we have seen, the advent of video technology was a godsend to the Maharishi; he could now give lectures wherever and whenever he wanted. He was by no means camera shy, and entered into the spirit of the new age with dedicated enthusiasm, giving performance after performance on any topic that took his fancy. Was it the worry that his teachings might one day be lost to the world that drove him on, or merely the novelty of a new toy? Whatever his motives, countless miles of tape were being amassed. To the watching, waiting world the Maharishi was no longer a man of flesh and blood, but a two-dimensional image, 625 lines high and compacted to fit inside a television screen. For many, this prepackaged Master was as close as they would ever get to the real Maharishi, who spent the major part of his time in the secure stronghold of the Capital of the Dawn of the Age of Enlightenment in Seelisberg, Switzerland, a virtual recluse.

Latecomers to the world of the Maharishi and his meditation had an unenviable task before them. The promise of an easy path to happiness was certainly alluring, but what were they to make of all the talk of an Age of Enlightenment and the recent formation of a World Government? Although the attempts to nail down the verifiable aspects of the meditation were bold and imaginative, it was easy to become overwhelmed by the plethora of charts and statistics. Whilst it was apparent that the TM movement was intent on promoting the Maharishi and his views, new converts found themselves unable to gain access to any information about the man; there were no biographies and no commercial tapes of his lectures available. Another dilemma was that although meditation had traditionally been linked with spirituality, the main thrust of the Movement's promotion now lay in seductive promises of greater material prosperity. To resolve any questions new meditators might have, most of the available information lay within the grasp of the movement itself. Personal and historical data on the

Maharishi being all but impossible to acquire, the only way to find out more about the Maharishi was to go on a TM course and see the videos. And those who, having immersed themselves in the aspiration to become cosmically conscious, unable to resist the temptation to become a latter day Peter Pan enrolled for lessons in miracle working.

The roller-coaster ride of declarations, conferences, inaugurations and assemblies that had filled the Maharishi's diary carried on unabated. The meditation business was booming, and yet a wave of envy, resentment and distrust was mounting. Disillusioned with the results of their meditations and disgruntled at the material trappings of the Movement, more and more voices were raised against it and, by implication, the Maharishi. When in late 1977 a rumour spread amongst meditators suggesting that the movement had lost the case brought against it in New Jersey, they did not know what to think. Up until then the Maharishi's sure touch had been taken for granted. Now it was a time for reflection.

On 19 October the federal court which had heard the case against TM decided to bar its teaching in schools in the state of New Jersey, believing that such teaching was in violation of the First Amendment to the Constitution, which requires separation of Church and State. The presiding judge, Judge Meanor concluded:

> The teaching of SCI/TM and the Puja are religious in nature, no other inference is permissible or reasonable ... although defendants have submitted well over 1500 pages of briefs, affidavits and deposition testimony in opposing plaintiffs' motion for summary judgement, defendants have failed to raise the slightest doubt as to the facts or as to the religious nature of the teaching of the Science of Creative Intelligence and the Puja. The teachings of SCI/TM courses in New Jersey violates the establishment clause of the First Amendment, and its teaching must be enjoined.[292]

On 13 October 1977, from the International Capital of the Age of Enlightenment in Seelisberg, the Maharishi launched the Inauguration of a Global Initiative for Invincibility to Every Nation, and on 21 October there was a celebration of this initiative. Addressing his World Government he skirted round the New Jersey judgement and announced with characteristic optimism:

> The celebration of Invincibility to Every Nation is a proof of rising purity in world consciousness, brought about by the Transcendental Meditation and TM-Sidhi programme. The world has changed. The conches and bells and trumpets which, in the past, were sounded to announce preparedness for war, are now being blown and rung to announce Invincibility to Every Nation – to announce the end of wars, the end of conflicts, the end of fears, and the end

of hostility in life.[293]

To the ageing Maharishi in the seclusion and beauty of his lakeside retreat, everything appeared rosy and bright. Truly remarkable and not a little disturbing was a new aspect to the Maharishi's thinking, his search for perfection and quest for absolutes. These ambitions were unusual for one coming from a highly religious culture where devotion, humility and resigned acceptance are seen as the indications of spiritual greatness.

The Maharishi's cohorts kept him informed about everyday news and global affairs and some of the bleakness and suffering therefore seeped into his dreams of an ideal world. He weighed up ideas like age-reversal and immortality with a vested interest, and must have understood that life is not all a bowl of cherries. But within a celebratory speech lay a clue to his continued, if not compulsive, flow of optimism:

> When we inaugurated the dawn of the Age of Enlightenment three years ago, it was still dark and there was great intensity of economic depression and inflation, and there were cries from everywhere. But we saw the forthcoming sunshine of the Age of Enlightenment, and we declared it -someone has to say what is going to come tomorrow. We have that golden vision to see only the right things, because we know the power of good is greater than any other power, and we see the power of good rising in the world.[294]

One cannot deny the simple sincerity of his sentiments, but it is an unfortunate fact that many who have held such views have not been spared great personal tragedy. The crucial issue really lay in whether or not he could vouchsafe his followers' welfare. Were the magic *mantras* really powerful enough to ensure their invincibility, their immortality even? He remained unequivocal, declaring: 'Life is immortal and invincible. It is bliss.'[295]

The Maharishi continued his pastime of naming the years: 1978 became the 'Year of Invincibility to Every Nation', 1979 the 'Year of All Possibilities', 1980 the 'Year of Pure Knowledge', 1981 the 'Year of Vedic Science', 1982 the 'Year of Natural Law', 1983 the 'Year of Unified Field' and 1984 the 'Year of Unified Field Based Civilization'. They might also have been named the Years of the Real Estate for the Movement had by now adopted a policy of acquiring run-down stately homes, vacant plots, in fact anything that looked good in terms of utility and long-term investment. To the Maharishi goes the credit for negotiating down the asking price on the Fairfield, Iowa, site, and devotees followed his example by securing similarly good deals elsewhere. One might have thought that the long-desired inner-city centres which were to be set aside for the exclusive use of meditation, might now become a reality, but this was not the case. The majority of properties purchased were situated out of town, some deep in the country, and were destined to house only the most dedicated followers and provide accommodation for those on residential courses.

Many who helped the Maharishi's meteoric rise to fame were left on the sidelines as new policies ousted the old order. Some grassroots meditators were becoming disenchanted with the Movement. Charlie Lutes, the former head of the SRM in the USA took a dim view of the changes, especially when he found himself debarred from gaining access to the Maharishi. Returning home he fumed: 'Those idiots who surround him wouldn't let me in. They had me wait in the hallway.'[296] Apparently the Maharishi telephoned him to apologize, but Charlie was not easily pacified:

> God damn it, Maharishi, I wouldn't wait more than an hour for Jesus Christ! I'd like to talk to you in private, so don't have any of those jerks along.

Not all the changes were unwelcome to the old guard, however. News that an 'ideal village' was to be created attracted a great deal of interest especially from those without dependent relatives. Many had speculated on what life might be like in a society of meditators, and here, in Skelmersdale, Lancashire, England was their chance to find out.

The 'TM-Sidhi' programme referred to by the Maharishi (the Sanskrit word is actually *siddhi*, meaning 'one who has acquired supernatural powers') was not publicly demonstrated, but none the less attracted much attention from the press. Although not all the coverage was positive, the demand for higher experience being what it was, the arrival of new candidates continued without let-up. The release of *Superman: the Movie* produced an extra lift to meditators' interest in special powers, especially when they noticed the inclusion of the magic letters 'TM' (which actually stood for trade mark) on the billboards. Those who kept company with 'executive governors of consciousness', however, discovered to their surprise that the practice of the 'sidhis' required a launch-pad of aerated foam.

Not wishing to miss out on anything, many people were caught up with an insatiable curiosity to know what was happening in Switzerland. Nancy Cooke de Herrara was one of those who flew there to investigate. Whilst she was on the course she became disturbed at the activities of some of her fellow meditators:

> On one occasion, summoned downstairs to the phone, I heard ghastly sounds coming from the large conference room. It was as though cats, dogs, pigs,

chickens, and a cow or two were fighting.

'*Díos mio, qué es este ruido horrible?*' (My God, what is that horrible sound?) I asked the Spanish cleaning woman standing nearby.

In Spanish, she explained, 'This goes on all the time. Sometimes we see heads go up and down – this is what they call their "flying room".'[297]

There were other things to worry newcomers to the Capital of the Age of Enlightenment, not least the news that the Maharishi was now surrounded by a group of young Germans dubbed by meditators the 'Maharishi's gestapo'[298] Whilst in Switzerland Nancy was fortunate in running into old friend Jerry Jarvis, who, like Charlie Lutes before him, was astonished at the conduct of some of the new wave of devotees. He exclaimed:

> Why do they behave this way? They have driven all the intelligent older people away from the organisation.[299]

Jarvis also warned of some of the problems so far encountered in the experiments with the 'sidhi' techniques:

> Using the *sutras* is a strain on the nervous system and some people flip out.
> In the last course, we worked on invisibility. Several of us accomplished it on occasion, but Maharishi decided it took too much concentration.[300]

There was more. It seems the local chiropractor was doing brisk business in dealing with back disorders brought on during the 'sidhi' course.

In the wake of the Maharishi's pronouncements concerning ideals and order, certain unwelcome initiatives followed. The funding and planning for the building of Shankaracharya Nagar had been raised during the early years of the Movement from Western devotees. Since it had been envisaged that the *ashram* would forever be the international centre of the meditation movement, many looked forward to the time, when they might enjoy a visit there. Within a decade or so the site became more and more for the exclusive use of Indians, with the Maharishi only making the occasional appearance. The Academy of Meditation continued to draw visitors, both Eastern and Western, meditators and non-meditators, all intent on soaking up the atmosphere and feeling the 'good vibrations'. Indians were allowed ready access, but Westerners were shocked to find themselves barred entry. Even those who had earned themselves a place in the Movement's hierarchy were summarily refused admission. It would be hard to avoid the suspicion of racism at work, but this would not be a complete reflection of the situation. A statement from the Maharishi on 'Cultural Integrity – the Unshakeable

Foundation for Invincibility' goes some way to explain the underlying motives for vetting visitors at Shankaracharya Nagar:

> In the past, the mixing of cultures has been a drag on progress. People from one land, when they live in another's always miss their old habits and surroundings. This is not just a psychological weakness. The fact is that each land has a different culture according to its geographic and climatic conditions. So in each land the human nervous system is cultured differently, starting from birth. When a person moves to another land, his nervous system tries to adapt and often does succeed to a large extent. But even if the person fails to adapt to just one small factor, that will become a drag for him and for the host culture, because he will not be able to cohere fully with his environment. This mixing destroys cultures and hampers cultural integrity.[301]

One would have thought that he was referring to unwelcome foreign bodies rather than brethren. But he spoke from experience, for few had enjoyed the hospitality of a greater variety of 'host cultures' than he had. In view of the time he spent outside India, it was surprising he had not yet lost his Indian citizenship.

Within the perimeters of the *ashram*, the Maharishi's deputy, Satyanand ruled supreme. He complained of a hectic work schedule and was heard to admit that he hardly found time to meditate. The *ashram* swarmed with *sadhus* (religious mendicants) and other Indian male visitors (special courses were instituted for women), who by their upbringing had been taught to revere the *guru* as God. It was not unknown at the *ashram* for a meditator to prostrate himself in front of a of 'Guru Dev' and to touch the image of his feet.

Indian journalist Dinesh Khare, in his introduction to *Strange Facts About A Great Saint* clarified the position of 'Guru Dev' in the teaching of TM:

> The initiation took place in front of a picture of Guru Dev and I was told that I should consider neither my initiator nor Maharishi Mahesh Yogi as my spiritual teacher but the Guru Dev himself. It was a thrilling experience and the very first day my turbulent mind experienced such a serene calm that when I got up after practising TM for the first time, I bowed my head to the lotus feet of Guru Dev and since that day have regarded him as my spiritual teacher and guide.

Since religion is a way of life in the Indian subcontinent, it was not unnatural that religious customs surfaced at the academy too. *Shivalingas* (symbolic representations of the forces of cosmic energy) sprouted up on the *ashram* grounds, *sadhus* (religious mendicants) gathered together for *kirtan*, the singing of devotional songs to God.

According to Satyanand, one of the *sadhus* given the 'TM-Sidhi' *sutras* 'leaned back and raised up several feet from the ground'. In an amusing contrast to the sycophantic attitudes adopted by the Maharishi's Western followers, a resident Indian teacher of meditation at the academy openly admitted that he did not wish to attend one of Satyanand's afternoon lectures, saying, 'It is Test Match cricket, I listen to wireless!'

For those who were unwilling to submit themselves to following the Maharishi's dictum but still keen on the underlying concepts of meditation, there was still the chance of obtaining an interview with his fellow disciple Shankaracharya Swami Shantanand Saraswati, who could always be relied on to redirect one's attention from the material to the spiritual, from the contemplation of the gross towards the subtler regions of existence:

> Everyone is free but thinks that they are bound. In fact all those things that bind them are the expression of their own ignorance. This is what everyone has to understand. Here is an example. A special trick is used to catch monkeys. A round earthen pot with a small mouth is buried in the ground. Pieces of tasty food are put inside. When the monkeys smell them, they come close and put their hands inside and clutch the food, and then they cannot pull them out. The monkey doesn't know that he can be free. He doesn't want to release the piece of food, and yet wants to be free, so he cries, and can't run away. At that moment the man appears from his hiding place and catches the monkey. Most people who think that they are not free are acting like the monkey. They are holding on to something, maybe things of beauty, of fragrance. If only they could release their hold, they would be free, because in truth they are free.[302]

But it has to be said that even to the Shankaracharya, for all his humility and wisdom, fate played its games of trick or treat. Just below the monastery in Joshimath the cave of Trottacacharya had been acquired for the use of one Swami Swaroopanand, an outspoken critic of the Maharishi and a claimant to the title of Shankaracharya. A local shopkeeper wrapped up the situation succinctly saying 'He (Swami Swaroopanand) has much money backing in Kashi (Benares), they have bought this *gupha* (cave) for him'. It is not unusual for disputes over succession to arise and the contoversy is unlikely to be easily resolved. A contributory factor might well be Shankaracharya Shantanand's association with the Maharishi which is not universally well received, in fact one of the Shankaracharya's disciples at Jyotir Math, at the mention of the Maharishi responded coolly, stating 'Here there is no need for *mantra*, meditation just comes'.

From time to time the Maharishi returned to India, where he tried to find time for all those wishing to speak with him. On one such visit the writer Gita Mehta sought him out, finding him at New Delhi's most expensive hotel, where he was holding court for a few days. Shown to his suite she joined the several hundred other people who were waiting to take audience with him in his bedroom. When Gita was shown in, she was joined by others, a pair of Italian countesses and two scientists, one from Britain, the other an Indian nuclear physicist. The younger of the two *contessas* had a problem with her meditation.

> 'But, Swami,' ended the Countess, 'my *mantra* is not working anymore.'
>
> 'Oh dear,' said the Maharishi, and continued to smile. 'Then we must give you another. Use the new *mantra* for four days, then let him know,' and he pointed to a man kneeling piously in the dark corner, 'whether it is working. I won't be here. I must fly back to Switzerland tomorrow. My work requires me there.'[303]

After the countesses had been dealt with, the Maharishi addressed the visiting scientists:

> 'You see, my friends,' said the *guru*, 'science is only beginning to catch up with the knowledge that we Indian mystics have had through the ages. Once you have scientific words for what we know and teach, then you will accept the truth of what we say. Until then you will consider us fools. What it amounts to is that you wish to make up your own *mantras*.'
>
> The Maharishi giggled wickedly at the scientists.
>
> 'For instance, anyone who is seriously interested and will not disturb, is welcome to come to Switzerland and see for themselves whether my students can levitate. But so many who come, go away and say they were hypnotized.'
>
> The Maharishi keeled over sideways in a fit of high-pitched laughter.[304]

The scientists did not know it, but they were privileged in not only being told about the floating populace of his centre in Switzerland, but also being offered an explanation as to the mechanics of levitation:

> We teach our students that by concentration through meditation they can create an impenetrable field of energy between the ground and their bodies. The greater the field of energy, the higher the meditating man can rise. It is simple QED.[305]

The Maharishi challenged the scientists to gain greater understanding of their disciplines by joining forces with him. When he paused to present them with some flowers, Gita, who had been carefully monitoring the proceedings, thought she detected a noticeable reluctance in the Indian Physicist:

> It was clear from the expression on his face that he suspected that the gift

might drain some of the power he had acquired from a lifetime of pursuing the rational.[306]

Before inviting the scientists to attend a conference to be held some months later, he decided to strengthen his links with them. In an impassioned plea he invited them to rid themselves of their reservations:

> 'Come gentlemen. Let us join hands. It is Kaliyug. The Age of Darkness. We have no time to wait thirty or forty years for scientists to find the right words. The moral issues are already clear.
>
> Look around you. See what it is possible to achieve. Look how the world is thirsty. People everywhere are crying "Show us the Way!" Is it not funny that they are asking this during Kaliyug, the most immoral of eras?' The Maharishi giggled in delight.
>
> 'But we can do it together, that is what is really funny. And only in these times when your knowledge is so close to our wisdom.'[307]

Those meditators who could not afford to travel to India in search of illumination and a new *mantra* or bring themselves to enrol on an SCI video course were left pretty much to their own devices. Those who browsed the shelves of bookshops in search of an inspirational book would find the odd TM title, sometimes useful, sometimes critical. In 1978 the brief appearance of *The Story of the Maharishi* by William Jefferson in the USA filled the gap for those who could find it. Another profile, *Maharishi, the Guru*, edited by Martin Ebon also came and went without leaving much trace. *The TM Cookbook*, which included an account and photographs of one of the last international teacher-training courses in Rishikesh India, was destined for a similar fate, soon becoming unavailable. Even rarer was a pink paperback in Hindi entitled *Shri Shankaracharya Upadeshamrita*, a reprint of 108 of Shankaracharya Brahmanand's spiritual *satsangs*. In covering the teaching of Transcendental Meditation, the odd author, in an attempt to add weight to his writings, would let slip a TM *mantra* or two.

Not all such books were anti-TM or even anti-Maharishi, but some most certainly were. Of these, few were informative or well researched, but there were occasional exceptions. From a number of directions their authors attacked what they saw as misconceptions about the Maharishi's teachings, challenged the findings of his scientific experiments, questioned his ethics, attempted to expose the religious connotations of his teachings and even went so far as to brand the teaching a mirage and a confidence trick. In all they presented a picture of the new Dawn of Enlightenment which greatly contrasted to that given out by the Movement.

Not all the authors who were critical of TM dismissed the benefits to be derived from its practice. The central question for most of them was not whether TM was a practical method of relaxation but whether it was in fact a religion by any other name. Armed with a transcript of the Sanskrit *puja* and a list of over a dozen *mantras*, they sought to dissuade upright Christian people from associating with the Maharishi or his messengers. The lists of *mantras* had, they claimed, been divulged by disaffected initiators. In disclosing these *mantras* they also gave attention to the manner of selection, which was believed to be based on one criteria alone, the age of the initiate. Having convinced themselves that the *mantras* were just the names of the principal gods and goddesses of the Hindu faith, they contended that their repetition was proof that TM constituted a form of Hindu worship. It was a reasonably powerful argument.

The Maharishi's representatives were unhappy at this interpretation of their practice, and strenuously denied all charges, in particular that of being branded a religion. In order to evaluate this situation an unbiased definition of 'religion' is useful. *The Concise Oxford English Dictionary* offers an example of current thinking by defining religion as:

> Human recognition of superhuman controlling power and esp. of a personal God entitled to obedience; effect of such recognition on conduct and mental attitude.

From this it can safely be assumed that involvement in religion is a conscious act and not something that can be undertaken unwittingly as a result of, say, chanting, making a gesture or hearing of someone else's religious convictions. However, the moment one ascribes religious attributes to any such actions, it might reasonably be said that one was involving oneself in religion.

On the basis of this definition, therefore, it would be unreasonable to suggest that meditators, many of whom profess no religion, are involved in religion. The suggestion that by attending a ceremony conducted in a foreign tongue followed by instruction in the use a sound 'Meaningless to us' one might become embroiled in a fledging offshoot of the Hindu religion is a little hard to accept. Few meditators would agree with this assertion since for the most part, they view TM as nothing more than a useful self-help technique, a way to relax after the upheavals that beset their everyday life. Having learned to meditate, only a small proportion then trouble themselves to make further contact with the Movement. It is unlikely that many practitioners of TM have more than a scant awareness of the Maharishi's philosophy and fewer still a knowledge of his religious convictions.

Although it does not easily fall into the category of religion, it would be mistaken to infer that TM and its attendant philosophy is not a religion for any of its followers. If by the practice of TM a 'recognition' of a 'superhuman controlling power' came to the meditator, or if a meditator perceived the Maharishi to be such a being, then TM could be considered a religion. Somebody who has given the subject considerable thought is Peter Russell. In one of his books, *The Awakening Earth* he explains the function of the *mantra* in meditation:

> In Transcendental Meditation (TM), one of the most widespread practices in the West at present, the person sits down quietly and silently repeats a '*mantra*', which as far as TM is concerned is just a meaningless sound, although in some other practices the *mantra* may have a specific meaning. In this meditation one attends to the *mantra* in a passive manner, not forcing it into any particular form or rhythm. This passive mode of attention is greatly helped by the fact that the *mantra* has no meaning; it does not, in itself, set you thinking on long trains of associative thought.[308]

Certainly this view of the TM technique is in perfect accord with the corporate standpoint and echoes the Maharishi's comments on the subject. But things were not always thus.

Before surveying some of the Maharishi's earlier allusions to the religious nature of his teachings, which meditators are largely ignorant of, it would be appropriate to look at his views on the right to freedom of information. Although he sometimes appeared cautious and highly selective about what information he chose to impart, it is unlikely that he would ever have agreed with the old maxim that 'ignorance is bliss'. At the Inauguration of the Dawn of the Age of Enlightenment on 12 January 1974 he put across his viewpoint very forcefully: 'Individuals don't have to remain in ignorance. Ignorance is the worst sin that a man can ever commit.'[309]

And to ignore the lessons of history would be to live a life in ignorance.

The Maharishi's earliest recorded lectures were those published under the title *Beacon Light of the Himalayas* in October 1955. In the course of his expositions on 'the dawn of a happy era in the field of spiritual practices, mind control, peace and *atmananda*' he explained to his audience a little about the techniques he was imparting:

> We do not select any sound like mike, flower, table, pen, wall etc. because such ordinary sounds can do nothing more than merely sharpening the mind; whereas there are some special sounds which have the additional efficacy of producing vibrations whose effects are found to be congenial to our way of life. This is the scientific reason why we do not select any word at random. For our practice we select only the suitable *mantras* of personal Gods. Such

mantras fetch to us the grace of personal Gods and make us happier in every walk of life.[310]

The following day he elaborated on this theme, explaining that a householder, in addition to his concerns for 'wife, children, friends, relatives, money, name and fame' might also do well to undertake devotion to 'his "ISHTAM" – his personal God – his beloved Deity - Almighty. "SAT-CHIT-ANANDAM".'[311]

This suggests that a householder might readily cultivate devotion for supposed personal gods by repeating the *mantras* given by the Maharishi. He explained:

> When he devotes himself and meditates on the name and form (NAMA AND RUPA) of the LORD, he begins to experience some ANANDAM and also the Grace of the Lord in every walk of life.[312]

But is this 'Grace of the Lord' a 'recognition' of a 'superhuman controlling power'? He appeared to be suggesting that the vital ingredient in securing this link was the power of love, the love of the deity:

> Love for the ISHTAM enables the Grihastha [householder] to feel the presence of his 'ISHTAM' always with him, in all his ways of life, in all his thought, speech and action.[313]

Apparently, in a publication printed three years later in Hawaii entitled 'Meditation: easy system propounded by Maharishi Mahesh Yogi' there is to be found a series of questions which includes the following:

> Q. How does meditation improve the fortune of a man?

> A. Our system of meditation involves the All Mighty Power. We take the 'MANTRA' of some God according to our faith and meditate on that. The power of the 'MANTRA' brings to us the Almighty

Closer inspection of the published booklet of 'Beacon light' lectures reveals on page fifty-nine, four Sanskrit verses forming a variant of a well known prayer in veneration of the *guru* or more particularly the *guru's* sandals, popularly known as the *Guru Paduka-Panchakam* and attributed to Adi Shankara, the founder of the Shankaracharya tradition of monks. Interestingly, one of these verses contains no fewer than three TM-style *bij mantras*. This is seemingly compelling evidence of a connection between an older tradition of *bij mantra* meditation and the Maharishi's Transcendental Meditation. Transliteration of the particular Sanskrit verse is as follows:

aimkaara hriimkaara rahasyayukta shriimkaara

guudaartha mahaavibhuutyaa,
omkaara marma pratipaadiniibhyaam namo namah
shrii gurupaadukaabhyaam.

In case anyone assumes that the Maharishi departed from the views he had expressed in 1955 they should be aware that many years later, when reflecting on that historic set of lectures, he was heard to comment:

> As time goes on it looks as if it's just the more expanded commentary of what that book contains. The same message, the same thing.[314]

Although all the foregoing might appear to be conclusive evidence that TM is a religion, it is not necessarily the case. At the 'Beacon Light' lectures the Maharishi was addressing an audience that in all probability consisted entirely of anchorites of the Hindu faith. By offering them a method by which they might deepen their faith, he was not offering them a religion, but an adjunct to their existing convictions. When years later he offered his techniques to those without religious beliefs, could it reasonably be said that he was therefore offering them a religion, that he was pulling the wool over their eyes? Perhaps not, but the presence of the following passage from his commentary on the *Bhagavad-Gita*, published some twelve years after the 'Beacon Light' lectures, appears to confirm that his meditation has an essentially religious basis:

> By taking the name or form of the god and experiencing it in its subtler states until the mind transcends the subtlest state and attains transcendental consciousness. Those who are highly emotional, however, may even transcend through an increased feeling of love for the god during the process of making offerings.[315]

The debate as to whether or not the Maharishi's meditation method is totally unconnected with the Hindu faith has persisted throughout the years of his ministry. As long ago as 1964, when he participated in the celebrated 'Meeting Point' debate,[316] the presenter Robert Kee asked:

> Maharishi, I'm very struck by the apparent similarity of approach between you and the Abbot, but of course the basis of your meditation technique is the Hindu religion isn't it?

It took more than this exceedingly direct question to goad the Maharishi into impatience. Side-stepping the question he directed Kee's attention to the non-religious aspects of his teaching:

> The basis of my meditation is the desire of mind to go to a field of greater happiness the innate tendency of the mind to go to a field of greater happiness; and the Being is of blissful nature.

Although it is obvious that the Maharishi disliked his meditation technique being linked with the Hindu religion, he was happy enough to admit its religious potential. The Abbot of Downside took him up on this topic:

> But there is one thing which I would really like to ask you about, Maharishi, if I may, because I think you would not entirely reject the statement that the condition which is reached in meditation is a condition in which we find God.

The Maharishi was surprisingly and spectacularly forthcoming: 'Yes, yes. That is the only way to find God. The only way to find God.'

23

★

QUEST FOR UTOPIA

Someone once asked what interests, other than meditation, the Maharishi pursued in his spare time, suggesting that perhaps he might be a collector or a connoisseur of antique furniture. Although most of us have leisure interests and hobbies, the prospect of the founder of Transcendental Meditation, the Science of Creative Intelligence and the TM-Sidhi programme and the mastermind behind a host of other initiatives, finding satisfaction in the contemplation of a collection of Chippendale chairs or porcelain plates is somehow faintly ludicrous. However he was, in his own way, an avid collector of sorts. The themes of his collections were extremely diverse, and his appetite for acquiring new additions apparently insatiable, but the subject was always the same – people. At the start of his movement, the hunt was on to find willing and eager individuals ready to take up his meditation, then the emphasis moved to find volunteers with organizational skills and then to those who would be willing to teach. Those were simple, relatively carefree years when he was relatively unknown and giggled his way through interviews, apparently enjoying himself.

His involvement with The Beatles and the uneven publicity this generated did not deter a great many celebrities from exploring his teachings. Over the years rumours have circulated in the media about who might be using the Maharishi's *mantras*. Some were unlikely contenders, such as Mick Jagger of the Rolling Stones, who is reputed to have been fairly disparaging in his remarks about the Maharishi. On the other hand, two of the Beach Boys, Mike Love and Al Jardine, became so committed as to become teachers of meditation. Others, altogether less public about their spiritual lives, included Canadian Premier Pierre Trudeau, Emperor Haile Selassie of Ethiopia, various musicians and singers including Stevie Wonder, his ex-wife Syreeta and Cher, actors Clint Eastwood, Burt Reynolds, Efrem Zimbalist Jr and Robert Powell, actresses Jane Fonda, Shirley McLaine, Faye Dunaway and Anna

Massey, sportsmen and women, and entertainers.

After his run-in with The Beatles, it was not the celebrities but the scientists that the Maharishi looked to 'collect'. And the scientists collected findings, and the findings collected new meditators and new helpers who in time became recruited as new initiators and so the process continued, forming circles within circles. Fresh inspirations led to new avenues, new themes to explore, creating newer ways of luring in candidates for initiation, leading to more donations. With an expanding source of revenue the organizations the Maharishi had founded acquired printing presses, video technology, scientific technology and real estate and even went so far as entering the arena of industry. What had started as an innocent, possibly naive attempt to regenerate the world spiritually was fast gaining the attention of the business community. Boardroom interest in meditation began to flourish; instead of investing in new equipment, some companies calculated that better dividends would accrue from getting workers meditating. It seems a German cement manufacturer was amongst the first to harness meditation for profit, allegedly quadrupling its production. John Lennon, in an interview for a teen magazine in 1967 jokingly announced:

> Tventy minutes a day is prescribed for ze verkers. Tventy minutes in the morning and tventy minutes after verk. Makes you happy, intelligent and more energy.[317]

It is commonly assumed that the Maharishi neither indulged in sensual pursuits nor had any interest in such matters. 'He is above these things' it was claimed. Certainly, there is no evidence that he was involved in licentious or lascivious behaviour, or is there any record of his telling ribald jokes. The Maharishi's disinclination to speak of matters sexual could make one suspect that he was of a Puritanical bent. However, it is said that in response to a question concerning sex in marriage, he offered a veritable gem of an answer, directing the questioner to 'water the fruit and enjoy the fruit'. One is tempted to say that if he did not really utter these words then he definitely should have!

According to a British initiator, one of the Maharishi's *brahmacharin* lapsed in his celibacy and had sexual intercourse.

'But, did you enjoy?' asked his master.

'Oh yes,' the *brahmachari* answered unreservedly.

Apparently, instead of admonishing the monk, the Maharishi suggested that a *puja* should be performed.

And had the Maharishi himself actually undertaken vows of celibacy? Leslie Smith of the BBC asked him in October 1969:

> LS: What is the vow you have taken?
> MMY: To refrain from the worldly joys of life – that is a monkish way of life.
> LS: Have you renounced the world?
> MMY: I did renounce the world
> I had the idea that I must renounce the world in order to be really a spiritual man, a *yogi*. But what I found out is that this spiritual life is not dependent on the renunciation of the world.

Largely as a result of the undisputed allegations of Beatle John Lennon to rock magazine *Rolling Stone*, the Maharishi had acquired a reputation for being something of a ladies' man. It is true that many young women easily became besotted with the man and his teaching, but so did a great many young men.

Rumours have a limited life span, however, and this was no exception. It was almost dead when someone kicked over the dying embers and rekindled speculation about his interest in matters carnal:

> One of the maharishi's foremost disciples, Linda Pearce, revealed that she had been seduced by the *guru* when she first went to India as a twenty-two-year-old virgin. 'When I asked him about his celibacy,' Mrs. Pearce recalled, 'he said: "There are exceptions to every rule." We made love regularly, and I don't think I was the only girl.'[318]

Allegedly there are other women too who claim that the Maharishi made sexual advances towards them and also that it became serious. If we were to start to believe these allegations we would soon recognise that, if such behaviour did occur, and it became public knowledge, it would seriously reflect upon his reputation and thus even make him a potential victim to blackmail.

But were the women offering the truth, the scorn of disaffected devotees or simply make-believe tales told in order to attract attention? Whatever it was, Ms Pearce's allegations caused quite a stir and the meditation teachers, attempting to uphold the Maharishi's reputation as a saint must have puzzled at his continued silence and wondered how one young woman could, with so few words, cause so much discomfort for them, with the Age of Enlightenment apparently so close at hand.

Rumours have also circulated about another aspect of his 'private' life, about the prescence of members of the family holding posts in his various organisations. The following report is said to have been carried by *The Illustrated Weekly of India* :

> Among the yogi's relatives, his brother J P Srivastava's sons, Anand and Ajay Prakash, seem to be in charge of accounts and administration. The [Maharishi's] brother, reportedly, is not given much importance in the family hierarchy, for reasons that date back to the illustrious younger sibling's youth. Mahesh Yogi, apparently, had early in life forsaken hearth and home after being allegedly ill-treated by his brother....

> The yogi, is reportedly, fondest of his niece, Kirti, his sister Indira's daughter.... She has two brothers, Praful and Pramod. While Pramod has settled in West Germany through the benevolence of his uncle [the Maharishi], Praful operates from India, say sources. The Maharishi's munificence extends to more distant relatives as well. Girish Varna, the son of one of the yogi's paternal uncles, has comfortably settled at NOIDA....

The main instruction when one is learning the TM technique, which is emphasized again and again, is 'Take it easy, take it as it comes, it is a simple natural innocent process, we do not expect anything.' But the suggestion that meditation is likely to bring wonderful improvements to one's life and that such improvements are happening to thousands upon thousands of meditators, is surely enough to make people expect *something*! The TM-Sidhi courses took the situation beyond belief, with people expecting to fly, hoping to materialize objects at will, to walk through walls and eventually to become immortals.

One of the many enticements offered to those adopting the method was the promise of improved health. His views on the relationship of mind and body immediately put one in mind of those of the Christian Science Church whose adherents assiduously avoid contact with doctors and drugs, preferring to neutralize disease by deliberately purging 'erroneous' thoughts. The contention that stresses and strains not only exacerbate existing symptoms of illness but are sometimes the very cause of them, has received considerable backing from the medical profession over the years. The Maharishi asserted that not only would disorders originating from mental tension be eliminated but so too would those of an organic origin. In his book *Science of Being and Art of Living* he had thrown down the gauntlet, calling on the medical establishment to adopt the practice of his Deep Meditation as a means of eradicating physical and mental problems. He painted a compelling picture of a life lived in bliss, a life where suffering had no place, where negativity could take no hold. Unlike other mortals his meditators would not have to endure the ups and downs of mundane reality; they would live a life free of headaches and heartaches, they would have no colds, no internal disorders, no problems at all!

But where was the evidence upon which he based these promises? At that time he had only been teaching his TM technique for a few years. How could he have been so certain of its benefits? The answer was twofold. First he advocated that contact with Being could bring about a state of completeness and grace; this was his belief, his religious creed. If someone had been conscientiously following his guidance but had not been freed from the anguish of disease or mental disorders, the Maharishi would not have accepted this as disproving his claims. His faith concerning the preventative and curative powers of Being was so unshakeable that it is unlikely that anyone could have prevailed on him to change his beliefs, whatever the proof.

The other reason for his utter confidence in the healing power of meditation was more obvious. He himself enjoyed the rudest of health and saw no reason to doubt that this condition would continue. He *expected* it to be so.

Some people see more than their fair share of suffering. One such person is Dr Deepak Chopra a fellow countryman of the Maharishi who lived in the USA. In 1980 he happened to purchase a book on TM and became profoundly interested in its message. Coming as he did from a similar cultural background to the Maharishi it is interesting to note the preconceptions he brought to the subject of mystic practices:

> It is impossible to come from India and not have a set of strong impressions about meditation. To me, meditation meant controlling the mind. The saying we all heard growing up was that the mind is like a drunken monkey, leaping this way and that in its maddened desires. Or it is like a flame that wavers in the wind and cannot be still. Or it is a wild elephant that can only be tamed by tying it to a post and waiting until exhaustion wore out the wildness.[319]

Not long after purchasing the book, Dr Chopra decided to become initiated. He found the technique to his liking:

> In this meditation the first experience was remarkable. As the teacher had suggested, it was quiet and serene and without strain. You didn't seem to be doing anything. But something more personal was occurring, like a curtain being drawn aside at midnight.[320]

In 1985, the Maharishi's 'Year of Unified Field Based Education', Dr Chopra was offered his first opportunity to see the celebrated founder of TM, who as it happened was temporarily domiciled in Boston. Dr Chopra confesses to having grown unexpectedly shy at the prospect of meeting the Maharishi and acknowledges too the likely source of his reluctance; being a doctor he suspected he might find it particularly difficult to play the role of a patient follower. He also wished to retain the independence of thought and action that he valued so highly; he was concerned for his personal integrity. Perhaps unconsciously he understood the inherent dangers of becoming infatuated with the teacher and teachings that had already turned so many people's heads. Dr Chopra describes his first impressions on seeing the 'Man of La Mantra', as one magazine dubbed the Maharishi:

> I managed just barely to discern that the remote figure on the stage was indeed Maharishi, dressed in white silk and seated in lotus position on a divan. He rarely stirred, and even from a distance, one got the impression of immaculate stillness. As he talked, he gestured with a flower in his hand. His voice was unusually varied, rising and falling, often breaking out in a laugh.[321]

On this occasion, the topic of traditional Indian medicine was being presented by a variety of guest speakers including doctors and Indian *pandits*. For several hours, Dr Chopra and his wife listened, but since they had a plane to catch they slipped out early. Before going to the airport they stopped in the lobby for a glass of water.

> At just that moment, the doors to the hall opened and out came Maharishi. He walked very fast for such a small man. A group of people trailed behind him, but without warning he veered away from where they were going, towards the elevators, and walked to his left instead, right up to Rita and me.
>
> In his arms he carried a loose bundle of flowers, which had been given to him in the hail. He picked out a long-stemmed red rose and handed it to Rita, then another and handed it to me.
>
> 'Can you come up?' he asked us.[322]

Although initially hesitant, the specialist in endocrinology, who was also a writer and meditator, accepted the invitation and soon found himself flattered and pampered by his gleeful host.

With many volunteers to take care of the routine organizational tasks, the Maharishi was nowadays free to retire into the background and survey his empire at leisure. After so many years committed to peddling his philosophy and practices, he might well have run out of steam had it not been for his ready audiences, who waited on his every word. With time to play with, he was able to devote his attention to drawing out the strands of ideas suggested in his earlier lectures and in particular those pertaining to the *Vedas*. When the Maharishi attended functions, there would frequently be Vedic *pandits* with him, enveloped in intricately embroidered red woollen shawls, who would recite passages from these scriptures. Although their hymns were incomprehensible to most of those present, meditators were made to understand that the power of their chanting lay less in the meaning of the hymns than in the effects they produced (echoes of the *mantra* theory). Vedic *mantras* were also in vogue amongst those who practised the TM-Sidhi techniques. They were advised to listen to tape-recorded selections from the *Sama Veda* as part of their meditation programme.

In announcing the formation of his World Government the Maharishi cited the *Vedas* as the basis of its constitution. Those who took the trouble to investigate these texts – they managed to locate one of the few translations – were confronted with countless pages of largely unintelligible writings. The Maharishi is alleged to have suggested that before any study of such works, students would do well to gain a thorough grounding in mathematics, presumably to sharpen their facility for analytical thinking. The study of the *Vedas* became obligatory for those practising the TM-Sidhi techniques, and they were supplied with translations of sections of the ninth, and tenth *mandalas* of the *Rig Veda*. These translations had been undertaken from the viewpoint of the Maharishi's philosophy and were thus believed to reveal the true meanings of the texts. The justification for this view was that the *Vedas* had both exoteric and esoteric meanings and could therefore only be understood according to the level of one's consciousness. Thus only the approved translations and commentaries were to be used.

In July 1985 a World Assembly on Vedic Science was held in Washington DC, and attended by a collection of the Maharishi's aides. Such assemblies had already been conducted elsewhere during the previous year. The Taste of Utopia Assembly had been staged at MIU in Iowa, followed by others in Holland, the Lebanon and Yugoslavia. All of them proposed that as a direct result of fusing Vedic wisdom with the practising of the TM-Sidhi programme, a Utopian age would soon occur. In his inaugural address to the Washington assembly on 9 July 1985 the Maharishi declared:

> For centuries Vedic Science has been misinterpreted and misunderstood. But now modern science has dipped into the reality of the unity state of life at the basis of the infinite diversity in creation. If human intelligence is to proceed on the more fulfilling levels of knowledge and existence on earth, now is the time for the complete knowledge of life to be brought to human awareness. Vedic Science is that most fundamental, complete value of science, which has in store all the future progress of the world.[323]

He had exceedingly high hopes for his new meditation method, the TM-

Sidhi programme, with its mixture of meditation and the mental murmuring of Patanjali's *sutras*.

> Inaugurating this World Assembly on Vedic Science, I am so hopeful for the world. These thousands of experts in the Technology of the Unified Field are practical exponents of Vedic Science. They are assembled to understand thoroughly all the implications of this technology for human society throughout the world. When I started the Transcendental Meditation movement, I was one man who knew this is something which people need, which the world needs. I am very happy that those inspirations of the past 30 years, which took me around the world many times, are lively as we inaugurate the World Assembly of Vedic Science. The whole human race is now being set on the platform of perpetual, complete progress for living all possibilities in daily life. This is my great, great satisfaction.[324]

By referring to those who practised these techniques as 'experts in the Technology of the Unified Field' he was making both implicit and explicit claims for them. How much did they know of the *Vedas*, how much of this unified field? Surely it was time for these 'experts' to speak up and demonstrate their supposed abilities.

In his bid to convince audiences that his Vedic 'science' was no illusion, this thoroughly modern mystic frequently had recourse to a mass of charts, graphs and statistics. The Maharishi was not actually at the assembly. In order to plumb the depth of meaning behind India's ancient scriptures, he had surrounded himself by those who might best help him. The building of the Capital of the Age of Enlightenment, in the 'land of the Ved', had brought the Maharishi back home to India and it was from there that he spoke to the assembly in Washington:

> I would have liked to have participated in the Assembly, but I am digging deeper and deeper into Vedic Science here in India with the Vedic Pandits. India is very fortunate to have preserved this total knowledge of natural law in the ancient traditions, and each day I am busy enjoying different values of Vedic Science.[325]

The Maharishi answered questions from the media by telephone. Someone asked him what effect the presence of certain religious leaders had on world consciousness. The master of evasion felt the need to be especially careful in his reply:

> As positivity grows in the world consciousness, the Pope will enjoy more success with his followers and the Ayatollah Khomeini also will enjoy more harmony in his country. I'm sure he must be worried about all that is going on with his own religious people, and he must not be very happy with the differences with Iraq. And the Pope, of course, will never be happy with the violence on earth.[326]

According to one newspaper the Maharishi predicted that 'the time is closing fast when the media will not report anything negative in world events'. The statement is consistent with the Maharishi's policy of giving but scant attention to negative issues, but the *Christian Science Monitor* had long ago beaten him to it, with its policy of good news reportage. Nevertheless, the tragedies still continue.

Amongst the many besuited speakers who took part in the assembly were the master of ceremonies, President and Chairman of the Board of Trustees, Maharishi International University, Chief Minister of the Ministry of Education and Enlightenment, World Government of the Age of Enlightenment, Dr Bevan Morris, and a fresh new face, the President of the American Association of AyurVedic Medicine and President and Chief of Staff of New England Memorial Hospital, Dr Deepak Chopra. In 1981 Dr Chopra had gained a great interest in the possibilities offered by alternative medicine after meeting a respected *ayurvedic* practitioner Dr Brihaspati Dev Triguna (who was also present at the Washington assembly). At the news conference Dr Chopra elucidated his views of *ayurveda:*

> As Maharishi has beautifully brought out, the basic premise of Ayurveda is very simple: nature is intelligent. As scientists we are able to study nature because it is intelligent. If nature were not intelligent, we would not get consistent results. Looking around us we can see the infinite organizing power of nature as it performs its operations with elegant simplicity. An individual is healthy to the extent that he allows nature to function spontaneously and effortlessly through his physiology. When he violates the laws of nature he creates stress, which obstructs the spontaneous flow of nature's creative intelligence. Ayurveda is a profound knowledge which allows one to live life spontaneously in accord with natural law.[327]

Dr Chopra had not taken long to master Maharishi-speak, and was already making his mark on the organization.

Meanwhile, back in 'the land of the Ved', at the new town of Maharishi Nagar, Noida, Ghaziabad, near Delhi a new nerve-centre of the organization was emerging. In 1985, 'Maharishi's World Plan for Perfect Health' had come into being along with a World Centre for Ayurveda. No longer was the Maharishi associated only with his introduction of meditation into the Western world, for now he was spearheading a massive promotion of a variety of Indian belief systems under the umbrella of his movement.

It was now some thirty-two years since Swami Shantanand Saraswati had succeeded to the title of Shankaracharya of Jyotir Math. It came as a surprise when he announced his intention of retiring in favour of his foremost disciple Swami Vishnu Devanand Saraswati. The criticisms of his association with the Maharishi might well have contributed to his decision to take to a quieter existence. Swami Vishnu Devanand, although not exactly young himself – his beard was already bleach white – would have greater stamina to endure the responsibilities of the post. One of Vishnu Devanand's first decisions as Shankaracharya was to become better acquainted with his master's fellow pupil. In order to take full advantage of the Maharishi's presence in India, he made haste in arranging an extended stay with him at Maharishi Nagar.

It had been decided to release a limited set of publicity photographs showing practitioners of the TM-Sidhi programme apparently hovering above the ground. As yet, however, there had been no public demonstration of these apparently extraordinary powers. It was now approximately seven years since the *siddhi sutras* had first been taught; surely this was time enough to test the 'Vedic technology'. Since the Maharishi and his movement were by no means averse to publicity, it had to be only a matter of time before the world was able to witness it in practice. After all, there was still time for a pre-emptive strike by a rival organization. The Sivananda Yoga Vedanta Centre released pictures of some of their young students levitating, presumably to prove that the Maharishi had no monopoly on mystical practices. There were also people who, having learned the TM-Sidhi techniques, had since dropped out of the organization and were ready to reveal all.

A steady stream of disaffected meditators, and even teachers, had already left the meditation movement, some to Satya Sai Baba, some to work alongside the South African Guru Raj in attempting to evolve an improved TM technique, others to join rival factions such as Mata Ji's Sahaja Yoga group, to go it alone or even to give the whole thing up altogether. Since the introduction of the TM-Sidhi courses there had been an increase in open criticism of the organization, the magnitude of its claims, and the apparent lack of personal progress. The lack of spiritual progress might have been tolerable if there had been more evidence of material gains. The corporate message was that meditators were successful people in every task they performed: successful in their careers, content in their family life and able to make lots of friends. Now some of the meditators were prepared to admit to themselves that it just wasn't working out as well as they had hoped; that the oft-quoted claim, that in meditation lay the key to realizing all one's desires, was becoming harder to believe in. Most people put this inability to realize their dreams down to personal failings, concluding either that their *karma* must be incredibly bad or simply that they were not worthy of higher experiences. Either way, they were not about to bite the hand that appeared so giving, and so they kept their reservations to themselves.

Nevertheless, the time was more than ripe for the Maharishi to either 'put up or shut up' and in 1986, the 'Year of Unified Field Based Perfect Health for All Mankind', plans were laid for mobilizing groups of *sidhas* to perform for the masses. As a prelude to the first unaided human fly-past, the Maharishi, on 25 May 1986, announced his latest plan, a programme designed to bring about world peace:

> Time demands the rise of the supreme power in the world which can have authority over the dangerous rivalry of the superpowers and can act like a dear mother to all nations. Ten thousand experts in the Technology of the Unified Field together in India can create coherence in world consciousness, which will positively dominate over the dangerous rivalry of the superpowers. Everyone in the world family will rise together under an indomitable strength of evolutionary power of natural law. Every nation coming to the level of fulfilment will be no damage to the fulfilment of any other nation. This is what will establish a permanent state of world peace.[328]

24

─ ★ ─

AT THE HOP

On Wednesday, 9 July 1986 over 120 journalists gathered at the Capital Convention Center in Washington DC to witness the first official display of the TM-Sidhi techniques. As with TM, the TM-Sidhi techniques were aimed at bringing the meditator to a state of 'restful alertness'. Dr Chopra, who was by now a leading light of the Maharishi's worldwide organization, clarified the connection between the practices of meditation and levitation:

> When he has meditated and reached this silent, even state, the person must next apply the mental technique that will allow him to lift up from the ground. The phrase 'mental technique' simply means a correct thought. At first his body will not co-operate with the thought. If one sits in an armchair and thinks, 'I want to fly', the body will not co-operate, but if the mind is in *samadhi*, there will be a result.[329]

The Maharishi's own explanation of the deeper value of experiencing this phenomenon is also worth noting:

> 'Yogic flying' demonstrates the ability of the individual to act from the unified field and enliven the total potential of natural law in all its expressions – mind, body, behaviour, and environment. 'Yogic flying' presents in miniature the flight of galaxies in space, all unified in perfect order by natural law.[330]

On 8 July 1986, the day before the 'yogic flying competition', 3,000 *sidhas* gathered for the World Assembly on Perfect Health in Washington to listen to an inaugural pep-talk from the Maharishi, courtesy of the latest time-lapse technology, explaining his latest initiative, a Programme to Create World Peace. Having at last learned that it was ill-advised to continue to skirt around negative issues in the way he had in the 1960s and 1970s, he now acknowledged an awareness of specific contemporary fears:

> The political history in the world has not been very worthwhile, with all the wars and now with something worse than war – the present state of terrorism. Terrorism can burst out at any place at any time, and terrorism involving the superpowers has created a terrible time for the whole human race.[331]

This was a very different Maharishi from the old days. Rumour had it that he now employed a bodyguard to protect him. What had happened to his theories concerning the infallible laws of *karma*? Surely one reaps only that which one has sown. Were not the recipients of violence only receiving their just desserts? Apparently not, for he declared:

> Whatever wars are seen here and there – the Iran-Iraq war, so much misfortune in South Africa and in Lebanon – all these negative things which should not be there will simply disappear.[332]

One is tempted to ask how this idyllic state of affairs was to be achieved. Was he seriously suggesting that he could undertake to deliver world peace on the strength of research into the TM-Sidhi programme? The days had long gone when the Maharishi would extol the virtue of simple innocence; nowadays he would have everyone believe that he knew the answers.

> Already, trends are seen in this direction. This has resulted from the purifying influence in world consciousness generated by such world assemblies as we have here today.[333]

These words were as music to his docile devotees' ears, for they believed that out of a world population of many many millions, only they and their kind held the secret of improving life on earth for others.

The day of the 'yogic flying' demonstrations arrived and the press gathered to witness the spectacle. They were primed for the big moment by a panel of sharp-suited men thoroughly conversant with Maharishi-speak, who indulged in lengthy explanations about the theories connecting the practice of the TM-Sidhi programme with the goal of world peace. But the media had only come to watch the 'flying', and the cameramen waited impatiently to determine once and for all the truth of the Movement's claims. Giving themselves a preliminary booster, 'experts in the Technology of the Unified Field' dressed in athletic costumes and seated on foam mattresses arranged across the auditorium, took part in a brief meditation. The cameramen steadied their cameras and waited, fingers itching, waiting for the first signs of flight. And then it happened.

It took a while for the reality of the event to sink in, for the sight of 22 young people hopping about like frogs, trying to project themselves across the vast expanse of the hall was a long, long way from the long-awaited act of flying.

It was difficult to understand why anyone should wish to be filmed bouncing along in such a manner, or even why they should wish to participate in the first place. What of the increased brain coherence that might be generated by these exercises? What about the feelings of bliss that apparently coursed through participants' bodies impelling them to take their next jump.

> The Washington Post reported, 'When the final race, the 50-metre dash was completed, the contestants were utterly animated. While the audience rose to their feet in applause, the hoppers remained seated, hopping vigorously amongst themselves ...'[334]

It is thought that the audience referred to was about 1,000 strong, and composed exclusively of meditators.

The name of His Divinity Swami Brahmanand Saraswati Maharaj, Jagadguru Shankaracharya of Jyotir Math, Himalayas was still murmured with reverence by the faithful, and he was worshipped as 'the supreme teacher'. Each July, on the day of full moon (known to Hindus as *Guru Purnima*), the Maharishi's closest disciples offered their devotions to a man of whose life story and philosophy they were largely ignorant. In 1986 *Guru Purnima* fell on Monday, 21 July and this auspicious day was chosen for the First International 'Yogic Flying' Competition at the Indira Gandhi Indoor Stadium in New Delhi, India. Surrounding the foam-mattressed arena were advertisements proclaiming 'Maharishi's Programme to Create World Peace' and 'Maharishi Ayurveda Perfect Health for All Mankind'. To a capacity audience of 10,000 the seventy-odd *sidhas* came from across the world to exhibit their ability to defy gravity. The new Shankaracharya, Swami Vishnu Devanand opened the proceedings, his arrival prompting a group of Vedic *pandits* to begin their recitations. Following on from the Shankaracharya's appearance came Dr Bevan Morris and a succession of other speakers, mainly Indian.

Then it was time for the show to commence. The 'levitating' athletes, after a few minutes of *mantra* meditation, sprang about like Chinese crackers. Earnestly they hop-jumped, hop-raced and hurdle-hopped in their bid to demonstrate the 'Mechanics to Create Coherence in World Consciousness, the Basis of World Peace'. Whilst waiting for the results, the audience was entertained by a series of 'inaugurations' by senior people from institutions connected with the Maharishi. The man himself however was not to be seen. He had decided to miss the event, possibly because he had seen it all before. Dr Brihaspati Triguna spoke on behalf of the Maharishi World Centre for Ayurveda and World Hospital of Ayurveda, and Dr B V Raman appeared for the World Centre for Jyotish (Indian Astrology), whilst the Maharishi World Centre for Gandharva Veda was represented by of its performers, who gave a recital of some selections of Indian classical music.

The moment of truth had arrived. The results had been calculated and were announced by Dr Paterson, Governor General of the World Government of the Age of Enlightenment for North America. He first offered his view of the Maharishi's place in the scheme of things:

> Maharishi's activity in the world mirrors the sequential and spontaneous character of nature's functioning. This functioning is described by unified quantum field theories in terms of 'sequential dynamical spontaneous symmetry breaking', whereby the unified field creates from within its own self-referral dynamics.[335]

And the verdict on the day's flying? The best results of the hopping races were: 25-Metre Hurdles Race, 14.81 seconds; Long Jump, 163 cm; High Jump, 60 cm; 50-Metre race, 25.89 seconds. For their efforts these best performers were awarded gold medals, with others taking silver and bronze.

It is said that a *sidha's* capacity to produce 'increased coherence' and assist world peace is calculated at 100 times that of one who practises the regular TM technique. With approximately 50,000 supermeditators available worldwide, a plan was devised which would both draw greater attention to the phenomenon of 'yogic flying' and generate cash contributions for the peace initiative. With a penchant for magic numbers, the movement targeted no fewer than 1,008 cities in 108 countries in order to allow the world's press a thorough understanding of the theory and practice of 'yogic flying'. On Friday, 15 August 1986, across the world *sidhas* twitched, convulsed and hopped their way to short-term fame. The ambitious goal of raising $100 million for the World Peace Fund was not achieved, but the still photographs portraying lotus positioned peaceniks seeming to float above *terra firma* did make it look as if magic had that day been done.

For Dr Morris, the Maharishi's right-hand man, August was a very busy month. He had appeared at numerous gatherings and press conferences; in fact, so ubiquitous was he becoming, that one might have thought he possessed some of the extraordinary powers that had been promised but so far not seen. As he faced the press in London's Royal Garden Hotel, one sensed that here was a man who was unusually honest, one who found it difficult if not impossible to tell a lie. He told BBC Radio 4's Trevor Barnes:

> When the person practises Transcendental Meditation their mind settles down to a completely silent state, a state of pure consciousness. Then they begin to practise a technique from the ancient *Yoga Sutras* of Patanjali which is supposed to produce flying. The brain becomes intensely coherent, and inside what you feel is an incredible surge of energy and great waves and thrills of bliss from head to toe and then the mind -

At this point he was interrupted by Barnes who, spotting the first signs of activity, wanted to keep his radio listeners informed:

> The first one has started to hop towards us. It looks like a physical thing. He could just be propelling himself along with his hands.[336]

It fell to Dr Morris to answer the central question of whether the 'yogic flying' had yet progressed past the phase of hopping. With visible reluctance he said that, of the three postulated stages of levitation - hopping, hovering and floating – only examples of the first stage had been witnessed amongst practitioners of the TM-Sidhi programme. He did, however, emphasize his conviction that it would one day be possible to go beyond this stage, and pointed to the historical wealth of accounts of such phenomena. This man, dedicated to the Maharishi and his teaching, appeared pained that he could not offer the world better proof of his master's message, but remained true to his faith without resorting to tactics of evasion and convoluted reasoning.

One might wonder why people expected so much from the 'flyers' if it were not for the Maharishi's forecast that his disciples would soon be flying over Lake Lucerne. Dr Chopra supplies further evidence of his capacity for predictions. He remembered the occasion when a young man said that 'yogic flying' would never be used as a method of transport. On hearing this, the Maharishi contradicted him: ' "Oh, no," he said, "we will fly outside the buses, even if just for fun." '[337]

When the 12 January celebrations came around again, 1987 was declared the 'Year of World Peace'. The Maharishi still contended that everyone should become blissful, but nowadays he seemed less concerned about how they should do so:

> Enjoy your life and be happy. Being happy is of the utmost importance. Success in anything is through happiness. More support of nature comes from being happy. Under all circumstances be happy, even if you have to

force it a bit to change long standing habits.[338]

He no longer seemed to believe that meditation cured all man's ills. Those as yet unable to radiate the bliss he spoke of were eager to hear his advice:

> Just think of any negativity that comes at you as a raindrop falling into the ocean of your bliss. You may not always have an ocean of bliss, but think that way anyway and it will help it come. Doubting is not blissful and does not create happiness. Be happy, healthy and let that love flow through your heart.[339]

He told of his hopes that by amassing large groups of *sidhas*, world peace would occur. On hearing this announcement at least some people must have had a strange feeling of *déjà vu.* They had heard it before. Almost a decade before, one of the Movement's magazines had announced the triumph of the Maharishi's peace forces in having created world peace. The *World Government News* was an unnecessarily lavish production which left the hands of readers smeared with specks of gold ink – at least one meditator is said to have become so incensed about what he felt to be a waste of donations that he determined to discontinue practising TM forthwith. In the January 1979 issue of the magazine, under a gilt-framed photograph of the Maharishi, the text ran:

> During October, in a historically unprecedented global initiative, the World Government of the Age of Enlightenment sent Governors of the Age of Enlightenment to restore peace in the five most troubled areas of the world. Through this initiative, inspired by His Holiness Maharishi Mahesh Yogi, founder of the World Government of the Age of Enlightenment, world peace has been achieved and large-scale violence and conflict, and consequent mass pain and suffering of humanity, have been vanquished from the face of the earth.[340]

The Maharishi really did seem to believe that his 'flying circus' could, if it were expanded to 10,000 *sidhas* and maintained by a $100 million World Peace Fund, create a situation where world peace might become an all-time reality:

> 10,000 Vedic Scientists in one place on earth, Maharishi Nagar, India, will enliven the supreme power of natural law in world consciousness, which will nourish all nations and disallow the rise of any negative or destructive influence in any part of the world.[341]

Whether the Maharishi liked it or not, whether he acknowledged it or not, the world beyond his movement could not easily be brought under the control of 'orderly thinking'. However he must have been warmed to hear from his teachers that approximately 3½ million people had by now received instruction in TM and to know that he could rely on others to spread the word. In one of the Movement's books, *Feel Great With TM*, the eminent doctor Desmond Kelly, MD, FRCP, FRCPsych, endorsed the technique, saying amongst other things:

> Setting aside 20 minutes twice a day for Transcendental Meditation enables the brain to be quiet and tranquil. It helps people think more clearly and positively, to have creative ideas, and to cope with the stress of a busy life. People sleep more soundly. TM also elevates the good-mood neurotransmitters in the brain, and because it acts on the brain directly it is much more than just another relaxation technique …[342]

The Fourteenth and Fifteenth 'Years of Enlightenment', the 'Second Year of World Peace' (1988) and the 'Year of Heaven on Earth' (1989), established nothing like world peace, although this did not stop the Maharishi from continuing to talk about the better times to come:

> Heaven on Earth has been the most laudable aspiration of the wise throughout the ages. Creation of Heaven on Earth is the most desirable project in entire history of the human race.
>
> Everyone can now enjoy Heaven on Earth through perfect alliance with natural law, through the enlivenment of the total potential of natural law in one's own consciousness. Perfect alliance with natural law is now available to every individual and every nation through my Vedic Science and Technology – the perfect science and technology of life which offers to enrich and raise to perfection all fields of daily life and create Heaven on Earth.[343]

In earlier lectures and writings the Maharishi had assiduously avoided the use of the words 'I' and 'my' in favour of 'we' and 'our'. The names of his movements were similarly impersonal until his university in Iowa was named Maharishi International University. Then, virtually everything he associated with himself took on his name. In 1989 he inaugurated Maharishi's Global Green Revolution, Maharishi's Global Rural Development, Maharishi's Global Urban Renewal and Maharishi's Global Industrial Revolution: programmes aimed at eradicating poverty. His previous achievements also became retroactively embellished with his name, as with Maharishi's Transcendental Meditation and Maharishi's Science of Creative Intelligence. Recently the market diversification had led to the introduction of Maharishi AyurVedic preparations and Maharishi Gandharva music cassettes, products to ring in the new Age of Enlightenment or Heaven on Earth:

> The inspiration to create Heaven on Earth comes from the great
> achievements of my Movement around the world during the last thirty years
> and above all from the discovery of the Ved, the infinite creative intelligence
> of natural law, in the self-referral consciousness, transcendental
> consciousness of everyone.[344]

The Maharishi might well have intended his 'Heaven on Earth' to be
literally just that. Each year the Maharishi would 'go into silence' for
about ten days at the beginning of January and again in July to recharge
his energies. In her book *Beyond Gurus* Nancy Cooke de Herrara
recounts that Charlie Lutes knew of another reason for these periods of
seclusion:

> It's also a time when he gets to talk with the Hierarchy. It [the Hierarchy] is
> the government of the cosmic force which controls the universe. Maharishi
> consults it in his silences when he needs guidance for his world mission. He
> obeys Mother Divine and honors this force, although the name is not
> mentioned in public.[345]

In May 1987 Benjamin Creme, the representative of an Eastern
missionary known as Maitreya, was asked:

> Q Which position does Maharishi Mahesh Yogi hold in the hierarchy of the
> Masters?
> A He is a disciple of a 6th ray Master of the 6th degree known as Guru Dev,
> Who is not in incarnation.[346]

In September 1987 he was again asked about the Maharishi, this time
less directly:

> Q Is Swami Brahmananda Saraswati [Guru Dev] now on Sirius and
> connected through Maharishi Mahesh Yogi to planet Earth?
> A No. Guru Dev still works on the inner [higher] planes of this Earth.[347]

On 12 January 1990 from the World Capital of the Age of
Enlightenment, Maharishi Nagar, Delhi, India, Maharishi Mahesh Yogi,
refreshed from some days spent in silence, proclaimed to his audience,
and to all the devotees who were viewing him across the world on
satellite link-up, that the Sixteenth Year of the Age of Enlightenment
would be the 'Year of Alliance with Nature's Government'. The Master
of Ceremonies, Dr Bevan Morris, opened the proceedings to announce
that the Maharishi was about to make his entrance. In the company of
some half dozen of his *brahmacharin*, amongst them Satyanand, and to
the sound of Vedic chanting, the Maharishi made his way across the
hall. His face (remarkably aged) beamed with a particularly joyous
expression as with palms placed together he acknowledged the crowds

of disciples. Amongst the assembled throng sat row upon row of young Brahmin boys in Nehru hats, known as the 1000 Headed Purusha; perhaps out there too were the 1000 young girls collectively known as Divine Mother. Also there to witness the celebrations were the VIPs, who had been allotted comfortable orange armchairs, and others, presumably lesser beings, the rank and file, who stood beside their white tubular chairs. Marked with the Hindu ritual red *tilak* upon his forehead with garlands of seasonal flowers around his neck, the Maharishi stood before a painting of his 'Guru Dev' placed upon a long altar replete with fruit, flowers and other symbolic offerings such as candles and incense. All present joined together in singing the *puja*, the prayer to the Masters of the Holy Tradition.

When everyone was seated and after the Vedic *pandits* had recited some more ancient chants, the speeches commenced. A succession of Indian speakers came and went, with Dr Triguna and Dr Chopra amongst them. Dr Chopra had come with some news, on hearing which the Maharishi became unusually animated:

> I was just waiting for this news today. Just this morning thought came to me 'How cruel is the health law of USA which prohibits things for health which have worked for thousands of years?' but that idea has now got this beautiful beautiful news and I am going to congratulate America for this. I congratulate the Medical Association of America, you have taken a timely stand for perfect health of human race. America has proved to be the most creative country in the world and now I see my feeling for years that USA is the most creative country in the world is materialized now in this news, if the news is true. If the news is true.[348]

Dr Chopra assured him that the news was true: the American Medical Association was giving credit for a course on Maharishi Ayurveda. This pleased its founder no end:

> Then from today I'll cease to think that American Medical Association have been and is continuing to be a puppet of the multinationals. I'll change my views.[349]

Then he launched into praise for those leading his *ayurveda* initiative and the promotion of its value, holding that the fundamental strength of *ayurveda* lay in its ability to prevent illness.

He was in particularly good form, his delivery bubbly and enthusiastic. As he glanced around him his eyes danced and sparkled. This was not to say he never hesitated or found himself grasping for words. The name he had applied to the year of 1990 for some moments eluded him, but after quickly referring to his notes he continued undaunted, stating that he perceived 'an upsurge in friendliness in the world today' which he attributed to the practice of accessing transcendental consciousness:

> Freshness is blossoming in world consciousness, negativity is subsiding in the world behaviour. It is a very good time for the human race, that this knowledge is fully enlivened. Today we have the total knowledge of natural law in our fingertips. This is the time that we feel, we are the custodians of heaven and earth so we want to bring them together. We want to create heaven on earth because we have that knowledge, that pure knowledge, that total knowledge of natural law. That reigns life in heaven just as much as it reigns life on earth.
>
> A common intelligence which reigns the whole universe is available now through my Vedic science to every individual in his own self-awareness, in his transcendental consciousness.[350]

He continued his marathon speech. He was in high spirits and in especially confident mood. Although his outer appearance showed his age, his strength of purpose and his capacity to express himself told another story. With head and body bobbing up and down, his toothsome, smiling face emitted hope and generosity. His words tumbled amidst bubbles of humour. The man seemed to be on a perpetual 'high'. Was it any wonder that, on the strength of his personality, so many had taken to his teachings? His passion and optimism flowed out in seemingly endless torrents of speech. One could really believe that such a man would have his own universities, with numerous scientists and specialists working for him, and would be able to form his own government and even to live in his own capital. He had the power, he had the charisma, he had that certain something, a magnetism that drew people near.

In a passing reference to world peace, he mentioned that it had already been gained, confiding:

> I am very happy today that those days should now be over for those powerful governments. That they hush up the great discoveries in order that 'no other government can have it and I will have a more powerful weapon'. The days of weapons are over.
>
> We have achieved the first year of the heaven on earth and now what will prevail in the world? Friendliness, sincerity, protection, nourishment, motherly and fatherly affection towards human race.[351]

One can only assume that his followers had been forbidden to pass on any bad news, for how else could he be so ill-informed? Nevertheless one might have been forgiven for believing his assurances, he sounded so knowledgeable, so convincing, so right, and with so much more to say. Many more speakers were to have their say, but the star of the show, as always, was still the Maharishi.

A novel twist to the proceedings came with a guest appearance of sorts, a pre-recorded video statement from the Delhi Police Commissioner, Raja Vijay Karan. He looked an intelligent man, conscientious but beleaguered with the problems of running an overworked police force of over 52,000 (believed to be the largest metropolitan force in the world)). His concern was that his officers had to work very long hours, seven days a week, and were therefore subjected to unbearably high levels of stress, and he was looking for a way to assist them. Presumably he was unable to offer his staff shorter working hours and so had to find an alternative way of keeping them fresh. It is unlikely that such a down-to-earth sort of person would have given much credence to the Movement's claims about being able to create an ideal society, but he was happy enough for his staff to give the meditation a try:

> So we hope with the introduction of Transcendental Meditation in the Delhi Police, the Delhi policeman will be less stressful, will suffer from less anxiety. He will be more fresh in his duty and will be able to perform the 12-14 hours of duty every day with greater cheer, with greater energy and with greater happiness and service to the people. Thank you.[352]

Another surprise speaker was one Anil Anatha Krishna, President of a division of a major Maharishi endeavour, the Maharishi Heaven on Earth Development Corporation. The topic of his presentation was the provocatively named Electric Chariots Project:

> Maharishi has given me this opportunity to exercise my technological capabilities to initiate and implement an electric vehicle project, to bring about a pollution-free world. With the blessings and guidance of Maharishi, we are gearing up for massive commercial production and marketing of pollution-free electric vehicles scheduled for commercial release by March 1990.
>
> In March we march to bring about heaven on earth with the introduction of pollution-free personal and public transportation system electric vehicles in the classes of two-, three- and four-wheelers.[353]

Until such time as the 'yogic flying' could be perfected, the organization's sights had been lowered somewhat to navigate a path more assured of results.

25

— ★ —

CORPORATE STRUCTURE

During the 12 January 1990 celebrations, the Maharishi accorded Dr Deepak Chopra generous praise; Dr Chopra, he said, had given up a highly lucrative career in medicine to involve himself in the study and promotion of Maharishi Ayur-ved. What he did not mention however, was that Dr Chopra was now so highly placed within the Movement that he was tipped as the most likely contender for succession to the leadership of the Maharishi's organizations. The new year saw the publication of another of Dr Chopra's books, the fourth in as many years, and the release of a package of six tape recordings under the title *Magical Mind, Magical Body.* Both his written and his recorded material were heavily promoted within the Movement, with Dr Chopra himself in ever greater demand. Reading between the lines it seemed as though the Maharishi wished Dr Chopra to have greater exposure, and therefore that he was gently divesting himself of his responsibilities in order to retire at last.

It is ironic that after several decades in which the Maharishi and his spokespeople strenuously upheld the all-embracing nature of meditation's benefits, the Movement should evince such sudden interest in 'alternative' medicine. Maharishi Ayur-Ved and its principal product *Amrita Kalash* 'Known in the ancient Vedic civilisation as the nectar of immortality'[354] had first surfaced in 1986. By 1991 the Maharishi's 'Year of Support of Nature's Government', the promotion of Maharishi Ayur-Ved had burgeoned to the point where a 500-room Maharishi Ayur-Ved Prevention Centre was to be set up in every continent, with 1,000 Maharishi Ayur-Ved Health and Rejuvenation Centres in North America alone. In pursuance of the Maharishi's commitment to his belief in the merits of 'yogic flying' a permanent group of 7,000 'Vedic scientists' was to be established at Maharishi Ved Vigyan Peeth, Maharishi Nagar, Delhi.

The new upsurge of interest in *ayurveda* centred around the names of

Dr V. M. Dwivedi, Dr Brihaspati-Dev Triguna and Dr Balraj Maharshi, Dr Han Sharma and Dr Deepak Chopra. The Maharishi offered his unreserved and unconditional support for ayurvedic medicine:

> Ayur-Ved is that simple, natural program for perfect health that eliminates all imbalances – in the physiology, psychology, behaviour, and environment. All the different health systems of the world are going to be fulfilled with support and enrichment from Ayur-Ved.[355]

The Maharishi's style of ayurvedic medicine offered more than just a range of herbal preparations, it offered 'pulse diagnosis' and the intriguingly named 'primordial sound techniques'. According to Dr Chopra, whilst he was staying at Maharishi Nagar once, the Maharishi had summoned him to his quarters and told him:

> I have been waiting a long time to bring out some special techniques. I believe they will become the medicine of the future. They were known in the distant past but were lost in the confusion of time; now I want you to learn them, and at the same time I want you to explain, clearly and scientifically, how they work.[356]

The Maharishi then revealed certain simple sounds to him and explained how they should be used. He ended their meeting on a note of caution:

> 'This knowledge is extremely powerful,' he repeated. 'By comparison, the drugs and surgery you are used to using are very crude. It will take time, but people will grow to realize this.'[357]

Apparently Dr Chopra was convinced of the healing potential of these sounds, for they soon came to be offered as part of the Maharishi's package of measures designed to usher in his dream of a perfect society:

> Through the application of the prevention value of Maharishi Ayur-Ved, we envision a time in which life is lived in perfect health, free from sickness and suffering, and every nation, on the basis of perfect health, enjoys self-sufficiency, cultural integrity, and invincibility in the perpetual sunshine of the Age of Enlightenment.[358]

Having entered the field of alternative medicine, it was perhaps only natural that the Maharishi would not stop at *ayurveda*. Meditators had become involved in a whole series of commercial endeavours, ranging from selling air-freshening ionizing units to putting in a bid for the construction toy giant Meccano, playing with stocks and shares and selling precious gems. With the introduction of Maharishi Ayur-Ved, the scope for new businesses seemed unlimited. There seemed to be no good reason why they should not go the whole hog and explain all the other magical possibilities offered by ancient thought (making sure of course, that they were offered in a scientific way).

Had anyone given any serious consideration to the environment we live in? Why not dabble in a few ancient ideas about architecture and planning? Enter Maharishi Sthapatya-Ved:

> 'Our homes should be celestial, highly artistic homes worthy of Heaven on Earth,' says a spokesman for the World centre for Sthapatya-Ved. 'Using good materials is not enough. All the surfaces should be richly carved inside and out. The artists and the architect should work together to create a formidable, magical piece of art, stunning to the senses and fulfilling to the heart.'[359]

Armenia, recently the victim of severe earthquakes, was to serve as a model for this new architecture, and the town of Leninakan was chosen to be a City of Immortals.

Astrology was also brought into service, suitably approved and branded:

> Maharishi Jyotish is that precious and intimate aspect of Vedic Science representing the inner light of consciousness which brings the full knowledge of past, present and future.[360]

A lesser-known field of Indian philosophy is the practice of ritual performances known as *yagya:*

> Maharishi Yagyas are ancient precise performances by specially trained Vedic *pandits* at Maharishi Ved Vigyan Vidya Peeth in India which create specific life-supporting influences from the field of pure consciousness, the source of natural law, to counteract any negative effects which are going to come from our past actions.[361]

In effect it was a sort of dial-a-prayer service for those with problems with their past *karma.*

After years of concern about his movement's image, this swing towards wholesale Hindu revivalism seems to suggest that the Maharishi had finally given up his dreams of gaining support from Western scientists. Perhaps sceptics like author James Randi were right:

> Ever since I heard that the Maharishi Mahesh Yogi of Transcendental Meditation fame has a doctorate in physics, I've been wary of scientists who have lots of education but aren't very scientific. This yogic person, in common with most amateur philosophers, gropes about for a simple analogy to demonstrate a novel notion, failing to recognize that analogies are only for purposes of illustration and simplification, and do not often represent parallels. The Maharishi actually equates the solar system, with its planets

orbiting about central Sun, with the atom and its accompanying electrons orbiting a central nucleus. It doesn't take much science to recognize that not only is His Holiness thereby ignorant of the actual state of the atom, but that his parallel is ludicrous.

The Maharishi's solar system-atom analogy is not only crackpot, it is very bad crackpot.[362]

In January 1992, from his new top-security base in a converted monastery in Vlodrop, Holland, the Maharishi broadcast his new year's message. With the help of satellite technology the scrambled signals made their way to his faithful supporters clustered around television monitors around the world. Speaking from the Maharishi Continental Capital of the Age of Enlightenment for Europe, he announced that the Eighteenth Year of the Age of Enlightenment was to be 'Maharishi's Year of the Constitution of the Universe'.

On 1 April 1992 the former Beatle George Harrison announced his intention to perform at the Royal Albert Hall, London, in a benefit concert for a new political party, the Natural Law Party. At the inspiration of the Maharishi, the Natural Law Party was to field over 300 candidates in the British General Election. Few would be able to remain ignorant of this new political force, as the Natural Law Party's manifesto had been dropped through letterboxes across the land. George Harrison's involvement seems to have been spurred by his attendance at a lecture on Ayur-Ved by Dr Chopra some weeks earlier in London. When he was approached to lend his support to the campaign he unhesitatingly agreed and set about rehearsing. He was obviously still prepared to stand up and be counted as one of the Maharishi's meditators, but did he seriously believe that the practice of meditation automatically endowed practitioners with the ability to govern others?

> I believe this Party offers the only option to get out of our problems and create the beautiful nation we would all like to have. The General Election should be a celebration of democracy and our right to vote. The Natural Law Party is turning this election into a wonderful, national celebration and I am with them all the way.[363]

His appearance, billed as his first UK show since leaving The Beatles, proved hugely successful for his reputation and for the meditators. Before the concert he announced:

> I still practice Transcendental Meditation and I think it's great. Maharishi only ever did good for us, and although I have not been with him physically, I never left him.[364]

But it was going to take more than the return of this quiet superstar to win over the voters. The fledgling offshoot of the World Government of the Age of Enlightenment had its headquarters in rural Buckinghamshire, at the splendid country mansion of Mentmore Towers. Geoffrey Clements, the leader of the party, was asked what would happen if the Natural Law Party won no seats. 'That's a scenario that isn't going to unfold,' he replied confidently.[365]

But not everyone was 'with them all the way'. Simon Garfield of the *Independent* newspaper wrote:

> There appears to be nothing illegal about the activities of the Natural Law Party, but there is a vaguely sinister air to its HQ; amid dripping candles and incense, secret doors and dank passageways, cracked masonry and tarnished gilt, it is as though New Agers were making gothic horror movies. Visitors to Mentmore may arrive with an open mind, but they will almost certainly come away converted. The problem is, they will be converted to Conservatism.[366]

The Party had approached George Harrison to become a candidate, but he was unwilling to go that far. They met with more success with Canadian magician Doug Henning. Henning was at the time involved in a $1.5 billion scheme to open up a 1,400 acre theme park at Niagara Falls to promote the Maharishi's teachings. Although several other similar projects had been mooted in Florida, California, India and Holland, and substantial plots of land had been purchased, none had yet been developed. The theme park ideas seem to stem from the Maharishi's visit to Disneyland some years before. The park at Niagara Falls, in addition to educational facilities, planned to offer such attractions as the Seven States of Consciousness, a Ride into the Molecular Structure of a Flower, and a 'levitating' building referred to as the Courtyard of Illusions. Henning was interviewed for Canadian radio and asked what involvement the Maharishi had in these projects:

> Oh he isn't in the corporate structure. He's ... you might say the knowledge aspect and the enlightenment aspect. He's a sage. He is a monk. He doesn't make money. He doesn't have any money. He just is there and he gives the knowledge.[367]

Doug Henning's bid to become a Member of Parliament for Blackpool South appeared somewhat flawed, for he had never even been there:

> But I've read all about it, I'll be going in a few days. My platform in Blackpool is to beautify it with beautiful fountains and flowers and trees and waterfalls, and create more high-quality attractions and improve life for everybody and phase out VAT.[368]

He was not the only 'out-of-town' candidate; amongst the others were Australians Byron Rigby and President of Maharishi International University Dr Bevan Morris, who had been flown in specially for the election. Most of the candidates, however, were British residents and teachers of meditation, not all of them unknown.

> Dr Henning has recently been seen on BBC television, presenting his magic shows, as have Leslie Davis and Roger Chalmers, two members of the party's executive council. But their appearance was rather less glamorous, coming as it did on the BBC news last October after being struck off the medical register for offering herbal treatments for AIDS. The treatment was part of the Ayur-Ved health programme, practised and promoted by the Natural Law Party.[369]

Heaven on earth sounded attractive enough, but some of the voters were left unconvinced of the NLP's ability to provide 'perpetual sunshine of the Age of Enlightenment; always and everywhere a rainbow in the sky – coherent light of good luck for everyone'. Even meditators were divided about it, wondering whether the Movement's involvement in politics was not ill-advised. The Party's main appeal was to the floating voter, but it won no seats; indeed, none of it's candidates came anywhere close to being elected. In Southport, where Geoffrey Clements, the leader, stood for election, of the 55,440 people who turned out to vote only 159 supported him. Doug Henning fared a little better, gaining 173 votes out of 43,941 cast, but all candidates lost their deposits. Many of the Maharishi's followers must have wished that he had not suggested getting embroiled in the mundane and pressurized world of politics. One would have thought that this débâcle would mark the end of the Maharishi's involvement with politics, but he tried again in May 1992 in Israel and again in August 1992 in the USA, with no better results.

When 1993 came, the Maharishi had still not returned to his native India, but was still in Vlodrop, Holland. Rumour had it that he had fled on hearing that tax officials were to raid his *ashram*, but the Maharishi himself offered a rather different reason for his departure:

> The leaders in Europe have been trying to integrate, so I thought to establish a Vedic Science university here to help integrate the collective consciousness of all the countries in Europe.[370]

His continued presence in Holland did not, however, prevent him from attending numerous assemblies or from speaking with his followers all over the world by conference telephone and satellite broadcasts.

The image of the laughing, bouncing, giggling *guru* with the long, flowing hair and twinkle in his eye had, by repeated exposure, become etched in the minds of his followers. His oft-repeated claim that his techniques contribute to perfect health and a reversal of the ageing process justified expectation that he at least, would demonstrate these benefits. But the 12 January 1993 broadcast belied these promises. The Maharishi was almost totally bald, his forehead furrowed with deep lines, and his eyes no longer darted about as he spoke. They now appeared unseeing, the pupils all but permanently veiled by his heavily-hooded eyelids. In the three-quarters of an hour that he spoke, he gave the impression of one who had great difficulty rising to the occasion. Subdued beyond belief, his words no longer bubbled up spontaneously from a well of inspiration. He delivered his annual speech hesitantly and almost without humour. Naming 1993 the 'Year of Administration Through Natural Law', the Maharishi spoke at length of the greatness of nature's government, saying that it:

> ... maintains perfect order in the infinite diversity of the universe, whole galactic life, infinite dynamism in all directions, all the time. With such speed everything is moving in the empty space, but no collisions, no problems for anyone.[371]

His latest message to the world was that it was possible for life on earth to exemplify the qualities of order and perfection:

> It's a very great joy for us today with this ability that it's completely within our reach, to create a perfect government, as competent as the government of the universe, absolute government. And on that basis have the life of every individual in the nation and the collective life of the nation as a whole to be fully alert, and this will be the society that we envision now. Because of the ability of this pure knowledge.[372]

He declared that some time in the distant past, earth had witnessed ideal or perfect civilizations:

> We have great records of such times when such societies existed. Our ancient record of knowledge, not speaking of the modern historians, but our ancient record of civilizations has given us beautiful records and the golden records of ideal civilizations that existed. Golden records of ideal governments that have existed. So we know from the ability of knowledge that we have to make life great, fully according to natural law.[373]

The belief was that if sufficient numbers achieved transcendental consciousness, then an administration governed by natural law would result in which all good to everybody would prevail. He described his vision of the panorama of cosmic life:

> The whole universe, infinite number of galaxies moving in empty space with infinite speed, all the time, but well ordered.
>
> Empty space permeates the universe and there is the performance of that infinite creative intelligence which maintains order at every moment in the huge, expanding universe.[374]

The thrust of his present initiative was that each nation should be encouraged to maintain a group of individuals (supported by 'donations' rather than by taxes) dedicated to making contact with 'nature's government'. Governments in the countries which housed these groups would then, he assured, be able to function with a 'cool head' and 'warm heart':

> It is a very great joy to inaugurate that administration, that global administration through natural law today that is going to transform the history of mankind. The history of so many thousands of years is now going to be transformed into a golden age.[375]

During 1993 the Natural Law Party continued to try to gain influence, contesting elections in Canada, New Zealand and Australia, but without success. Apparently the Maharishi was still keen to see some results from his initiative to join the political scene. According to *Maharishi European Sidhaland News*, on 24 October 1993 (dubbed Invincibility Day), he proclaimed:

> The Natural Law Party is purifying the last and deepest layer of ignorance in the world – the field of politics.[376]

The publicity generated by the campaigns must have gained the Movement at least a few new converts, but not enough to leave initiators feeling self-satisfied. A suggested remedy, which would do away with the need for people to pay substantial fees for initiation was that the teaching of Transcendental Meditation might be offered in Great Britain as part of the National Health Service.

The Twentieth Year of the Age of Enlightenment, 1994, started with the announcement that 'donations' for learning to meditate were to be increased to £470. On 12 January, the Maharishi once again came onto the television screens of meditation centres equipped with decoding devices and satellite dishes. Once again his appearance was prefaced by a preamble from his number one devotee, Dr Bevan Morris, from whom viewers learned that this was to be the Maharishi's 'Year of Discovery of Veda in Human Physiology'. The man himself, now seventy-seven years of age looked in better shape than in the previous year. As he sat, surrounded by a veritable garden of flowers, plants, birthday cakes, Vedic *pandits* and devotees, he spoke at length on the meaning of the 'Veda in Human Physiology'. Interspersed with his explanations of this new 'discovery', he spoke of the 'dawn of perfection for every individual', of the 'vision or the reality of the fabric of immortality' and of the 'fruit of knowledge', that 'knowledgeable life will be mistake-free life'. He provided an answer to the eternal question: 'It is the basic violation of natural law that is the cause of all kinds of disorders and suffering ...'[377]

With an estimated four million people so far having been taught Transcendental Meditation, there can be little doubt that it will continue to occupy the attention of many people for years to come, but it is unlikely that the world will ever again witness a public appearance by the Maharishi. And when he finally dies, his teachings will probably continue, although not necessarily under the monopoly of his movement. One is tempted to suspect that the *mantras* will not remain secret for long. Divisions over the true nature of his teaching – whether they are secular or religious – will in time most certainly split the ranks of his followers. Perhaps he will nominate a successor, an individual who will inherit the mantle of leadership and preside over all the various branches of his empire. And who would this be? Dr Chopra perhaps? But the star of Maharishi Ayur-Ved, once the main contender for the seat of power, appears no longer to be available. The *Journal of the American Medical Association* published an extremely positive profile of Maharishi Ayur-Ved, and then changed its stance, following it with an article which sought to expose alleged malpractice. It has been reported that the writer of the later article, along with his editor, are being sued for somewhere in the region of $200 million plus legal expenses. Since then Dr Chopra appears to have severed his connections with the Movement.

The year of 1995 became the Year of Silence, 1996 the Year of Awakening with the following years starting from 1997 collectively labelled the Years of Global Administration Through Natural Law. India has seen no return of the Maharishi who remains in the Netherlands. Plans and schemes have become ever more grandiose and the cost of learning TM ever rises (in spite of suggestions to the contrary). Then again, some breakaway teachers offer meditation at a budget price whilst others teach it for free. With the explosion of personal computer usage giving ever wider access to the internet, many websites have been created to promote TM and the many commercial ventures of the movement.

News of the crowning of one of his aides as 'Raja Ram' and the opportunity for others with enough wealth to also become a *'Raja'* looks preposterous to outsiders. But even insiders must be shocked that teachers will need to become re-certified before being able to continue teaching TM. This initiative is more likely to produce a wave of renegade teachers than it is to strengthen an already divided organisation.

If the Maharishi wishes to surrender his power, a likely successor could be found in the present Shankaracharya of Jyotir Math, Swami Vasudevanand Saraswati, who would have the strength of the Shankaracharya Tradition behind him. This could be a problem since succession to the throne of Shankaracharya has for many years been contested and the outcome will not necessarilly be in favour of this particular *swami*. On the other hand, perhaps he might wish to offload the responsibility to one of his *brahmacharin*, to Dr Morris or another of the Western disciples. Alternatively he could always nominate a board of trustees and empower them to oversee his affairs. When questioned directly about this issue, the Maharishi responded:

> Heaven on Earth will have lots of people as successors of this knowledge. By now there are about 40,000 teachers of Transcendental Meditation and they're all the successors of this beautiful Vedic wisdom.[378]

Some teachers will no doubt go there own way. This is understood. It is reported that at a press conference back in 14th May 2003 the Maharishi answered a question relating to this very issue:

> What I have taught, because it has it's eternal authenticity in the Vedic literature and you should know that, how many? 30 – 40 thousand teachers of TM I have trained and many of them have gone on there own and they may not call it Maharishi's TM but they are teaching it in some different name here and there. So there's a lot of these, artificial things are going on, doesn't matter, as long as the man is getting something useful to make his life better, we are satisfied.

Even before his death, the Maharishi's life and work is already frequently being misrepresented and distorted, as can be seen from the following example, an extract from a potted biography:

> The Yogi was unknown till he got himself a public relations expert, who arranged for his trip to England and booked the ball-room of the elegant Claridges Hotel for his show. Complete with a specially tailored saffron outfit, flowers and proper lighting, the Yogi with his soft-spoken syllables,

enthralled the audience among whom were the world famous pop singers –
the fabulous Beatles ... Once the Yogi captured the interest of the group
there was no turning back. They came to India followed by other artists,
including Mr Farrow [sic]. This was in 1967.[379]

Actually, it was in 1968 that The Beatles journeyed to India, after their
initial meeting with him at the London Hilton, not Claridges. And a
saffron-coloured outfit? Not the Maharishi! Other popular
misconceptions are that he amassed a huge fleet of Rolls Royce cars and
private aeroplanes, but, people easily confuse him with other Indian
teachers, such as Bhagwan Rajneesh and Guru Maharaj Ji.

He is not without critics amongst his peer group, there are others,
coincidentally also from the Jabalpur area of India, who have openly
disparaged him. According to Osho World Online Magazine- June
2004, Osho (formerly Bhagavan Rajneesh) had this to say:

> A *Sudra* can be a *yogi*, and the name Maharishi is something to replace
> "*Swami*," because in India things are such that if the name "*Swami*" is
> missing, then people would suspect something is wrong. You have to put
> something else there just to cover up the gap. He invented "Maharishi." He is
> not even a *rishi*; *rishi* means "seer," and *maharishi* means "great seer." He
> can't even see beyond his nose. All he can do when you ask him relevant
> questions is giggle. In fact, I will call him "Swami Gigglananda," that will fit
> him perfectly. That giggling is not something respectable, it is really a
> strategy to avoid questions. He cannot answer any question.

More serious are the allegations said to have been made by a fellow-
disciple of Guru Dev and now himself a Shankaracharya in his own
right, Shankaracharya of Dwarka, Swami Swaroopanand Saraswati in an
interview with a former TM teacher:

> Q: Mahesh Yogi claims that he preaches *yoga* according to the instruction of
> his *guru*. The truth of the matter, however, is that Guru Dev never asked
> anyone who is not a *Brahmin* by birth to go and spread his teachings. What is
> your opinion?

> Shankaracharya: This is true. In reality, preaching, initiating, guiding people
> engaged in spiritual pursuits, is the duty of those who are born in a *Brahmin*
> family. If he is a follower of *Sanatan Dharma* (the Hindu religion), he should
> not do what he is doing. This is against the orders of his *guru*. Moreover,
> making others write *puujya* (revered), calling himself Maharishi (a great
> seer) is totally inappropriate. No assembly of saints has either conferred upon
> him a title of Maharishi nor has announced him *puujya*. In the ashram he was
> doing the work of typing and writing and translation. Then he became a
> *sadhu*. However, he has never practiced *yoga*. It is said that Guru Dev was
> given poison. Who gave that poison we don't know but we know that there

was poison in his body. When Guru Dev's body became unwell, then we wanted him to go to Kashi to rest. But he (Mahesh) removed him from that trip forcibly and took him to speak in Calcutta. There he died.

Who knows what posterity will make of the Maharishi? Opinions about him will very likely become polarized. Some will probably dismiss him as a crank, whilst others are likely to hallow him as a religious Messiah the very moment he stops breathing. It would be unjust to suggest that he ever encouraged his followers to worship him or that he has created a religion around himself. The object of his mission appears simply to have been to try to spread happiness, even if the message lost a little in the telling. A journalist once put it to him that he was 'working on a very high state' and asked whether or not this was his last incarnation:

Last incarnation? I think I leave a better world than what I found it, and then I have done my duty to the world – don't have to come back. Sure I'm going to leave a better world than what I found it.[380]

The following observations are attributed to the Maharishi's teacher 'Guru Dev':

The one who has come, has to go. Nobody can stay here. Every moment keep your luggage packed. Nobody knows when death will call. The warrant of death is like the arrest warrant. One cannot think of appealing against it. Quickly one should leave off everything and leave. Whatever is, wherever is, we have to leave and go. So, if you are ready before, there will be not much of a difficulty, while leaving.

Whatever man does while living, be it good or bad, it comes to be remembered at the moment of death. At the time of death, remembering the dreadful results of ones evil actions, the soul starts repenting and hence becomes very sad. Therefore one should always be cautious, such that no sin happens, so that one has no regrets at the time of death.

It is a waste to make much of your activity, so try to live quietly as long as you have to live. Even emperors like Chakravarti Dasaratha could not get all that they desired. That is why, it is a great mistake to be distressed by involving oneself day and night in trying to satisfy ones desires. One should not forget, one day it is certain for us to move out of here!

Whatever program and in whatever condition it might be, and wherever it is we are involved in, we have to leave it as it is and go. Everyone has to travel alone. So do not be sad about things that we have no choice, but to leave.

As long as one has to live, live peacefully. It is certain, the work here can never be completed. So do not make much out of doing. Work as it is, is a waste. Lead this life with a peaceful mind, doing your duty and always remembering *Paramatma*.

The Creator is Vishvambhara. He shoulders the duty to sustain and protect us. And so, he will make arrangements. Without having faith in His support, if you depend on your intellect and cleverness, deceit and craftiness, you will lead a life of turbulence and the future path will also be darkened.

So, lead life in such a way, that you will be peaceful while living and making your future path bright as well.

Glossary

Adharma Vice, sin
Amrita Nectar
Ananda Joy, bliss
Arya Noble
Ashram Hermitage
Ashrama Stage of life
Atma, Atman Soul
Avataar Incarnation
Bhagavan Bhagwan God
Bhajan Hymn
Bhakti Devotion
Bharat India
Bhavateet Transcendental
Bij Seed
Brahma Hindu god of creation
Brahmanand, Brahmananda Absolute bliss
Brahmachari Celibate student
Brahman The Absolute
Brahmin Learned or priestly caste
Charan Ray of sun or moon
Chela Disciple
Chit Consciousness
Darshan Holy look
Deepak Light, lamp
Dharma Duty
Dhoop Sticky incense, fragrant lamp
Dhoti Sheet
Dhyan Meditation
Diksha Initiation
Ganapati Ganesha Hindu god with elephant trunk
Gandharva-Ved Indian classical music
Gandharvas Celestial musicians
Ganja Marijuana
Gita Song

Grihastha Householder
Guna Quality
Hare Lord
Gupha Cave
Guru Teacher, master
Gurudwara Sikh temple
Gyan, Gyaan, Gnan, Jyaan Knowledge
Hansa Swan
Hawaii Pertaining to the air
Jai, Jay, Jaya Hail, glory
Japa Repetition of *mantra*
Ji Term of respect
Jyotir Light
Jyotishi Indian astrology
Kalpa Period of time
Kamandalu Wooden pot
Karma Law of action and reaction
Kashi Benares, Varanasi
Kaupeen Loincloth
Krishna Dark, name of principal character of *Mahabharata* poem
Kshatriya Caste of warriors, administrators
Lingam Phallus
Maharaj(ah) King
Maharishi (*Maharshi*) Great sage
Mahesh Name of Hindu god Shiva
Mala Rosary
Mandir Hindu temple
Mantra Word or words of spiritual power
Manu Smriti or *Manu Samhita* Law book
Math Monastery
Mukti Liberation
Nagar Town
Pandit Learned man
Paramatma Supreme Spirit, God
Prana Breath
Pranava Name of om *mantra*
Prasad Blessing
Puja Ceremony, ritual
Purnima Full moon night
Raj Royal
Rajasic, Energetic, passionate

Rama Name of hero of *Ramayana* poem
Rishi Wise man
Rudra Name of Hindu god Shiva
Sadhana Spiritual discipline
Sadhu Wandering holy man
Samadhi Stillness of the mind
Sannyas Vow of renunciation
Saraswati Name of Hindu goddess of learning, name of river
Satsang To take the company of the good or pious
Sattvic Pure
Satya Truth
Shankar Name of Hindu god Shiva
Shanti Peace
Shiva Name of Hindu god of destruction, lord of the *yogis*
Shivalinga Symbol of creative forces
Shivaratri Night(s) dedicated to worship of Hindu deities Shiva and his consort Shakti
Shloka Verse
Shri Blessed
Siddha Perfected being
Siddhi One who has acquired supernatural powers
Smriti Remembered texts
Swami Renunciate
Swaroop Divine form
Tilak Mark of sandalwood paste applied to forehead
Tri Three
Upadesh Lecture
Upanishad Texts on *yoga*, to sit near
Vanaprasthas Forest dwellers
Varna Caste
Vishnu Hindu god of preservation
Yagya, Yajna Ritual, sacrifice
Yatra Tour, pilgrimage
Yuga Period of time

Notes

CHAPTER 1

1. *Intro*, issue 1, September 1967, p. 7.
2. Maharishi Mahesh Yogi, *Thirty Years Around the World*, vol. 1, p. 244.
3. Elsa Dragemark, *The Way to Maharishi's Himalayas*, p. 257.
4. Rameshwar Tiwari, *The Whole Thing – The Real Thing*, p. 12.
5. ibid., p. 22.
6. ibid., p. 33.
7. ibid., p. 34.
8. ibid., p. 42.
9. Swami Rama, *Living with the Himalayan Masters*, pp. 257-8.
10. Maharishi Mahesh Yogi, *Meditations of Maharishi Mahesh Yogi*, pp. 39-40.
11. Maharishi Mahesh Yogi, *Science of Being and Art of Living*, p. 181.
12. Maharishi Mahesh Yogi, *Meditations*, p. 61.
13. *MIU World*, vol. 1, no. 2, 1991.
14. Maharishi Mahesh Yogi, *Thirty Years*, p. 184.
15. ibid.
16. *International Times*, 15 December 1967.

CHAPTER 2

17. Elsa Dragemark, *The Way to Maharishi's Himalayas*, p. 259.
18. Maharishi Mahesh Yogi, *Thirty Years*, p. 185.
19. Swami Rama, *Living with the Himalayan Masters*, p. 260.
20. Rameshwar Tiwari, *The Whole Thing*, p. 68.
21. Elsa Dragemark, *The Way to Maharishi's Himalayas*, p. 238.
22. Herbert Tichy, *Himalaya*, p. 50.
23. Elsa Dragemark, *The Way to Maharishi's Himalayas*, p. 261.
24. Maharishi Mahesh Yogi, *Love and God*, p. 10.
25. Elsa Dragemark, *The Way to Maharishi's Himalayas*, pp. 261-2.
26. ibid., p. 262.

27. Rameshwar Tiwari, *The Whole Thing*, p. 73.
28. Maharishi Mahesh Yogi, *Thirty Years*, p. 186.
29. Helena Olson, *Hermit in the House*, p. 67.
30. Robert Hollings, *Transcendental Meditation*, p. 83.
31. ibid.
32. Maharishi Mahesh Yogi, *Thirty Years*, p. 189.

CHAPTER 3

33. Jack Forem, *Transcendental Meditation*, p. 209.
34. Maharishi Mahesh Yogi, *Beacon Light of the Himalayas*, p. 43.
35. ibid., p. 46.
36. ibid., p. 62.
37. ibid.
38. Maharishi Mahesh Yogi, *Thirty Years*, p. 40.
39. Maharishi Mahesh Yogi, *Beacon Light*, p. 66.
40. ibid.
41. ibid., p. 76.
42. ibid., introduction.
43. ibid., p. 77.
44. Maharishi Mahesh Yogi, *Thirty Years*, p. 208.
45. Maharishi Mahesh Yogi, *Bhagavad-Gita*, p. 9.
46. *International Times*, 15 December 1967.
47. Maharishi Mahesh Yogi, *Thirty Years*, p. 211.
48. Elsa Dragemark, *The Way to Maharishi's Himalayas*, p. 40.
49. ibid.
50. Maharishi Mahesh Yogi, *Thirty Years*, p. 213.
51. ibid., pp. 217ff.
52. ibid., p. 223.
53. ibid., p. 227.
54. ibid., p. 229.
55. ibid.
56. *International Times*, 15 December 1967.

CHAPTER 4

57. ibid.
58. Maharishi Mahesh Yogi, *Thirty Years*, p. 242.
59. ibid., p. 243.
60. Helena Olson, *Hermit in the House*, pp. 21-2.
61. ibid., p. 33.

62. ibid., p. 43.
63. ibid., p. 44.
64. ibid.
65. ibid., p. 50.
66. ibid., p. 51.
67. ibid., p. 53.
68. ibid., p. 79.
69. ibid., p. 160.
70. Maharishi Mahesh Yogi, *Deep Meditation*.
71. Helena Olson, *Hermit in the House*, p. 104.
72. ibid., p. 148.
73. Maharishi Mahesh Yogi, *Thirty Years*, p. 252.
74. Helena Olson, *Hermit in the House*, pp. 160-1.
75. ibid., p. 165.
76. Maharishi Mahesh Yogi, *Thirty Years*, p. 264.
77. Maharishi Mahesh Yogi, *Maharishi Mahesh Yogi*.
78. ibid.
79. Josh McDowell, *Understanding the Cults*, p. 107.

CHAPTER 5

80. Maharishi Mahesh Yogi, *Thirty Years*, p. 301.
81. Maharishi Mahesh Yogi, *Deep Meditation*.
82. Maharishi Mahesh Yogi, *Thirty Years*, p. 314.
83. Elsa Dragemark, *The Way to Maharishi's Himalayas*, pp. 43-4.
84. ibid., p. 44.
85. ibid., p. 351.
86. ibid., p. 352.
87. ibid., p. 354.
88. Maharishi Mahesh Yogi, *Love and God*, p. 50.
89. *A Six Month Course in Yoga Asanas*, p. 3.
90. Maharishi Mahesh Yogi, *Meditations*, p. 143.
91. ibid., p. 185.
92. ibid., p. 123.

CHAPTER 6

93. Maharishi Mahesh Yogi, *Science of Being*, revised edition, p. xv.
94. *Science of Being*, first edition, p. xviii.
95. *Science of Being*, revised edition, p. 97-8.
96. ibid., p. 271.

97. ibid., p. 272.
98. ibid., p. 238.
99. ibid.
100. ibid., p. 259.
101. ibid., p. 240.
102. ibid., p. 300.
103. Rameshwar Tiwari, *The Whole Thing*, p. 65.
104. Maharishi Mahesh Yogi, *Maharishi Mahesh Yogi* (gramophone record).
105. Maharishi Mahesh Yogi, *Thirty Years*, p. 542.
106. Maharishi Mahesh Yogi et at., *The Maharishi and the Abbot*.
107. Elsa Dragemark, *The Way to Maharishi's Himalayas*, p. 45.
108. ibid., p. 46.

CHAPTER 7

109. Maharishi Mahesh Yogi, *Thirty Years*, p. 572.
110. Maharishi Mahesh Yogi, *Meditations*, pp 13ff.
111. ibid., p. 15.
112. ibid., pp. 17-18.
113. ibid., p. 32.
114. ibid., p. 50.
115. Maharishi Mahesh Yogi, *Science of Being*, pp. 98-9.
116. Etsa Dragemark, *The Way to Maharishi's Himalayas*, p. 259.
117. Maharishi Mahesh Yogi, *Meditations*, p. 64.
118. ibid., pp. 110-11.
119. Maharishi Mahesh Yogi, *Bhagavad-Gita*, p. 8.
120. Maharishi Mahesh Yogi, *Meditations*, pp. 187-8.

CHAPTER 8

121. ibid., p. 134.
122. Maharishi Mahesh Yogi, *Love and God*, pp. 7-8.
123. ibid., p. 6.
124. Atdous Huxley, *The Doors of Perception*, pp. 16-17.
125. ibid., p. 18.
126. John Densmore, *Riders on the Storm*, p. 32.
127. ibid., p. 33.
128. ibid.
129. ibid.
130. Ved Mehta, *Portrait of India*, p. 94.

131. ibid., pp. 95-6.
132. ibid., p. 96.
133. ibid., p. 97.
134. Nancy Cooke de Herrara, *Beyond Gurus*, p. 165.
135. ibid., p. 175.
136. Paul Horn, *A Special Edition*.
137. Paul Horn, *Paul Horn in India*.
138. Maharishi Mahesh Yogi, *Seven States of Consciousness*.

CHAPTER 9

139. Author's transcript from recording.
140. Maharishi Mahesh Yogi, *Bhagavad-Gita*, p. 8.
141. ibid., p. 184.
142. ibid.
143. ibid., p. 185.
144. ibid., p. 340.
145. ibid., p. 342.
146. ibid., p. 88.
147. ibid., p. 169.
148. ibid., pp. 139-40.
149. ibid., p. 93.
150. ibid., p. 144.
151. ibid.
152. ibid., p. 94.

CHAPTER 10

153. *Observer*, 26 November 1967.
154. ibid.
155. ibid.
156. *International Times*, 13 May 1967.
157. *Intro*, issue 1, September 1967.
158. Peter Shotton and Nicholas Schaffer, *John Lennon – In My Life*, pp. 137-8.
159. ibid., p. 138.
160. ibid., p. 139.
161. Albert Goldman, *The Lives of John Lennon*, pp. 324-5.
162. *Daily Express*, 27 August 1967.
163. Author's transcript from radio broadcast.
164. *Daily Express*, 27 August 1967.

165. Derek Taylor, *Thirty Years Ago Today*, p. 132.
166. *Intro*, issue 1, September 1967.
167. ibid.
168. Author's transcript from recording.
169. ibid.
170. ibid.
171. The quotations that follow are taken from the author's transcript from the broadcast.
172. Author's transcript from recording.

CHAPTER 11

173. The quotations that follow are taken from the author's transcript from the broadcast.
174. Richard Neville, *Playpower*, p. 79.
175. Peter Brown and Steven Gaines, *The Love You Make*, p. 249.
176. Peter Shotton and Nicholas Schaffer, *John Lennon – In My Life*, p. 161.
177. ibid.
178. ibid.
179. Steven Gaines, *Heroes and Villains*, pp. 238-9.
180. ibid., p. 239.
181. *International Times*, 26 February 1968.
182. Maharishi Mahesh Yogi, *Meditations*, p. 32.

CHAPTER 12

183. Elsa Dragemark, *The Way to Maharishi's Himalayas*, pp. 169ff.
184. Author's transcript from recording.
185. Albert Goldman, *The Lives of John Lennon*, p. 351.
186. Elsa Dragemark, *The Way to Maharishi's Himalayas*, p. 170.
187. Denny and Kathleen Somach, *Ticket to Ride*, p. 122.
188. Cynthia Lennon, *Twist of Lennon*, pp. 154-5.
189. Author's transcript from recording.
190. *Rave*, May 1968.
191. Elsa Dragemark, *The Way to Maharishi's Himalayas*, p. 170.
192. ibid., p. 178.
193. *The Beatles Book*, issue 58, May 1968.
194. Paul Horn, *Special Edition*.
195. Cynthia Lennon, *Twist of Lennon*, pp. 156-7.
196. ibid., p. 160.

197. Philip Norman, *Shout*, p. 320.
198. Jonathon Greene, *Days in the Life*, pp. 160-1.
199. Peter Brown and Steven Gaines, *The Love You Make*, p. 253.
200. ibid.
201. ibid.
202. Cynthia Lennon, *Twist of Lennon*, pp. 159-60.
203. Jan Wenner, *Lennon Remembers*, p. 56.
204. ibid.
205. Cynthia Lennon, *Twist of Lennon*, p. 161.
206. ibid.
207. Peter Shotton and Nicholas Schaffer, *John Lennon – In My Life*, p. 162.

CHAPTER 13

208. Nancy Cooke de Herrara, *Beyond Gurus*, p. 281.
209. ibid., p. 282.
210. Peter McCabe and Robert D. Schonfield, *Apple to the Core*, p. 95.
211. Steven Gaines, *Heroes and Villains*, p. 243.
212. ibid., p. 244.
213. Rameshwar Tiwari, *The Whole Thing*, p. 48.
214. ibid., p. 46.
215. ibid., pp. 46-7.
216. ibid., p. 47.
217. Author's transcript from recording.
218. Nancy Cooke de Herrara, *Beyond Gurus*, p. 298.
219. ibid., p. 299.

CHAPTER 14

220. Alistair Shearer and Peter Russell, *The Upanishads*, p. 65.
221. ibid., p. 33.
222. Maharishi Mahesh Yogi, *Love and God*, p. 10.
223. Author's transcript from recording.
224. ibid.
225. Jean Le Mee and Ingbert Gruttner, *Hymns from the Riq-Veda*, RV. IX. 112. 1-4.
226. *Vedic Hymns and Prayers*, RV. I. 2. 15.
227. This and the quotations that follow are taken from the author's transcript from a recording.

CHAPTER 15

228. *International Times*, 15 December 1967.
229. Lyall Watson, *Supernature*, pp. 178-9.
230. This and the quotations that follow are taken from the author's transcript from a recording.

CHAPTER 16

231. This and the quotations that follow are taken from the author's transcript from a recording.

CHAPTER 17

232. Author's transcript from a recording.
233. Maharishi Mahesh Yogi, *Meditations*, p. 95.
234. This and the quotations that follow are transcript from a recording.
235. *International Times*, 15 December 1967.
236. This and the quotations that follow are taken from the author's transcript from a recording.

CHAPTER 18

237. This and the quotations that follow are taken from the author's transcript from a recording.
238. Swami Sivananda, *Triple Yoga*, p. 3.
239. This and the quotations that follow are taken from the author's transcript from a recording.
240. *International Times*, 15 December 1967.
241. This and the quotations that follow are taken from the author's transcript from a recording.

CHAPTER 19

242. *International Times*, 29 August 1969.
243. ibid.
244. Maharishi Mahesh Yogi, *Science of Being*, revised edition, p. 155.
245. Author's transcript from recording.
246. ibid.
247. Shankaracharya Shantanand, *Good Company*, p. 128.
248. ibid., pp. 129-30.

249. Author's transcript from a recording.
250. ibid.
251. ibid.
252. Shankaracharya Shantanand, *Good Company*, p. 43.
253. Swami Sivananda, *The Bhagavad Gita*, p. 80.
254. Author's transcript from a recording.
255. Wendy Doniger and Brian K. Smith, *The Laws of Manu*, p. 87.
256. ibid., p. xxiii.
257. Author's transcript from a recording.
258. ibid.

CHAPTER 20

259. Jan Wenner, *Lennon Remembers*, p. 55.
260. ibid.
261. Jack Forem, *Transcendental Meditation*, p. 108.
262. ibid.
263. ibid., p. 15.
264. Harold Bloomfield et al., *TM**, p. 224.
265. Peter Russell, *The TM Technique*, p. 171.
266. Photocopied and circulated transcript.
267. ibid.
268. Robert Hollings, *Transcendental Meditation*, p. 57.
269. Harold Bloomfield et al., *TM**, p. 162.
270. ibid., p. 165.
271. ibid., p. 166.
272. ibid., pp. 183-4.
273. ibid., p. 184.
274. ibid., p. 228.

CHAPTER 21

275. Peter Russell, *The TM Technique*, p. 85.
276. ibid., p. 85.
277. Richard Tames, *William Morris – Lifelines 3*, p. 11.
278. *Inauguration of the Dawn of the Age of Enlightenment*, p. 23.
279. ibid.
280. ibid., p. 25.
281. ibid.
282. ibid., p. 27.
283. ibid., p. 47.

284. *Creating an Ideal Society: A Global Undertaking*, p. 96.
285. ibid., p. 109.
286. *Enlightenment and Invincibility to Every Individual and to Every Nation*, p. 254.
287. Maharishi Mahesh Yogi, *Deep Meditation*.
288. ibid.
289. Shree Purohit Swami and W.B. Yeats, *Aphorisms of Yoga Bhagwan Shree Patanjali*, p. 48.
290. Nancy Cooke de Herrara, *Beyond Gurus*, p. 432.
291. *Creating an Ideal Society*, p. 5.

CHAPTER 22

292. *United States District Court, District of New Jersey, Civil Action No. 76-341,* quoted in Josh McDowell and Don Stewart, Understanding the Cults, p. 108.
293. *Enlightenment and Invincibility*, p. 51.
294. ibid., p. 59.
295. ibid., p. 51.
296. Nancy Cooke de Herrara, *Beyond Gurus*, p. 432.
297. ibid., p. 438.
298. ibid.
299. ibid., pp. 452-3
300. ibid., p. 456
301. *Enlightenment and Invincibility*, p. 141.
302. Shankaracharya Shantanand, *Good Company*, p. 88.
303. Gita Mehta, *Karma Cola*, pp. 110-11.
304. ibid., p. 112.
305. ibid., p. 113.
306. ibid.
307. ibid., pp. 113-14.
308. Peter Russell, *The Awakening Earth*, p. 148.
309. *Enlightenment and Invincibility*, p. 386.
310. Maharishi Mahesh Yogi, *Beacon Light of the Himalayas*, p. 65.
311. ibid., p. 75.
312. ibid., p. 76.
313. ibid.
314. Maharishi Mahesh Yogi, *Thirty Years*, p. 194.
315. Maharishi Mahesh Yogi, *Bhagavad-Gita*, pp. 213-14.
316. Maharishi Mahesh Yogi et al. *The Maharishi and the Abbot.*

CHAPTER 23

317. *Intro*, issue 1, September 1967.
318. Albert Goldman, *The Lives of John Lennon*, p. 351.
319. Deepak Chopra, *Return of the Rishi*, p. 123.
320. ibid., p. 127.
321. ibid., p. 139.
322. ibid., pp. 139-40.
323. *Life Supported by Natural Law*, p. 35.
324. ibid., p. 36.
325. ibid.
326. ibid., p. 165.
327. ibid., p. 182.
328. *Maharishi's Programme to Create World Peace*, p. 2.

CHAPTER 24

329. Deepak Chopra, *Return of the Rishi*, p. 183.
330. *Maharishi's Programme to Create World Peace*, p. vii.
331. ibid., p. 4.
332. ibid., p. 8.
333. ibid.
334. ibid., p. 33.
335. ibid., p. 37.
336. ibid., p. 301.
337. Deepak Chopra, *Return of the Rishi*, p. 185.
338. Displayed at the London centre, 1993.
339. ibid.
340. *World Government News*, issue 11, November/December 1978, January 1979.
341. *Maharishi's Programme to Create Heaven on Earth*, p. 39.
342. Bill Stevens and Jim Anderson, *Feel Great with TM*, p. 7.
343. *Maharishi's Programme to Create Heaven on Earth*, p. 5.
344. ibid.
345. Nancy Cooke de Herrara, *Beyond Gurus*, p. 111.
346. Benjamin Creme, *Maitreya's Mission*, vol. 2, p. 79.
347. ibid.
348. Author's transcript from a recording.
349. ibid.
350. ibid.
351. ibid.

352. ibid.
353. ibid.

CHAPTER 25

354. *Maharishi's Programme to Create Heaven on Earth*, p. 126.
355. ibid., p. 46.
356. Deepak Chopra, *Quantum Healing*, p. 3.
357. ibid., p. 4.
358. *Maharishi's Programme to Create Heaven on Earth*, p. 52.
359. Rachel Storm, *In Search of Heaven on Earth*, p. 111.
360. Maharishi's *Programme to Create Heaven on Earth*, p. 54.
361. ibid., p. 56.
362. James Randi, *Psychic Investigator*, p. 32.
363. Press release.
364. ibid.
365. *Independent*, 4 April 1992.
366. ibid.
367. Author's transcript from radio broadcast.
368. *Independent*, 4 April 1992.
369. ibid.
370. *MIU World*, vol. 1, no. 2, 1991, p. 19.
371. Author's transcript from a recording.
372. ibid.
373. ibid.
374. ibid.
375. ibid.
376. *Maharishi European Sidhaland News*, December 1993.
377. Author's transcript from recording.
378. *MIU World*, vol. 1, no. 2, 1991, p. 18.
379. *Tourist Guide to Dehradun-Mussoorie (Haridwar-Rishikesh)*, p. 21.
380. *International Times*, 15 December 1967.

Bibliography

Bloomfield, Harold, Michael Cain and Dennis Jaffe. *TM* * Delcarte, 1976.

Brown, Peter and Steven Gaines. *The Love You Make*. Macmillan, 1983.

Chopra, Deepak. *Quantum Healing*. Bantam New-Age Books, 1990.

Chopra, Deepak. *Return of the Rishi*. Houghton Mifflin, 1991.

Collin-Smith, Joyce. *Call No Man Master*. Gateway, 1988.

Cooke de Herrara, Nancy. *Beyond Gurus*. Blue Dolphin, 1992.

Creating an Ideal Society: A Global Undertaking. International Association for the Advancement of the Science of Creative Intelligence, 1976.

Creme, Benjamin. *Maitreya's Mission, vol. 2*. Share International Foundation, 1993.

Das, A.C. *R.g Vedic India*, Motilal Banarsidass, 1920.

Densmore, John. *Riders on the Storm*. Bloomsbury, 1991.

Doniger, Wendy and Brian K. Smith. *The Laws of Manu*. Penguin, 1991.

Dragemark, Elsa. *The Way to Maharishi's Himalayas*. Stockholm, 1972.

Enlightenment and Invincibility to Every Individual and to Every Nation. International Association for the Advancement of the Science of Creative Intelligence, 1978.

Forem, Jack. *Transcendental Meditation*. Allen & Unwin, 1974.

Gaines, Steven. *Heroes and Villains*. Grafton, 1986.

Goldman, Albert. *The Lives of John Lennon*. Bantam, 1989.

Greene, Jonathon. *Days in the Life*. Minerva, 1988.

Hollings, Robert. *Transcendental Meditation*. Aquarian, 1982.

Horn, Paul. *Paul Horn in India*, record sleeve notes. Blue Note BN-LA529-H2, 1975.

Horn, Paul. *Special Edition*, record sleeve notes. Island Records ISLD6, 1974.

Huxley, Aldous. *The Doors of Perception*. Penguin, 1972. *Inauguration of the Dawn of the Age of Enlightenment*. Maharishi International University, 1975.

Le Mee, Jean and Ingbert Gruttner. *Hymns from the Rig- Veda*. Cape, 1975.

Lennon, Cynthia. *Twist of Lennon.* Star, 1978.

Life Supported by Natural Law. Age of Enlightenment Press, 1988.

McCabe, Peter and Robert D. Schonfield. *Apple to the Core.* Sphere, 1973.

McDowell, Josh and Don Stewart. *Understanding the Cults.* Here's Life, 1982.

Maharishi's Programmes to Create Heaven on Earth. Global Video Productions, 1992.

Maharishi's Programme to Create World Peace. MERU and Age of Enlightenment Presses, 1987.

Mahesh Yogi, Maharshi Bala Brahmachari. *Beacon Light of the Himalayas – The Dawn of the Happy New Era.* Adhyatmic Vikas Mandal, Kerala, 1955.

Mahesh Yogi, Maharishi. *Bhagavad-Gita.* International SRM Publications, 1967.

Mahesh Yogi, Maharishi. *Deep Meditation.* IMS Records WP1420, 1962.

Mahesh Yogi, Maharishi. *Love and God.* SRM Oslo, 1965.

Mahesh Yogi, Maharishi. *Maharishi Mahesh Yogi.* World Pacific Records WPS21446/Liberty Records LBS83075, 1967.

Mahesh Yogi, Maharishi. *Meditations of Maharishi Mahesh Yogi.* Bantam, 1968.

Mahesh Yogi, Maharishi. *Science of Being and Art of Living.* First edition, Allied Publishers (Private) India, 1963.

Mahesh Yogi, Maharishi. *Science of Being and Art of Living.* Revised edition, Signet, 1968.

Mahesh Yogi, Maharishi. *Seven States of Consciousness.* World Pacific Records WPS21446, 1968.

Mahesh Yogi, Maharishi. *Thirty Years Around the World – Dawn of the Age of Enlightenment, vol. 1 1957-64.* Maharishi Vedic University, 1986.

Mahesh Yogi, Maharishi, Abbot of Downside and Robert Kee. *The Maharishi and the Abbot.* International SRM Publications, 1964.

Mehta, Gita. *Karma Cola.* Cape, 1980.

Mehta, Ved. *Portrait of India.* Weidenfeld & Nicolson, 1970.

Neville, Richard. *Playpower.* Paladin, 1971.

Norman, Philip. *Shout.* Penguin, 1993.

Olson, Helena. *Hermit in the House.* Los Angeles, 1967.

Purohit Swami, Shree and W.B. Yeats. *Aphorisms of Yoga Bhagwan Shree Patanjali.* Faber & Faber, 1987.

Rama, Swami. *Living with the Himalayan Masters.* Himalayan Institute of Yoga Science and Philosophy of the USA, 1978.

Randi, James. *Psychic Investigator.* Boxtree, 1991.

Russell, Peter. *The Awakening Earth.* Routledge & Kegan Paul, 1982.

Russell, Peter. *The TM Technique.* Routledge & Kegan Paul, 1976.

Shantanand, Shankaracharya. *Good Company.* Element, 1992.

Shearer, Alistair and Peter Russell. *The Upanishads.* Wildwood, 1978.

Shotton, Peter and Nicholas Schaffer. *John Lennon – In My Life.* Coronet, 1984.

Sivananda, Swami. *The Bhagavad Gita.* Divine Life Society, 1939.

Sivananda, Swami. *Triple Yoga.* Divine Life Society, 1986.

A Six Month Course in Yoga Asanas. International SRM Publications, 1962.

Somach, Denny and Kathleen. *Ticket to Ride.* Macdonald, 1989.

Stevens, Bill and Jim Anderson. *Feel Great with TM.* Golden Arrow Publications, 1988.

Storm, Rachel. *In Search of Heaven on Earth.* Bloomsbury, 1991.

Tames, Richard. *William Morris – Lifelines 3.* Shire, 1972.

Taylor, Derek. *Thirty Years Ago Today.* Bantam, 1987.

Tichy, Herbert. *Himalaya.* Vikas, 1970.

Tiwari, Rameshwar. *Shri Jyotishpeethaddharaka*, Biography of Swami Brahmanand Saraswati (in Hindi) 1965 (transcreated into English by Prem Pashrica and re-titled as *The Whole Thing – The Real Thing,*. Delhi Photo Studio, 1977).

Tiwari, Rameshwar. *Shri Shankaracharya Upadeshamrita*, A Collection of 108 of Swami Brahmanand Saraswati's Satsangs (in Hindi), 1969

Tourist Guide to Dehradun-Mussoorie (Haridwar-Rishikesh). Nest & Wings, India, 1989.

Varma, Raj. *Strange Facts About a Great Saint*, 1980.

Vedic Hymns and Prayers. All India Arya (Hindu) Dharma Sewa Sangha, 1978.

Watson, Lyall. *Supernature.* Coronet, 1971.

Wenner, Jan. *Lennon Remembers.* Penguin, 1975.

Index